Vocabulary

FOR THE

High School Student

Vocabulary books by the authors

Vocabulary and Composition Through
Pleasurable Reading, Books I–VI

Vocabulary for Enjoyment, Books I–III

Vocabulary for the High School Student, Books A, B

Vocabulary for the High School Student

Vocabulary for the College-Bound Student

The Joy of Vocabulary

Vocabulary
FOR THE
High School Student

Third Edition

HAROLD LEVINE
Chairman Emeritus of English,
Benjamin Cardozo High School, New York

NORMAN LEVINE
Associate Professor of English,
City College of the City University of New York

ROBERT T. LEVINE
Professor of English,
North Carolina A & T State University

AMSCO SCHOOL PUBLICATIONS, INC.
315 Hudson Street / New York, N.Y. 10013

Please visit our Web site at:

www.amscopub.com

When ordering this book, please specify:
R 597 S *or* VOCABULARY FOR THE HIGH SCHOOL STUDENT, SOFTBOUND
  or
R 597 H *or* VOCABULARY FOR THE HIGH SCHOOL STUDENT, HARDBOUND

ISBN 1-56765-008-2 (Softbound edition)
NYC Item 56765-008-1

ISBN 1-56765-015-5 (Hardbound edition)
NYC Item 56765-015-4

Printed in the United States of America

8 9 10   02 03 04 05 06

Preface

The principal aim of this updated and enlarged edition is to help high school students build a superior vocabulary and learn the skills of critical thinking, close reading, and concise writing. The exercises in this edition have been written expressly to teach these and other desirable skills at the same time as vocabulary.

Like its predecessors, this edition involves students in a variety of vocabulary-enriching activities in chapter after chapter.

Learning New Words From the Context (Chapter 1) presents one hundred sixty short passages in which unfamiliar words can be defined with the help of clues in the context. By teaching students how to interpret such clues, this chapter provides them with an indispensable tool for vocabulary growth and, at the same time, *makes them better readers.*

Enlarging Vocabulary Through Central Ideas (Chapter 2) teaches twenty groups of related words. In the EATING group, students learn *condiment, glutton, palatable, succulent, voracious,* and other *eating* words. Each word studied in such a group helps with the learning of some other words in the group.

Enlarging Vocabulary Through Anglo-Saxon Prefixes (Chapter 3) teaches words beginning with eight Anglo-Saxon prefixes, like FORE-, meaning "before," "beforehand," or "front." Knowing FORE-, students can more readily understand *forearm, forebear, foreboding, foreshadow, foreword,* etc.

Enlarging Vocabulary Through Latin Prefixes (Chapter 4) does the same with twenty-four Latin prefixes. It is easier for students to understand *discontent, discredit, disintegrate, dispassionate,* and *disrepair* when they know that the prefix DIS- means "opposite of."

Enlarging Vocabulary Through Latin Roots (Chapter 5) teaches words derived from twenty Latin roots. If students, for example, know that the root HERE- means "stick," they can better understand *adhere* ("stick to"), *cohere* ("stick together"), *incoherent* ("not sticking together"; disconnected), etc.

Enlarging Vocabulary Through Greek Word Elements (Chapter 6) teaches derivatives from twenty Greek elements, like AUTO-, meaning "self." Among the ten AUTO- words taught in this chapter are *autocrat* (ruler exercising self-derived power), *automation* (technique for making a process self-operating), and *autonomy* (self-government).

Expanding Vocabulary Through Derivatives (Chapter 7) teaches students how to convert one newly learned word into several—for example, *literate* into *illiterate, semiliterate, literacy, illiteracy*, etc. The chapter also provides an incidental review of some basic spelling rules.

Understanding Word Relationships and Word Analogies (Chapter 8) supplements the numerous explanations and hints given throughout the book on dealing with analogy questions. This chapter is principally for students who are unfamiliar with analogy questions, or are having difficulty with them.

Dictionary of Words Taught in This Text (Chapter 9) is intended as a tool of reference and review.

Whenever something is learned, it is likely soon to be forgotten unless it is used. Therefore, students must be encouraged to use—in their writing and class discussions—the words and skills they are learning in this book. If a wordy paragraph can be made more concise—or if undesirable repetition can be avoided by use of a synonym—they should be expected to do so because they have been using these very same skills hundreds of times in the exercises of this book. When a strange word can be understood from a knowledge of its root or prefix—or from clues in the context—they should be challenged to define it, and to verify their definition in the dictionary. Above all, they should be encouraged to own a good dictionary and to develop the dictionary habit.

The Authors

Contents

CHAPTER 2.   ENLARGING VOCABULARY THROUGH CENTRAL IDEAS   72

CHAPTER 3. ENLARGING VOCABULARY THROUGH ANGLO-SAXON PREFIXES 123

CHAPTER 4.   ENLARGING VOCABULARY THROUGH LATIN PREFIXES   148

CHAPTER 5. ENLARGING VOCABULARY THROUGH LATIN ROOTS 207

CHAPTER 6.   ENLARGING VOCABULARY THROUGH GREEK WORD ELEMENTS   240

Why study Greek word elements?   240
Purpose of this unit   240

CHAPTER 7. EXPANDING VOCABULARY THROUGH DERIVATIVES 279

CHAPTER *1*

Learning New Words From the Context

What is the context?

The *context* is the part of a passage in which a particular word is used and which helps to explain that word. Suppose you were asked for the meaning of *bear*. Could you give a definite answer? Obviously not, for *bear*, as presented to you, has no context.

But if you were asked to define *bear* in the phrase "polar *bear*," you would immediately know it refers to an animal. Or, if someone were to say, "Please stop that whistling—I can't *bear* it," you would know that in this context *bear* means "endure" or "stand."

Why is the context important?

An important point for those of us who want to enlarge our vocabularies is this: *the context can give us the meaning not only of familiar words like bear, but also of unfamiliar words.*

Suppose, for example, you were asked for the meaning of *valiant*. You might not know it, unless, of course, you already have a fine vocabulary. But if you were to meet *valiant* in the following context, you would have a very good chance of discovering its meaning:

> "Cowards die many times before their deaths;
> The *valiant* never taste of death but once."
> —William Shakespeare

From the above context, you can tell that the author is *contrasting* two ideas—"cowards" and "the valiant." Therefore, "the valiant" means the *opposite* of "cowards," namely "brave people." *Valiant* means "brave."

In what ways will this unit benefit you?

This unit will show you how to get the meaning of unfamiliar words from the context. Once you learn this skill, it will serve you for the rest of your life in two important ways: (1) it will keep enlarging your vocabulary, and (2) it will keep making you a better and better reader.

Part 1

Contexts With Contrasting Words

Each passage below contains a word in italics. If you read the passage carefully, you will find a clue to the meaning of this word in an opposite word (antonym) or a contrasting idea.

For each passage, enter on your paper (*a*) the clue that led you to the meaning and (*b*) the meaning itself. The answers to the first two passages have been inserted as examples.

Do not write in this book. Enter all answers on separate paper.

---

1. "In the meantime, we could never make out where he got the drink. That was the ship's mystery. Watch him as we pleased, we could do nothing to solve it; and when we asked him to his face, he would only laugh, if he were drunk, and if he were *sober*, deny solemnly that he ever tasted anything but water."—Robert Louis Stevenson

    a. CLUE: *sober* is the opposite of "drunk"

    b. MEANING: *sober* means "not drunk"

2. One sandwich for lunch usually *suffices* for you, but for me it is not enough.

    a. CLUE: *suffices* is in contrast with "is not enough"

    b. MEANING: *suffices* means "is enough"

3. Plastic dishes last a long time because they are unbreakable. Ordinary china is very *fragile*.

4. Our tennis coach will neither *confirm* nor deny the rumor that she is going to be the basketball coach next year.

5. Don't *digress*. Stick to the topic.

6. Your account of the fight *concurs* with Joanne's but differs from the accounts given by the other witnesses.

7. "I greatly fear your presence would rather increase than *mitigate* his unhappy fortunes."—James Fenimore Cooper

8. Roses in bloom are a common sight in summer, but a *rarity* in late November.

9. The tables in the restaurant were all occupied, and we waited more than ten minutes for one to become *vacant*.

10. There are few theaters here, but on Broadway there are theaters *galore*.
11. "I do not *shrink* from this responsibility; I welcome it."
    —John Fitzgerald Kennedy
12. Ruth is an experienced driver, but Harry is a *novice*; he began taking lessons just last month.
13. A bank clerk can usually tell the difference between *genuine* $100 bills and counterfeit ones.
14. When I ask Theresa to help me with a *complicated* assignment, she makes it seem so easy.
15. On the wall of my room I have a copy of Rembrandt's "The Night Watch"; the *original* is in the Rijks Museum in Amsterdam.
16. "Friends, Romans, countrymen, lend me your ears;/I come to bury Caesar, not to praise him./The evil that men do lives after them;/The good is oft *interred* with their bones;/So let it be with Caesar."
    —William Shakespeare
17. In some offices, work comes to a halt at noon and does not *resume* until 1 p.m.
18. When we got to the beach, my sister and I were *impatient* to get into the water, but Dad was not in a hurry.
19. Off duty, a police officer may wear the same clothes as a *civilian*.
20. "No matter what time of day his [the pony express rider's] watch came on, and no matter whether it was winter or summer, raining, snowing, hailing, or sleeting, or whether his 'beat' was a level, straight road or a crazy trail over mountain crags and precipices, or whether it led through peaceful regions or regions that swarmed with *hostile* Indians, he must always be ready to leap into the saddle and be off like the wind."—Mark Twain

Study Your Lesson Words, Group 1

WORD	MEANING AND TYPICAL USE
civilian (*n.*) sə'vil-yən	person who is not a member of the military, or police, or fire-fighting forces Eight of the passengers were soldiers and one was a marine; the rest were *civilians*.
complicated (*adj.*) 'käm-plə,kāt-əd	hard to understand; elaborate; complex; intricate If some of the requirements for graduation seem *complicated*, ask your guidance counselor to explain them to you.
concur (*v.*) kən'kə(r)	agree; coincide; be of the same opinion The rules of the game require you to accept the umpire's decision, even if you do not *concur* with it.
confirm (*v.*) kən'fərm	state or prove the truth of; substantiate; verify My physician thought I had broken my wrist, and an X-ray later *confirmed* his opinion.
***confirmation** (*n.*)	proof; evidence; verification
digress (*v.*) dī'gres	turn aside; get off the main topic; deviate At one point, the speaker *digressed* to tell of an incident in her childhood, but then she got right back to the topic.
fragile (*adj.*) 'fraj-əl	easily broken; breakable; weak; frail The handle is *fragile*; it will easily break if you use too much pressure.
galore (*adj.*) gə'lò(r)	aplenty; in abundance; plentiful; abundant (*galore* always follows the word it modifies) There were no cabs on the side streets, but on the main street there were cabs *galore*.
genuine (*adj.*) 'jen-yə-wən	actually being what it is claimed or seems to be; true; real; authentic Jeannette wore an imitation fur that everyone thought was *genuine* leopard skin.

*Note that *confirmation* is a bonus word—you can understand it instantly if you know *confirm*. Useful bonus words, like *confirmation*, will be introduced from now on.

hostile (*adj.*)
'häs-təl

of or relating to an enemy or enemies; unfriendly; inimical
In the heat of battle, allies are sometimes mistaken for *hostile* forces.

impatient (*adj.*)
im'pā-shənt

not patient; not willing to bear delay; fretful; anxious
Five minutes can seem like five hours when you are *impatient*.

inter (*v.*)
ən'tə(r)

put into the earth; bury; entomb
Many American heroes are *interred* in Arlington National Cemetery.

interment (*n.*)

burial; entombment; sepulture

mitigate (*v.*)
'mit-ə,gāt

make less severe; lessen; alleviate; soften; relieve
With the help of novocaine, your dentist can greatly *mitigate* the pain of drilling.

novice (*n.*)
'näv-əs

one who is new to a field or activity; beginner; apprentice; neophyte; tyro
There are two slopes: one for experienced skiers and one for *novices*.

original (*n.*)
ə'rij-ənəl

work created firsthand from which copies are made; prototype; archetype
This is a copy of THANKSGIVING TURKEY by Grandma Moses. The *original* is in the Metropolitan Museum of Art.

original (*adj.*)

1. belonging to the beginning; first; earliest; initial; primary
Miles Standish was one of the *original* colonists of Massachusetts; he came over on the "Mayflower."

2. inventive; creative

originality (*n.*)

freshness; novelty; inventiveness

rarity (*n.*)
'rer-ət-ē

something uncommon, infrequent, or rare
Rain in the Sahara Desert is a *rarity*.

resume (*v.*)
rə'züm

1. begin again
School closes for the Christmas recess on December 24 and *resumes* on January 3.

2. retake; reoccupy
Please *resume* your seats.

shrink (*v.*)
'shriŋk

1. draw back; recoil; wince
Wendy *shrank* from the task of telling her parents about the car accident, but she finally got the courage and told them.

2. become smaller; contract
Some garments *shrink* in washing.

sober (*adj.*)
'sō-bə(r)

1. not drunk; not intoxicated
Our driver had avoided strong drink because he wanted to be *sober* for the trip home.

2. earnest; serious; free from excitement or exaggeration
When he learned of his failure, George thought of quitting school. But after *sober* consideration, he realized that would be unwise.

suffice (*v.*)
sə'fīs

be enough, adequate, or sufficient; serve; do
I had thought that $60 would *suffice* for my school supplies. As it turned out, it was not enough.

vacant (*adj.*)
'vā-kənt

empty; unoccupied; tenantless; not being used
I had to stand for the first half of the performance because I could not find a *vacant* seat.

vacancy (*n.*)

unfilled position; unoccupied apartment or room

Apply What You Have Learned

EXERCISE 1.1: SENTENCE COMPLETION

Write the required lesson word on your answer paper. *Resume* is the answer to question 1.

1. The showers have just stopped, but they may soon __?__ .
2. Their directions were __?__ ; yours were easy to follow.
3. Why are you __?__ to me? Aren't we friends?
4. We hope to move in as soon as there is a(n) __?__ apartment.
5. Experts can tell the difference between a copy and the __?__ .
6. How many more chairs do you need? Will five __?__ ?
7. Paul doesn't play tennis as well as Amy; he is a(n) __?__ .
8. If you __?__ , you will waste our time. Stick to the topic.
9. There is one __?__ in the cabinet; the rest are army officers.
10. It may be unpleasant, but we must not __?__ from doing our duty.
11. Jobs, then, were not plentiful; now, there are openings __?__ .
12. Is there a way to __?__ the pain? It is very severe.
13. What evidence do you have to __?__ your claim?
14. These cups are __?__ ; handle them with care.
15. At the gravesite, the relatives helped to __?__ the deceased.

EXERCISE 1.2: SYNONYMS

Eliminate repetition by replacing the boldfaced word or words with a **synonym** from your lesson words on pages 5–7. The answers to the first two questions are *original* and *sober*.

1. Who lived here first? Were you the **first** tenant?
2. He is **not drunk;** don't accuse him of drunkenness.
3. I wanted to wait a day, but they were **unwilling to wait.**
4. She has just begun to learn to swim. Are you a **beginner,** too?
5. Stick to the topic. Don't **get off the topic.**
6. A dozen is more than enough. Even six would **be enough.**
7. I tried to be friendly, though they seemed **unfriendly.**
8. You lack proof. There is no witness to **prove** your story.
9. All rooms are occupied; not a single one is **unoccupied.**
10. This is really a great buy. It's a **real** bargain.

EXERCISE 1.3: ANTONYMS

Enter the lesson word from pages 5–7 that is most nearly the **opposite** of the boldfaced word or words. The first answer is *original*.

1. This **copy** is so good that it looks like the __?__ .
2. Trees were once a **common sight** here; now they are a(n) __?__ .
3. The carpenter is a **veteran,** but his helper is a(n) __?__ .
4. Her __?__ attitude shows she is not **sympathetic** to our cause.
5. Is the auditorium **being used,** or is it __?__ ?
6. Our opinions now __?__ ; we no longer **disagree.**
7. I can neither __?__ your statement nor **deny** it.
8. Say nothing to **intensify** his fears; try to __?__ them.
9. Out of uniform, a **soldier** looks like an ordinary __?__ .
10. When we are **excited,** we are not capable of __?__ judgment.

EXERCISE 1.4: CONCISE WRITING

Express the thought of each sentence in **no more than four words,** as in 1, below.

1. The people living next door to us were unwilling to put up with delay.
   Our neighbors were impatient.
2. People who are new to a field or activity need a great deal of help.
3. Rita misplaced the document from which the copies were made.
4. Which is the apartment that no one is living in at the present time?
5. Jones is not a member of the military, or police, or fire-fighting forces.

EXERCISE 1.5: SYNONYM SUMMARY

Each line, when completed, should have three words similar in meaning. The parentheses indicate the number of missing letters. On your answer paper, write the complete words. Answers to the first line are **empty, tenantless,** and **vacant.**

1. em (1) ty	ten (1) ntless	v (1) cant
2. abund (1) nt	pl (2) t (1) ful	g (1) l (1) re
3. compl (1) x	intr (1) cate	com (2) ic (2) ed
4. pr (2) f	ev (1) dence	veri (2) cat (1) on
5. b (1) ry	ent (2) b	(3) er
6. neoph (1) te	t (1) ro	no (2) ce
7. nov (1) lty	inv (1) ntiveness	o (2) gin (2) ity

8. ser (1) ous	(2) rnest	sob (2)
9. an (1) ious	fr (1) tful	im (2) t (2) nt
10. br (2) kable	fr (2) l	frag (2) e
11. unfr (2) ndly	inim (1) cal	hos (2) le
12. all (1) viate	rel (2) ve	miti (1) ate
13. ver (1) fy	substant (2) te	con (2) rm
14. r (2) l	(2) thentic	gen (2) ne
15. rec (2) l	w (1) nce	sh (2) nk
16. proto (2) pe	arch (1) type	(1) riginal
17. agr (2)	coin (1) ide	con (2) r
18. anim (1) sity	u (1) fr (3) dly	hosti (2) ty
19. entom (1) ment	sep (1) lture	int (2) ment
20. s (1) rve	d __	su (2) ice

EXERCISE 1.6: ANALOGIES

Which lettered pair of words—*a, b, c, d* or *e*—most nearly expresses the same relationship as the capitalized pair? Write the letter of your answer on separate paper. The first three analogy questions have been explained to guide you, and their answers are (b), (a), and (e).

1. CONFIRM : DENY
   - (*a*) concur : agree
   - (*b*) succeed : fail
   - (*c*) greet : welcome
   - (*d*) disinter : unearth
   - (*e*) recoil : shrink

   Explanation: To **confirm** is the opposite of to **deny**. To **succeed** is the opposite of to **fail**.

2. NEOPHYTE : EXPERIENCE
   - (*a*) fool : judgment
   - (*b*) pedestrian : foot
   - (*c*) superstar : recognition
   - (*d*) motorist : license
   - (*e*) expert : skill

   Explanation: A **neophyte** lacks **experience**. A **fool** lacks **judgment**.

3. COMPLEX : UNDERSTAND
   - (*a*) painless : endure
   - (*b*) tasty : consume
   - (*c*) inexpensive : afford
   - (*d*) available : obtain
   - (*e*) vivid : forget

   Explanation: Something that is **complex** is hard to **understand**. Something that is **vivid** is hard to **forget**.

4. SOBER : INTOXICATED
- (a) weak : frail
- (b) fretful : restless
- (c) rude : impolite
- (d) inimical : friendly
- (e) weird : strange

harmful

5. IMPATIENT : WAIT
- (a) gossipy : talk
- (b) undecided : do
- (c) stubborn : compromise
- (d) industrious : work
- (e) obliging : assist

6. INTENSIFY : MITIGATE
- (a) prohibit : permit
- (b) deviate : digress
- (c) verify : substantiate
- (d) deny : contradict
- (e) relieve : alleviate

7. FRAGILE : BREAK
- (a) inflexible : bend
- (b) rubbery : chew
- (c) rare : find
- (d) uncomplicated : grasp
- (e) cumbersome : carry

8. CREATIVE : ORIGINALITY
- (a) hostile : rancor
- (b) selfish : generosity
- (c) sympathetic : ill will
- (d) unappreciative : gratitude
- (e) frail : stamina

9. INTRICATE : SIMPLE
- (a) vacant : unoccupied
- (b) abundant : scarce
- (c) authentic : genuine
- (d) pleasant : agreeable
- (e) uncommon : rare

10. CIVILIAN : COMBAT
- (a) runner : marathon
- (b) accomplice : guilt
- (c) passenger : navigation
- (d) singer : chorus
- (e) guest : celebration

Students who would like more help in answering analogy questions should consult Chapter 8, page 293.

Pretest 2

For each passage, write (*a*) the clue to the meaning of the italicized word and (*b*) the meaning itself.

21. "Then such a scramble as there is to get aboard, and to get ashore, and to take in freight and to *discharge* freight!"—Mark Twain

22. The dealer is giving up his gas station because the profit is too small. He hopes to go into a more *lucrative* business.

23. I tried reading Lou's notes but I found them *illegible*. However, yours were easy to read.

24. Debbie, who has come late to every meeting, surprised us today by being *punctual*.

25. As I hurried to the board, I *inadvertently* stepped on Alan's foot, but he thinks I did it on purpose.

26, 27. "When I was a boy, there was but one *permanent* ambition among my comrades in our village on the west bank of the Mississippi River. That was, to be a steamboatman. We had *transient* ambitions of other sorts. . . . When a circus came and went, it left us all burning to become clowns. . . . now and then we had a hope that, if we lived and were good, God would permit us to be pirates. These ambitions faded out, each in its turn; but the ambition to be a steamboatman always remained."—Mark Twain

28. When you chair a discussion, it is unfair to call only on your friends. To be *equitable*, you should call on all who wish to speak, without favoritism.

29. The only *extemporaneous* talk was Jerry's; all the other candidates gave memorized speeches.

30. "Your pal" may be a suitable closing for a friendly note, but it is completely *inappropriate* for a business letter.

31. If you agree, write "yes"; if you *dissent*, write "no."

32. "Mr. Hurst looked at her [Miss Bennet] with astonishment.
    " 'Do you prefer reading to cards?' said he; 'that is rather *singular* [strange].'
    " 'Miss Eliza Bennet,' said Miss Bingley, 'despises cards. She is a great reader, and has no pleasure in anything else.'
    " 'I deserve neither such praise nor such *censure*,' cried Elizabeth; 'I am not a great reader, and I have pleasure in many things.' "—Jane Austen

33. A child trying to squeeze through the iron fence became stuck between two bars, but luckily she was able to *extricate* herself.

34. When you let me take your bishop, I thought it was unwise of you; later I saw you had made a very *astute* move.

35. At first I was blamed for damaging Dad's typewriter, but when my sister said she was responsible, I was *exonerated*.

36. ''If you once *forfeit* the confidence of your fellow citizens, you can never regain their respect and esteem.''—Abraham Lincoln

37. Parking on our side of the street is *prohibited* on weekdays between 4 p.m. and 7 p.m. but permitted at all other times.

38. The caretaker expected to be praised for his efforts to put out the fire. Instead, he was *rebuked* for his delay in notifying the fire department.

39. If we can begin the meeting on time, we should be able to complete our business and *adjourn* by 4:30 p.m.

40. Before the new hotel can be constructed, the two old buildings now on the site will have to be *demolished*.

Study Your Lesson Words, Group 2

WORD	MEANING AND TYPICAL USE
adjourn (*v.*) ə'jərn	close a meeting; suspend the business of a meeting; disband; recess When we visited Washington, D.C., Congress was not in session; it had *adjourned* for the Thanksgiving weekend.
astute (*adj.*) ə'styüt	1. shrewd; wise, perspicacious; sagacious Marie was the only one to solve the riddle; she is a very *astute* thinker. 2. crafty; cunning; sly; wily An *astute* Greek tricked the Trojans into opening the gates of Troy.
censure (*n.*) 'sen-shə(r)	act of blaming; expression of disapproval; hostile criticism; rebuke; reprimand Bill was about to reach for a third slice of cake but was stopped by a look of *censure* in Mother's eyes.
demolish (*v.*) də'mäl-ish	tear down; destroy; raze; smash; wreck It took several days for the wrecking crew to *demolish* the old building.
demolition (*n.*)	destruction
discharge (*v.*) dəs'chä(r)j	1. unload After *discharging* its cargo, the ship will go into dry dock for repairs. 2. dismiss, fire One employee was *discharged*.
dissent (*v.*) də'sent	differ in opinion; disagree; object There was nearly complete agreement on Al's proposal. Enid and Alice were the only ones who *dissented*.
dissension (*n.*)	discord; conflict; strife
equitable (*adj.*) 'ek-wə-tə-bəl	fair to all concerned; just; impartial; objective; unbiased The only *equitable* way for the three to share the $600 profit is for each to receive $200.
inequitable (*n.*)	unfair; unjust

exonerate (*v.*)
eg'zän-ə,rāt

free from blame; clear from accusation; acquit; absolve

The other driver *exonerated* Isabel of any responsibility for the accident.

extemporaneous (*adj.*)
ek,stem-pə'rā-nē-əs

composed or spoken without preparation; offhand; impromptu; improvised

It was obvious that the speaker's talk was memorized, though she tried to make it seem *extemporaneous*.

extricate (*v.*)
'eks-trə,kāt

free from difficulties; disentangle; disencumber; release

If you let your assignments pile up, you may get into a situation from which you will not be able to *extricate* yourself.

forfeit (*v.*)
'fȯ(r)-fət

lose or have to give up as a penalty for some error, neglect, or fault; sacrifice

One customer gave a $150 deposit on an order of slipcovers. When they were delivered, she decided she didn't want them. Of course, she *forfeited* her deposit.

illegible (*adj.*)
i'lej-ə-bəl

not able to be read; very hard to read; not legible; undecipherable

It is fortunate that Roger does his reports on a word processor because his handwriting is *illegible*.

legible (*adj.*)

easy to read; readable

inadvertently (*adv.*)
,in-əd'vər-tənt-lē

not done on purpose; unintentionally; thoughtlessly; accidentally; carelessly

I finally found my glasses on the windowsill. I must have left them there *inadvertently*.

inappropriate (*adj.*)
,in-ə'prō-prē-ət

not fitting; unsuitable; unbecoming; not appropriate; improper

Since I was the one who nominated Bruce, it would be *inappropriate* for me to vote for another candidate.

appropriate (*adj.*)

fitting; proper

lucrative (*adj.*)
'lú-krə-tiv

money-making; profitable; advantageous; remunerative

This year's school dance was not so *lucrative*; we made only $70 compared to $240 last year.

permanent (*adj.*)
'pər-mə-nənt

lasting; enduring; intended to last; stable

Write to me at my temporary address, the Gateway Hotel. As soon as I find an apartment, I shall notify you of my *permanent* address.

prohibit (*v.*)
prō'hib-ət

forbid; ban; enjoin; interdict

The library's regulations *prohibit* the borrowing of reference books.

prohibition (*n.*)

ban; taboo; interdiction

punctual (*adj.*)
'pəŋk-chə-wəl

on time; prompt; timely

Be *punctual*. If you are late, we shall have to depart without you.

punctuality (*n.*)

promptness

rebuke (*v.*)
rə'byük

express disapproval of; criticize sharply; censure severely; reprimand; reprove

Our coach *rebuked* the two players who were late for practice, but praised the rest of the team for their punctuality.

transient (*adj.*)
'tran-shənt

not lasting; passing soon; fleeting; short-lived; momentary; ephemeral; transitory

It rained all day upstate, but down here we had only a *transient* shower; it was over in mintues.

transient (*n.*)

guest staying for only a short time

The hotel's customers are mainly *transients*; only a few are permanent guests.

Apply What You Have Learned

EXERCISE 1.7: SENTENCE COMPLETION

Write the lesson word that best fits the meaning of the sentence. *Rebuke* and *censure* answer question 1.

1. It is wrong to __?__ Sam only, with not one word of __?__ for the three others who are equally blameworthy.
2. As it was getting late, Lucy made a motion to __?__ the meeting.
3. A boxer who deliberately uses tactics that the rules of the ring __?__ will almost surely __?__ the bout.
4. A letter with a(n) __?__ address is undeliverable.
5. The complex has eighty unfurnished apartments to lease to __?__ tenants and four furnished ones to accommodate __?__ families.
6. Has the company agreed not to __?__ toxic wastes into the river?
7. Those who __?__ say they will not support the proposed settlement unless it is made more __?__ .
8. Her remarks were not __?__ ; they had been prepared in advance.
9. The corporation's __?__ new line of breakfast cereals should enable it to __?__ itself from its financial difficulties.
10. Martha dashed out, __?__ leaving her keys behind.

EXERCISE 1.8: SYNONYMS

Eliminate repetition by replacing the boldfaced word or words with a **synonym** from your lesson words on pages 13, 14.

1. Should we **ban** imports from nations that ban our products?
2. Cyclones **wreck** buildings, trapping victims in the wreckage.
3. The report clears them of blame, but it does not **clear** us.
4. The firm has fired two employees and may soon **fire** some more.
5. You are rarely on time; they are usually **on time.**
6. Low pr●fits are driving farmers into more **profitable** pursuits.
7. Wait for a suitable occasion; this one is **not suitable.**
8. The **lasting** peace we were supposed to have did not last long.
9. Pat's handwriting is hard to read; Anita's is more **readable.**
10. He is entangled in a web of lies and cannot **disentangle** himself.

EXERCISE 1.9: ANTONYMS

Enter the lesson word from pages 14–16 that is most nearly the **opposite** of the boldfaced word.

1. It makes no sense to __?__ a structure we may soon need to **build** anew.
2. People insist on __?__ treatment. **Unfair** practices must cease.
3. **Temporary** officers serve only until __?__ ones are chosen.
4. Clothes **suitable** for leisure wear may be __?__ for the office.
5. Many public places that used to **permit** smoking now __?__ it.
6. **Commendation** is much more pleasing to our ears than __?__ .
7. The new owner turned an **unprofitable** business into a(n) __?__ one.
8. I cannot **concur** with your conclusions. I must __?__ .
9. A **permanent** resident pays a lower daily rate than a(n) __?__ .
10. Our bus was **late** again today; it is seldom __?__ .

EXERCISE 1.10: CONCISE WRITING

Express the thought of each sentence in no more than four words, as in 1, below.

1. Jim strayed from the main topic without really intending to do so.
    Jim inadvertently digressed.
2. When are we going to bring our meeting to a close?
3. The laws by which we are governed must be fair to all concerned.
4. The comments she made were spoken on the spur of the moment, without any advance preparation.
5. The notes that you took are very hard to read.

EXERCISE 1.11: SYNONYM SUMMARY

Each line, when completed, should have three words similar in meaning. The parentheses indicate the number of missing letters. On your answer paper, write the *complete* words. The answers to the first question are **disagree, object,** and **dissent.**

1. disagr (2)	(2) ject	(3) sent
2. l (1) se	sacr (1) fice	forf (2) t
3. shr (2) d	w (1) ly	(2) tute
4. prom (2)	time (2)	punc (3) l
5. (1) reck	de (3) ish	r (1) ze

6. last (3)	(1) table	(3) man (3)
7. b (1) n	(2) boo	pr (1) hi (2) tion
8. accident (2) ly	care (4) ly	in (2) vertent (2)
9. impart (3)	(2) bias (2)	(1) quit (2) le
10. (3) charge	(3) miss	f (1) re
11. (2) proper	(2) becoming	(2) appropriate
12. (2) quit	(2) solve	(2) one (1) ate
13. fit (4)	prop (2)	(2) prop (2) ate
14. (2) cess	(3) band	(2) jour (1)
15. moment (3)	fleet (3)	t (3) sit (3)
16. (3) hand	(2) tempo (3) eous	(2) prompt (1)
17. profit (1) ble	remuner (1) tive	(2) crat (2) e
18. dis (2) tangle	rel (2) se	(2) tricat (1)
19. unread (1) ble	undecipher (1) ble	(2) leg (4)
20. (2) fair	(2) just	(2) eq (2) table

EXERCISE 1.12: ANALOGIES

Which lettered pair of words—*a, b, c, d,* or *e*—most nearly expresses the same relationship as the capitalized pair?

1. ADJOURN* : DISBAND
   - *(a)* win : lose
   - *(c)* raise : lower
   - *(e)* alleviate : intensify
   - *(b)* differ : agree
   - *(d)* bury : inter

2. DEMOLISH : BUILD
   - *(a)* prohibit : interdict
   - *(c)* sacrifice : forfeit
   - *(e)* absolve : exculpate
   - *(b)* discharge : hire
   - *(d)* rebuke : reprimand

3. ILLEGIBLE : DECIPHER
   - *(a)* audible : hear
   - *(c)* accessible : reach
   - *(e)* visible : see
   - *(b)* rare : find
   - *(d)* fragile : break

   Hint: Something **illegible** is hard to **decipher.**

4. FOOL : ASTUTE
   - *(a)* coward : valiant
   - *(c)* imitator : unoriginal
   - *(e)* accomplice : blameworthy
   - *(b)* inventor : creative
   - *(d)* neophyte : inexperienced

5. LUCRATIVE : UNREMUNERATIVE
- (a) barren : unproductive
- (b) scarce : unavailable
- becoming : inappropriate
- (d) unjust : inequitable
- extemporaneous : impromptu

6. EPHEMERAL : DURATION
- (a) spacious : capacity
- (b) priceless : value
- (c) enormous : size
- (d) lofty : height
- (e) insignificant : importance

Hint: Something **ephemeral** is of little **duration.**

7. LATECOMER : PUNCTUAL
- (a) liar : untrustworthy
- (b) invalid : frail
- (c) dictator : domineering
- (d) gossip : talkative
- (e) ally : inimical

8. OBJECTIVE : BIAS
- (a) dependent : domination
- (b) vengeful : hate
- (c) illiterate : ignorance
- (d) healthy : disease
- (e) hesitant : doubt

Hint: An **objective** person is free of **bias.**

9. FLEETING : STAY
- (a) boiling : evaporate
- (b) stable : disappear
- (c) complex : puzzle
- (d) amusing : entertain
- (e) mitigating : relieve

Hint: Something **fleeting** does not **stay.**

10. DYNAMITE : DEMOLITION
- (a) food : agriculture
- (b) fog : atmosphere
- (c) oil : heating
- (d) lumber : forest
- (e) temperature : refrigeration

Part 2.
Contexts With Similar Words

This section will show you how you may discover the meaning of an unfamiliar word or expression from a *similar* word or expression in the context.

1. Do you know the meaning of *remuneration?* If not, you should be able to learn it from passage *a:*

a. All school officials receive a salary except the members of the Board of Education, who serve without *remuneration.*

> Here, the meaning of *remuneration* is supplied by a similar word in the context, *salary.*

2. What is a *baker's dozen?* If you do not know, try to find out from passage *b:*

b. ''Mrs. Joe has been out a dozen times, looking for you, Pip. And she's out now, making it a *baker's dozen.*''—Charles Dickens

> A dozen plus one is the same as a *baker's dozen.* Therefore, a *baker's dozen* must mean ''thirteen.''

3. Let's try one more. Find the meaning of *comprehension* in passage *c:*

c. I understand the first problem, but the second is beyond my *comprehension.*

> The clue here is *understand.* It suggests that *comprehension* must mean ''understanding.''

Note that you sometimes have to perform a small operation to get the meaning. In passage *c,* for example, you had to change the form of the clue word *understand* to *understanding.* In passage *b,* you had to do some adding: twelve plus one equals a *baker's dozen.* In passage *a,* however, you were able to use the clue word *salary,* without change, as the meaning of *remuneration.*

Pretest 3

Write the meaning of the italicized word or expression. (Hint: Look for a *similar* word or expression in the context.)

1. "In the marketplace of Goderville was a great crowd, a mingled *multitude* of men and beasts."—Guy de Maupassant

2. When I invited you for a *stroll*, you said it was too hot to walk.

3. Jane's little brother has discovered the *cache* where she keeps her photographs. She'll have to find another hiding place.

4. The *spine*, or backbone, runs along the back of human beings.

5. "The king and his court were in their places, opposite the twin doors—those fateful *portals* so terrible in their similarity."—Frank R. Stockton

6. Ellen tried her best to hold back her tears, but she could not *restrain* them.

7. Why are you so *timorous?* I tell you there is nothing to be afraid of.

8. Harriet's *version* of the quarrel differs from your account.

9. Our club's first president, who knew little about democratic procedures, ran the meetings in such a *despotic* way that we called him "the dictator."

10. "The Hispaniola still lay where she had anchored, but, sure enough, there was the *Jolly Roger*—the black flag of piracy—flying from her peak."—Robert Louis Stevenson

11. The Empire State Building is a remarkable *edifice*; it has more than a hundred stories.

12. Some children who are *reserved* with strangers are not at all uncommunicative with friends.

13. The problems of the period we are living through are different from those of any previous *era*.

14. Why should I *retract* my statement? It is a perfectly true remark, and I see no reason to withdraw it.

15. CELIA [urging Rosalind to say something]. Why, cousin! Why, Rosalind! . . . Not a word?
    ROSALIND. Not one to throw at a dog.
    CELIA. No, thy words are too precious to be cast away upon *curs*; throw some of them at me.   —William Shakespeare

16. Jerry thought he saw a ship in the distance. I looked carefully but could *perceive* nothing.

17. Nina claims that I started the quarrel, but I have witnesses to prove that she *initiated* it.

18. "He praised her taste, and she *commended* his understanding."—Oliver Goldsmith

19. Students attending private schools pay *tuition*. In the public schools, however, there is no charge for instruction.

20. "His facts no one thought of *disputing*; and his opinions few of the sailors dared to oppose."—Richard Henry Dana

Study Your Lesson Words, Group 3

WORD	MEANING AND TYPICAL USE
cache (*n.*) 'kash	hiding place to store something After confessing, the robber led detectives to a *cache* of stolen gems in the basement.
commend (*v.*) kə'mend	praise; mention favorably; compliment The volunteers were *commended* for their heroic efforts to save lives.
commendable (*adj.*)	praiseworthy; laudable
cur (*n.*) 'kər	worthless dog Lassie is a kind and intelligent animal. Please don't refer to her as a *"cur."*
despotic (*adj.*) də'spät-ik	of a *despot* (a monarch having absolute power); domineering; dictatorial; tyrannical; autocratic The American colonists revolted against the *despotic* rule of George III.
despotism (*n.*)	tyranny; dictatorship
dispute (*v.*) də'spyüt	argue about; debate; declare not true; call into question; oppose; challenge Charley *disputed* my solution until I showed him definite proof that I was right.
disputatious (*adj.*)	argumentative; contentious
edifice (*n.*) 'ed-ə-fəs	building, especially a large or impressive building The huge *edifice* under construction near the airport will be a hotel.
era (*n.*) 'ē-rə or 'ir-ə	historical period; period of time; age; epoch The atomic *era* began with the dropping of the first atomic bomb in 1945.

initiate (*v.*)
ə'nish-ē,āt
	1. begin; introduce; originate; inaugurate
	    The Pilgrims *initiated* the custom of celebrating Thanksgiving Day.
	
	2. put through the ceremony of becoming a member; admit; induct
	    Next Friday our club is going to *initiate* three new members.

initiation (*n.*)	induction; installation

Jolly Roger (*n.*)
'jä-lē'räj-ə(r)

pirates' flag; black flag with white skull and crossbones

The *Jolly Roger* flying from the mast of the approaching ship indicated that it was a pirate ship.

multitude (*n.*)
'məl-tə,tüd

very large number of people or things; crowd; throng; horde; swarm

There was such a *multitude* outside the store waiting for the sale to begin that we decided to return later.

multitudinous (*adj.*)

many; numerous

perceive (*v.*)
pə(r)'sēv

become aware of through the senses; see; note; observe; behold; understand

When the lights went out, I couldn't see a thing, but gradually I was able to *perceive* the outlines of the larger pieces of furniture.

perception (*n.*)

idea; conception

portal (*n.*)
'pȯ(r)-təl

(usually plural) door; entrance, especially, a grand or impressive one; gate

The original doors at the main entrance have been replaced by bronze *portals*.

reserved (*adj.*)
rə'zərvd

1. restrained in speech or action; reticent; uncommunicative; tight-lipped; taciturn

Mark was *reserved* at first but became much more communicative when he got to know us better.

2. unsociable; aloof; withdrawn

restrain (*v.*)
rə'strān

hold back; check; curb; repress; keep under control

Mildred could not *restrain* her impulse to open the package immediately, even though it read, "Do not open before Christmas!"

retract (*v.*)
rə'trakt

draw back; withdraw; take back; unsay

You can depend on Frank. Once he has given his promise, he will not *retract* it.

spine (*n.*)
'spīn

chain of small bones down the middle of the back; backbone

The ribs are curved bones extending from the *spine* and enclosing the upper part of the body.

spineless (*adj.*)

having no backbone; weak; indecisive; cowardly

stroll (*n.*)
'strōl

idle and leisurely walk; ramble

It was a warm spring afternoon, and many people were out for a *stroll*.

timorous (*adj.*)
'tim-ə-rəs

full of fear; afraid; timid

I admit I was *timorous* when I began my speech, but as I went along, I felt less and less afraid.

tuition (*n.*)
tü'i-shən

payment for instruction

When I go to college, I will probably work each summer to help pay the *tuition*.

version (*n.*)
'və(r)-shən

1. account or description from one point of view; interpretation

Now that we have Vera's description of the accident, let us listen to your *version*.

2. translation

THE COUNT OF MONTE CRISTO was written in French, but you can read it in the English *version*.

Apply What You Have Learned

EXERCISE 1.13: SENTENCE COMPLETION

Write the lesson word that best fits the meaning of the sentence. The answers to question 1 are *multitude* and *portal*.

1. A(n) __?__ of desperate depositors gathered outside the closed __?__ s of the ailing bank.
2. If you prove me wrong, I will gladly __?__ my statement.
3. It is hoped that the settlement just reached will __?__ a new __?__ of cooperation between labor and management.
4. Most of us would be too __?__ to try sky-diving.
5. Since you __?__ my __?__ of what was said at today's meeting, I am eager to hear your interpretation.
6. Many college students hold part-time jobs to help pay their __?__ .
7. In our __?__ down Broadway, we passed one magnificent __?__ after another.
8. Sit up straight. Slouching tends to deform the __?__ .
9. It is hard to __?__ why any people would prefer to keep their savings in a(n) __?__ at home, instead of in an insured savings bank.
10. Why are you so __?__ today? Don't you have anything to say?

EXERCISE 1.14: SYNONYMS

Eliminate repetition by replacing the boldfaced word or words with a **synonym** from your lesson words on pages 23–25.

1. Her account of the incident is more believable than your **account.**
2. If he withdraws his objection to the plan, I will **withdraw** mine.
3. The malls were crowded. I had never seen such **crowds** there.
4. Why are they afraid of our dog? There is no reason to be **afraid.**
5. That **large building** was built just a year ago.
6. Your cousins must love arguments; they **argue about** everything.
7. It is hard to communicate with you if you are **uncommunicative**.
8. I knew the **hiding place** where my brother hid his baseball cards.
9. Teachers often **praise** us when we do something praiseworthy.
10. **Curb** your appetite for snacks. If uncurbed, it may cause problems.

EXERCISE 1.15: ANTONYMS

Enter the lesson word from pages 23–25 that is most nearly the **opposite** of the boldfaced word or words.

1. A **valuable poodle** like Muffin is certainly not a(n) _?_ .
2. **Censure** them for their faults, but also _?_ them for their merits.
3. Trained investigators _?_ details that others may **fail to notice.**
4. Nonswimmers are _?_ in a rowboat; swimmers are generally **unafraid.**
5. A **democratic** organization will not tolerate a(n) _?_ president.
6. Be **sociable.** Mingle with the other guests. You are too _?_ .
7. They received **few** complaints, but we got a(n) _?_ of them.
8. Please allow me to _?_ the regrettable statement I **made** earlier.
9. **Let go.** Do not _?_ me.
10. Nations that _?_ hostilities may find it difficult to **end** them.

EXERCISE 1.16: CONCISE WRITING

Express the thought of each sentence in no more than four words.

1. A number of very large and impressive buildings are not being used.
2. How much do you have to pay for the instruction that you are getting?
3. I question the truth of the interpretation that they have presented.
4. The supervisor that we worked for acted like an absolute monarch.
5. Avoid injury to the chain of small bones that runs down the middle of your back.

EXERCISE 1.17: SYNONYM SUMMARY

Each line, when completed, should have three words similar in meaning. The parentheses indicate the number of missing letters. On your answer paper, write the *complete* words. The answers to the first question are **behold, observe,** and **perceive.**

1. beh (1) ld	(2) serve	perc (2) ve
2. q (2) stion	challen (2)	dis (4)
3. c (1) rb	ch (1) ck	(2) strain
4. cr (1) wd	h (1) rde	(3) titude
5. pr (2) se	com (4)	compl (1) ment

6. dictator (4)	(2) ranny	(3) potism
7. orig (1) nate	intr (1) duce	init (2) te
8. (1) ge	epo (2)	(2) a
9. tac (1) turn	reti (1) ent	res (2) ved
10. (2) roll	(1) amble	w (1) lk
11. afr (2) d	(4) ful	(3) orous
12. acc (2) nt	interpr (1) tation	vers (2) n
13. (3) pot (2)	(2) tocratic	domin (2) ring
14. (1) ate	entr (1) nce	(3) tal
15. (2) say	with (4)	(2) tract
16. (2) ea	concept (3)	per (1) e (2) i (2)
17. (2) duction	(2) stallation	in (1) t (2) tion
18. m (1) ny	mu (3) tudinous	num (5)
19. (6) worthy	laud (4)	(3) mend (1) ble
20. arg (1) mentative	conten (2) ous	(3) puta (2) ous

EXERCISE 1.18: ANALOGIES

Which lettered pair of words—*a, b, c, d,* or *e*—most nearly expresses the same relationship as the capitalized pair?

1. CUR : DOG
   - (*a*) calf : cow
   - (*b*) lamb : sheep
   - (*c*) elk : deer
   - (*d*) nag : horse
   - (*e*) tadpole : frog

2. TUITION : INSTRUCTION
   - (*a*) dues : organization
   - (*b*) interest : bank
   - (*c*) rent : shelter
   - (*d*) fine : penalty
   - (*e*) tip : meal

   Hint: **tuition** is payment for **instruction.**

3. STROLL : WALK
   - (*a*) hum : sing
   - (*b*) drawl : speak
   - (*c*) gulp : swallow
   - (*d*) dash : move
   - (*e*) snore : sleep

   Hint: To **stroll** is to walk **slowly.**

4. DISPUTATIOUS : ARGUMENT
   - (*a*) obstinate : compromise
   - (*b*) sociable : company
   - (*c*) restless : delay
   - (*d*) indolent : exercise
   - (*e*) sober : exaggeration

   Hint: A **disputatious** person is fond of **argument.**

5. EDIFICE : BUILDING
- *(a)* apron : garment
- *(b)* closet : storage
- *(c)* canoe : vessel
- *(d)* glider : plane
- *(e)* banquet : meal

6. CACHE : CONCEALMENT
- *(a)* umbrella : rain
- *(b)* barrier : communication
- *(c)* oven : fuel
- *(d)* showcase : privacy
- *(e)* automobile : transportation

7. SPINELESS : WILLPOWER *(HALNO)*
- *(a)* impartial : prejudice
- *(b)* enthusiastic : zeal
- *(c)* inquisitive : curiosity
- *(d)* resentful : anger
- *(e)* dauntless : courage

8. TACITURN : SAY
- *(a)* disgruntled : complain
- *(b)* proficient : accomplish
- *(c)* timid : fear
- *(d)* literate : know
- *(e)* frank : conceal

    Hint: A **taciturn** person has **little** to say.

9. RESTRAINED : FREE
- *(a)* enlightened : educated
- *(b)* reserved : withdrawn
- *(c)* exonerated : guiltless
- *(d)* uninvited : welcome
- *(e)* contented : satisfied

10. JOLLY ROGER : PIRACY
- *(a)* green light : danger
- *(b)* full moon : illumination
- *(c)* white flag : truce
- *(d)* red carpet : hostility
- *(e)* yellow ribbon : cowardice

Pretest 4

Write the meaning of the italicized word or expression. (Look for a *similar* word or expression in the context.)

21. "When all at once I saw a crowd,/A *host* of golden daffodils,"—William Wordsworth

22. Choosing a career is a matter that calls for *reflection*, but I haven't yet given it enough thought.

23. How can Alice *tolerate* your whistling while she is studying? I would never be able to bear it.

24. We can't meet in the music room tomorrow because another group has reserved it. We shall have to *convene* somewhere else.

25. Some of the students who arrive early gather near the main entrance, even though they are not supposed to *congregate* there.

26. "'Ah, so it is!' Edmond said, and, still keeping Mercédès' hand clasped in his, he held the other one out in all friendliness to the Catalan. Instead, however, of responding to this show of *cordiality*, Fernand remained mute and motionless as a statue."—Alexandre Dumas

27. I can *dispense with* a midmorning snack, but I cannot do without lunch.

28. Up to now Diane has always started the disputes; this time Caroline is the *aggressor*.

29. Some pitchers try to *intimidate* batters by throwing fast balls very close to them, but they can't frighten a hitter like Joe.

30. "Rip now resumed his old walks and habits. He soon found many of his former *cronies*, though all rather the worse for the wear and tear of time; so Rip preferred making friends among the younger generation, with whom he soon grew into great favor."—Washington Irving

31. The English Office is at one end of the hall, and the library entrance is at the other *extremity*.

32. "'Slow, lad, slow,' he said. 'They might round upon us in a twinkle of an eye, if we was seen to hurry.'

    "Very *deliberately*, then, did we advance across the sand. . . ."
    —Robert Louis Stevenson

33. Two hours ago the weather bureau predicted rain for tomorrow; now it is *forecasting* rain mixed with snow.

34. The old edition had a *preface*. The new one has no introduction at all.

35. Patricia's dog ran off with our ball and would not *relinquish* it until she made him give it up.

36. By noon we had climbed to a height of more than 2000 feet. From that *altitude*, the housetops in the town below seemed tiny.

37. "He bade me observe it, and I should always find, that the *calamities* of life were shared among the upper and lower part of mankind; but that the middle station had the fewest disasters." —Daniel Defoe

38. Yesterday it looked doubtful that I could finish my report on time. Today, however, it seems less *dubious*.

39. The small fry always drew back in fear when the bully raised a fist, but this time they did not *recoil*.

40. Bears and bats *hibernate* in caves; frogs and lizards spend the winter in the earth, below the frost line.

Study Your Lesson Words, Group 4

WORD	MEANING AND TYPICAL USE
aggressor (*n.*) ə'gres-ə(r)	person or nation that initiates hostilities or makes an unprovoked attack; assailant; invader In World War II, Japan was the *aggressor*; its surprise attack on Pearl Harbor started the conflict in the Pacific.
aggression (*n.*)	unprovoked attack; assault; invasion
altitude (*n.*) 'al-tə,tyüd	height; elevation; high position; eminence Mount Washington, which rises to an *altitude* of 6,288 feet, is the highest peak in the White Mountains.
calamity (*n.*) kə'la-mə-tē	great misfortune; catastrophe; disaster The assassinations of John F. Kennedy and Martin Luther King, Jr. were national *calamities*.
calamitous (*adj.*)	disastrous; catastrophic
congregate (*v.*) 'kän-grə,gāt	come together into a crowd; assemble; gather Some homeowners near the school do not like students to *congregate* on their property.
convene (*v.*) kən'vēn	meet in a group for a specific purpose The board of directors will *convene* next Tuesday to elect a new corporation president.
convention (*n.*)	treaty; agreement
cordiality (*n.*) kȯ(r)'jal-ə-tē	friendliness; warmth of regard; amiability Pam's parents greeted me with *cordiality* and made me feel like an old friend of the family.
cordial (*adj.*)	warm and friendly; gracious; hearty
crony (*n.*) 'krō-nē	close companion; intimate friend; chum; associate Some students socialize only with their *cronies* and rarely try to make new friends.
deliberately (*adv.*) də'lib-ər-ət-lē	1. in a carefully thought out manner; purposely; intentionally We *deliberately* kept Glenda off the planning committee because we didn't want her to know that the party was to be in her honor.

2. in an unhurried manner; slowly
Dad was late because he had to drive *deliberately*; the roads were icy.

dispense (*v.*)
də'spens

1. deal out; distribute
Some charitable organizations *dispense* food to the needy.

2. (followed by the preposition *with*) do without; get along without; forgo
When our club has a guest speaker, we *dispense with* the reading of the minutes to save time.

dubious (*adj.*)
'dyü-bē-əs

doubtful; uncertain; questionable
There is no doubt about my feeling better, but it is *dubious* that I can be back at school by tomorrow.

extremity (*n.*)
ək'strem-ə-tē

very end; utmost limit; border
Key West is at the southern *extremity* of Florida.

forecast (*v.*)
'fȯ(r),kast

predict; foretell; prophesy; prognosticate
The price of oranges has gone up again, as you *forecasted*.

hibernate (*v.*)
'hī-bə(r),nāt

spend the winter
If Sue's grandparents had had the funds to *hibernate* in Florida, they would not have spent the winter at home.

host (*n.*)
'hōst

1. large number; multitude; throng; crowd; flock
The merchant had expected a *host* of customers, but only a few appeared.

2. person who receives or entertains a guest or guests at home or elsewhere (Note also: *hostess*—a woman who serves as a *host*)
Dad treats his guests with the utmost cordiality; he is an excellent *host*.

intimidate (*v.*)
ən'ti-mə,dāt

frighten; influence by fear; cow; overawe; coerce
A few spectators were *intimidated* by the lion's roar, but most were not frightened.

preface (*n.*)
'pre-fəs

introduction (to a book or speech); foreword; prologue; preamble; exordium
Begin by reading the *preface*; it will help you to get the most out of the rest of the book.

preface (*v.*)   introduce or begin with a preface; usher in; precede
　　　　　　　　　　Usually, I get right into my speech, but this time I *prefaced* it with an amusing anecdote.

recoil (*v.*)   draw back because of fear or disgust; shrink; wince; flinch
rə'koil
　　　　　　　　　　Marie *recoiled* at the thought of singing in the amateur show, but she went through with it because she had promised to participate.

reflection (*n.*)   1. thought, especially careful thought; cogitation; deliberation
rə'flek-shən
　　　　　　　　　　When a question is complicated, don't give the first answer that comes to mind. Take time for *reflection*.

　　　　　　　　　　2. blame; discredit; aspersion; slur
　　　　　　　　　　Yesterday's defeat was no *reflection* on our players; they did their very best.

relinquish (*v.*)   give up; abandon; let go; release; surrender; cede
rə'liŋ-kwəsh
　　　　　　　　　　When an elderly man entered the crowded bus, one of the students *relinquished* her seat to him.

tolerate (*v.*)   endure; bear; put up with; accept; permit
'täl-ə,rāt
　　　　　　　　　　Very young children will cry when rebuked; they cannot *tolerate* criticism.

tolerable (*adj.*)   bearable; endurable

Apply What You Have Learned

EXERCISE 1.19: SENTENCE COMPLETION

Write the lesson word that best fits the meaning of the sentence.

1. Many a(n) __?__ has occurred in the Alps on the Matterhorn, an almost unscalable mountain that rises to a(n) __?__ of 14,700 feet.
2. My teammates are confident of victory, but I am inclined to be __?__ .
3. We will __?__ no more delays because our patience has already been stretched to its __?__ .
4. The author's __?__ precedes the table of contents.
5. The United Nations has always called upon __?__ s to __?__ the territories they have seized.
6. If you stop to feed one pigeon, a flock of them will soon __?__ around you.
7. The candidate used to be a(n) __?__ of mine, but since our dispute there has not been much __?__ between us.
8. The __?__ greeted each of his guests with a cordial handshake.
9. Since this matter is important, let us proceed __?__ rather than hastily, with ample time for discussion and __?__ .
10. Lower winter air fares will probably encourage more Northerners to __?__ in the South this year.

EXERCISE 1.20: SYNONYMS

Eliminate repetition by replacing the boldfaced word or words with a **synonym** from your lesson words on pages 32–34.

1. They cannot **frighten** that reporter with threats; she is not easily frightened.
2. Cassandra was able to **predict** future events, but no one ever believed her predictions.
3. Will they **assemble** here or at some other place of assembly?
4. People have reluctantly put up with increases in taxes, but they refuse to **put up with** reductions in services.
5. All her guests were **close friends** with whom she has been friendly since grade school.
6. Our neighbor speaks **in an unhurried way**; he is never in a hurry.
7. We do not question your facts, but we think your interpretation of them is **questionable**.

8. The two are supposed to be friends, but sometimes there is no **friendliness** between them.
9. That family has had great misfortunes, but never such a **great misfortune** as this one.
10. Many youngsters will gladly forgo vegetables but are most reluctant to **forgo** dessert.

EXERCISE 1.21: ANTONYMS

Enter the lesson word that is most nearly the **opposite** of the boldfaced word or words.

1. When David saw others __?__ from the giant Goliath, he went out with his sling to **confront** him.
2. The crowds that __?__ at the scene of an accident are often slow to **disperse.**
3. Don't __?__ all your supplies; **keep** some for yourself.
4. I **inadvertently** neglected to say hello, but she thought I had done it __?__ .
5. The first **guest** arrived with a small present for the __?__ .
6. The __?__ is brief, but the **index** runs to more than six pages.
7. The **invaded nation** is fighting to repel the __?__ .
8. Sometimes what appears to be a(n) __?__ turns out to be a **boon.**
9. Some who **spend the summer** in Maine __?__ in Arizona.
10. We are **certain** about the election returns that have been verified, but we are __?__ about some of the others.

EXERCISE 1.22: CONCISE WRITING

Express the thought of each sentence in **no more than four words.**

1. I spoke without giving careful thought to what I was saying.
2. The one who had invited us to her home as guests was warm and friendly.
3. Has the individual who made the unprovoked attack offered an apology?
4. What is it that made you draw back in disgust?
5. Read the introduction to the book in an unhurried manner.

EXERCISE 1.23: SYNONYM SUMMARY

Each line when completed, should have three words similar in meaning. The parentheses indicate the number of missing letters. On your answer paper, write the *complete* words. The answers to the first question are **doubtful, questionable,** and **dubious.**

1. dou (1) tful	q (2) stionable	dub (4)
2. h (2) ght	el (1) vation	alt (2) ude
3. ab (2) don	c (1) d (1)	(2) linquish
4. pred (2) t	prophe (1) y	(4) cast
5. gath (2)	(2) semble	(3) gregate
6. b (2) rable	(2) durable	toler (4)
7. ch (1) m	as (2) ciate	(2) ony
8. (2) vasion	ass (2) lt	ag (1) r (2) sion
9. grac (4)	h (2) rty	cord (2) l
10. thr (2) g	(3) titude	h (2) t
11. dis (2) trous	(4) strophic	(2) lamit (3)
12. co (1) rce	(1) ow	(2) timid (3)
13. ac (1) ept	en (3) e	(2) lerate
14. p (2) posely	(2) tentionally	de (3) erately
15. shr (2) k	(2) nce	rec (2) l
16. (2) liberation	cog (1) tation	(2) flec (4)
17. fr (2) ndliness	am (2) bility	(3) diality
18. agr (2) ment	tr (2) ty	(3) vention
19. l (1) mit	b (2) der	ex (3) mity
20. pre (2) ble	ex (2) dium	(3) face

EXERCISE 1.24: ANALOGIES

Which lettered pair of words—*a, b, c, d,* or *e*—most nearly expresses the same relationship as the capitalized pair?

1. CALAMITY : MISFORTUNE
   - (a) hill : mountain
   - (b) deluge : rainfall
   - (c) crime : misdemeanor
   - (d) brook : river
   - (e) lake : ocean

   Hint: A **calamity** is a great misfortune.

2. PREFACE : INDEX
- *(a)* initiation : club
- *(b)* mouth : river
- *(c)* appetizer : dessert
- *(d)* sunrise : noon
- *(e)* lobby : edifice

Hint: A **preface** is the first part of a book; an **index** is the last.

3. RELINQUISH : ABANDON
- *(a)* wane : flourish
- *(b)* convene : adjourn
- *(c)* submit : defy
- *(d)* repel : attract
- *(e)* extinguish : quench

4. INVADER : AGGRESSION
- *(a)* burglar : arson
- *(b)* lawbreaker : arrest
- *(c)* liar : perjury
- *(d)* shoplifter : penalty
- *(e)* swindler : greed

Hint: An **invader** commits **aggression.**

5. CONGREGATE : DISPERSE
- *(a)* hesitate : waver
- *(b)* prognosticate : foretell
- *(c)* cow : coerce
- *(d)* flinch : wince
- *(e)* commend : reprimand

6. LOATHSOME : RECOIL
- *(a)* incredible : believe
- *(b)* irritating : relax
- *(c)* spectacular : gasp
- *(d)* interesting : yawn
- *(e)* illegible : understand

Hint: Something that is **loathsome** makes us **recoil.**

7. ALTITUDE : DEPTH
- *(a)* significance : importance
- *(b)* confidence : doubt
- *(c)* anxiety : worry
- *(d)* mitigation : relief
- *(e)* version : interpretation

8. INTOLERABLE : ENDURE
- *(a)* intelligible : comprehend
- *(b)* complicated : simplify
- *(c)* palatable : consume
- *(d)* inequitable : justify
- *(e)* accessible : approach

9. COGITATION : BRAIN
- *(a)* digestion : stomach
- *(b)* air : lungs
- *(c)* perspiration : exertion
- *(d)* backbone : spine
- *(e)* nutrition : food

10. HOST : MULTITUDE
- *(a)* novice : veteran
- *(b)* masterpiece : reproduction
- *(c)* crony : chum
- *(d)* cordiality : hostility
- *(e)* guest : courtesy

Part 3.
"Commonsense" Contexts

Do you know what *famished* means? If not, you should be able to tell from the following context:

> "The morning had passed away, and Rip felt *famished* for want of his breakfast."
>
> —Washington Irving

How do you feel when the morning has gone by and you have not had breakfast? Very hungry, of course, even starved. Therefore, *famished* in the above context must mean "very hungry."

Note that the above context is different from those we have had so far. It has neither an opposite word nor a similar word to help with the meaning of *famished*. It does, however, offer a clue in the words "for want of his breakfast," so that you can get the meaning by using *common sense*.

Here is another commonsense context. Can you tell what *inundated* means in the sentence below?

> As a result of a break in the water main, many cellars in the area were inundated.

What happens to cellars when a nearby water main breaks? They become flooded, naturally. Therefore, *inundated* in the above context must mean "flooded."

Pretest 5

Here are some more commonsense contexts. Each contains a clue or clues to the meaning of the italicized word. Discover the meaning by using common sense, as in the previous examples.

1. "Mrs. Linton's funeral was appointed to take place on the Friday after her *decease*."—Emily Brontë
2. The race ended in a tie when Paul and Abe crossed the finish line *simultaneously*.
3. If you stand up in the boat, it may *capsize*, and we'll find ourselves in the water.
4. I cannot tell you the secret unless you promise not to *divulge* it.

5. "I now made one or two attempts to speak to my brother, but in some manner which I could not understand the *din* had so increased that I could not make him hear a single word, although I screamed at the top of my voice in his ear."—Edgar Allan Poe

6. We had no use for our flashlights; the moon *illuminated* our path very clearly.

7. Sandra became *incensed* when I refused to return her library books for her, and she has not spoken to me since then.

8. The President heads our national government, the Governor our state government, and the Mayor our *municipal* government.

9. On February 12, 1809, in a Kentucky log cabin, there was born a boy who *subsequently* became the sixteenth President of the United States.

10. "All was dark within, so that I could *distinguish* nothing by the eye." —Robert Louis Stevenson

11. There was a noise like the explosion of a firecracker when Karen *punctured* the balloon with a pin.

12. President Franklin D. Roosevelt died in 1945, and his wife, Eleanor, in 1962; she *survived* him by seventeen years.

13. Every time you cross a busy street against the light, you are putting your life in *jeopardy*.

14. By automobile, you can *traverse* the bridge in two minutes; on foot it takes about half an hour.

15. "I was witness to events of a less peaceful character. One day when I went out to my woodpile, or rather my pile of stumps, I observed two large ants, the one red, the other much larger, nearly half an inch long, and black, fiercely *contending* with one another—Henry David Thoreau

16. The microscope is of the utmost importance in the study of biology because it can *magnify* objects too small to be seen by the naked eye.

17. At one point during the hurricane, the winds reached a *velocity* of 130 miles an hour.

18. Farmers will be in trouble unless the *drought* ends soon; it hasn't rained in six weeks.

19. The speaker should have used the microphone. Her voice was *inaudible*, except to those near the platform.

20. "However, at low water I went on board, and though I thought I had *rummaged* the cabin so effectually, as that nothing more could be found, yet I discovered a locker with drawers in it, in one of which I found two or three razors, and one pair of large scissors, with some ten or a dozen of good knives and forks. . . ."—Daniel Defoe

Study Your Lesson Words, Group 5

WORD	MEANING AND TYPICAL USE
capsize (*v.*) 'kap,sīz or kap'sīz	overturn; upset When Sam's canoe *capsized*, I swam over to help him turn it right side up.

contend (*v.*)
 kən'tend
	1. compete; vie; take part in a contest; fight; struggle
	    Every spring some baseball writers try to predict which two teams will *contend* in the next World Series.
	
	 2. argue; maintain as true; assert
	    Don't argue with the umpire. If he says you are out, it's no use *contending* you are safe.

contentious (*adj.*)	quarrelsome; belligerent
decease (*n.*) də'sēs	death; demise Shortly after President Kennedy's *decease*, Vice President Johnson was sworn in as the new Chief Executive.
din (*n.*) 'din	loud noise; uproar; clamor; racket I couldn't hear what you were saying because the jet plane that was passing made such a *din*.
distinguish (*v.*) də'stiŋ-gwish	tell apart; differentiate; recognize The twins are so alike that it is hard to *distinguish* one from the other.
divulge (*v.*) də'vəlj or dī'vəlj	make known; reveal; disclose Yesterday our teacher read us a composition without *divulging* the name of the writer.
drought (*n.*) 'draủt	long period of dry weather; lack of rain; dryness While some regions are suffering from *drought*, others are experiencing heavy rains and floods.
famish (*v.*) 'fam-ish	starve; suffer from extreme hunger; make extremely hungry The missing hikers were *famished* when we found them; they had not eaten for more than twelve hours.
illuminate (*v.*) ə'lyüm-ə,nāt	light up; lighten; brighten The bright morning sun *illuminated* the room; there was no need for the lights to be on.

inaudible (*adj.*)
in'ò-də-bəl

incapable of being heard; not audible
The only part of your answer I could hear was the first word; the rest was *inaudible*.

incense (*v.*)
in'sens

make extremely angry; enrage; madden; infuriate
Some of the members were so *incensed* by the way Ruth opened the meeting that they walked right out.

inundate (*v.*)
'in-ən,dāt

flood; swamp; deluge
The rainstorm *inundated* a number of streets in low-lying areas.

jeopardy (*n.*)
'je-pə(r)-dē

danger; peril
If you are late for the employment interview, your chance of getting the job will be in serious *jeopardy*.

jeopardize (*v.*)

endanger; imperil

magnify (*v.*)
'mag-nə-fī

cause to be or look larger; enlarge; amplify; exaggerate
The bacteria shown in your textbook have been greatly *magnified*; their actual size is considerably smaller.

municipal (*adj.*)
myü'nis-ə-pəl

of a city or town
Your mother works for the city? How interesting! My father is also a *municipal* employee.

puncture (*v.*)
'pəŋk-chə(r)

make a hole with a pointed object; pierce; perforate
Our neighbor swept a nail off his curb, and later it *punctured* one of his own tires.

rummage (*v.*)
'rəm-ij

search thoroughly by turning over all the contents; ransack
Someone must have *rummaged* my desk; everything in it is in disorder.

simultaneously (*adv.*)
,sī-məl'tā-nē-əs-lē

at the same time; concurrently; together
The twins began school *simultaneously*, but they did not graduate at the same time.

subsequently (*adv.*)
'səb-sə-kwənt-lē

later; afterward; next
When I first saw that dress, it was $49.95; *subsequently* it was reduced to $29.95; now it is on sale for $19.95.

survive (*v.*)
sə(r)'vīv

live longer than; outlive; outlast
    After landing at Plymouth, the Pilgrims suffered greatly; about half of them failed to *survive* the first winter.

traverse (*v.*)
trə'vərs

pass across, over, or through; cross
    The Trans-Siberian Railroad, completed in 1905, *traverses* the Asian continent.

velocity (*n.*)
və'lä-sə-tē

speed; swiftness; celerity; rapidity
    Do you know that light travels at a *velocity* of 186,000 miles a second?

Apply What You Have Learned

EXERCISE 1.25: SENTENCE COMPLETION

Write the lesson word that best fits the meaning of the sentence.

1. If that beached whale is to __?__ , we must get it back into the water.
2. At its maximum __?__ , the express train can __?__ the entire state in less than two hours.
3. Though she has a strong voice, her words were almost __?__d by the __?__ of the chanting crowd.
4. While Sal __?__d the attic, I __?__ searched the basement, but we failed to find the old comic books.
5. After the boat __?__d, we had to __?__ with the strong current as we swam shoreward.
6. The __?__ employees were __?__d when the Mayor refused to raise their salaries.
7. The doctor's __?__ put the health of the community in __?__ because no other physician was willing to practice in that remote area.
8. I know the Bakers well, but in their Halloween costumes I could not __?__ them from the other guests.
9. Driving is difficult on a moonless night when there are no street lights to __?__ the road.
10. The candidate attempted to __?__ his achievements, but his exaggerations were __?__d by the reporter's sharp questioning.

EXERCISE 1.26: SYNONYMS

Eliminate repetition by replacing the boldfaced word or words with a **synonym** from your lesson words.

1. Tanks can pass over terrain that civilian vehicles cannot **pass through.**
2. When he is in a rage, do not say anything that will **enrage** him further.
3. The forests are especially dry because we have had a **long period of dry weather.**
4. Those who drive today are putting their lives in **danger** because the roads are icy and dangerous.
5. If you lean over the side of the boat, you may **turn it over.**
6. Steve maintains that you started the fight, and you **maintain** that he did.
7. Even with flood control, the Mississippi will occasionally **flood** millions of acres.

8. The speeding vehicle was clocked at a **speed** of 90 miles an hour.

9. Many who had outlived previous earthquakes did not **outlive** this one.

10. The findings have not been disclosed; the committee will **disclose** them at the proper time.

EXERCISE 1.27: ANTONYMS

On your answer paper, enter the lesson word that is most nearly the **opposite** of the boldfaced word or words.

1. Savers are concerned about the **safety** of their deposits and do not want them to be put in __?__ .

2. In the flood, eighty-four people **perished,** nine are missing, and eleven __?__ d .

3. Let us neither __?__ our accomplishments nor **minimize** our failures.

4. The brightly __?__ d business district was momentarily **darkened** by a sudden power outage.

5. Skills **previously** acquired may __?__ serve us in good stead.

6. I often **confuse** one twin with the other. How are you able to __?__ them?

7. Admirers of the late leader faithfully observe the anniversaries of his **birth** and __?__ .

8. The **stillness** of the early morning was abruptly broken by the __?__ of wailing sirens.

9. Angela was so __?__ d that she could not be **placated.**

10. The two letters were mailed **at different times,** but they arrived __?__ .

EXERCISE 1.28: CONCISE WRITING

Express the thought of each sentence in **no more than four words**.

1. The long period of dry weather has come to an end.
2. Burglars searched through the cabinets, turning over all the contents.
3. The charges that they were making made her extremely angry.
4. Someone made a hole in that tank with a pointed instrument.
5. Light from the moon lit up the path that we were following.

EXERCISE 1.29: SYNONYM SUMMARY

Each line, when completed, should have three words similar in meaning. The parentheses indicate the number of missing letters. On your answer paper, write the *complete* words. The answers to the first question are **search, ransack,** and **rummage.**

1. s (2) rch	(3) sack	rum (4)
2. per (1) l	dan (3)	(3) pardy
3. sp (2) d	(2) lerity	(4) city
4. (2) set	(4) turn	caps (3)
5. quarrel (4)	bel (4) rent	conten (2) ous
6. d (2) th	(2) mise	(2) cease
7. (2) rage	in (3) se	(2) furi (3)
8. p (2) rce	per (6)	punc (4)
9. clam (1) r	(2) roar	(1) i (1)
10. bri (2) ten	(2) ghten	(2) lumin (3)
11. arg (2)	(3) tend	(2) sert
12. (2) gether	(3) currently	simul (4) ously
13. sw (1) mp	delu (2)	in (2) date
14. different (2) te	rec (2) nize	disting (2) sh
15. (3) live	out (2) st	surv (3)
16. di (3) ge	(3) close	rev (2) l
17. (2) terward	lat (2)	(3) sequently
18. (2) large	ampl (1) fy	magn (3)
19. (2) danger	imp (4)	j (2) pard (3)
20. muni (2) pal	(1) ity	t (2) n

EXERCISE 1.30: ANALOGIES

Which lettered pair of words—*a, b, c, d,* or *e*—most nearly expresses the same relationship as the capitalized pair?

1. AMPLIFY : ENLARGE
   (a) ban : allow
   (c) censure : commend
   (e) specify : incense
   (b) survive : perish
   (d) imperil : jeopardize

2. DROUGHT : RAIN
   (a) curiosity : interest
   (c) aloofness : privacy
   (e) frankness : honesty
   (b) famine : hunger
   (d) indifference : concern

3. HARE : CELERITY
  (a) lion : timidity   (b) chicken : courage
  (c) ant : industriousness   (d) bat : vision
  (e) spider : impatience

4. DECEASE : INTERMENT
  (a) cloudburst : inundation   (b) index : preface
  (c) inauguration : election   (d) evening : afternoon
  (e) childhood : infancy
    Hint: **Decease** is followed by **interment.**

5. CAPSIZE : RIGHT
  (a) raze : demolish   (b) suffice : do
  (c) perforate : puncture   (d) madden : incense
  (e) damage : repair
    Hint: To **capsize** is the opposite of to **right.**

6. TRESPASSER : TRAVERSE
  (a) builder : construct   (b) vendor : sell
  (c) pedestrian : walk   (d) transient : travel
  (e) thief : take
    Hint: A **trespasser traverses** another's property illegally.

7. RUMMAGE : SEARCH
  (a) vanquish : defeat   (b) scorch : burn
  (c) simmer : boil   (d) chill : freeze
  (e) whisper : shout

8. CONTENDER : VIE
  (a) emmissary : send   (b) aggressor : fear
  (c) outcast : reject   (d) victim : assault
  (e) dissenter : object

9. SECRET : DIVULGE
  (a) promise : keep   (b) thorn : remove
  (c) warning : ignore   (d) defect : correct
  (e) debt : pay

10. DIN : NOISE
  (a) garment : shirt   (b) vanilla : flavor
  (c) coin : dime   (d) color : purple
  (e) tool : saw
    Hint: A **din** is a **kind of noise.**

Pretest 6

By using the commonsense method, determine the meaning of the italicized words below.

21. "Now, the point of the story is this: Did the tiger come out of that door, or did the lady? The more we *reflect* upon this question, the harder it is to answer."—Frank R. Stockton

22. According to the rules, as soon as you lose a match, you are *eliminated* from the tournament.

23. In the midst of waxing the car, I became so *fatigued* that I had to stop for a rest.

24. Realizing that I was going the wrong way on a one-way street, I quickly *reversed* direction.

25. "And he took care of me and loved me from the first, and I'll *cleave* to him as long as he lives, and nobody shall ever come between him and me."—George Eliot

26. My father is a sales agent, but I plan to go into some other *vocation*.

27. Tenants usually do not stop complaining about the lack of heat until they are *content* with the temperature.

28. The speaker kept the audience laughing with one *facetious* remark after another.

29. Ms. Muldoon thought I was to blame for the whispering, unaware that the girl behind me was the true *culprit*.

30. "We set out with a fresh wind . . . never dreaming of danger, for indeed we saw not the slightest reason to *apprehend* it."—Edgar Allan Poe

31. In your sentence, "She refused to accept my invitation to the party," omit the words "to accept"; they are *superfluous*.

32. In New York City, Philadelphia, Chicago, Los Angeles, and most other large *urban* centers, traffic is a serious problem.

33. Room 109 is too small for our club; it can *accommodate* only 35, and we have 48 members.

34. Everyone makes a mistake once in a while; no one is *infallible*.

35. "Now, in the whale-ship, it is not every one that goes in the boats. Some few hands are reserved, called ship-keepers, whose *province* it is to work the vessel while the boats are pursuing the whale."—Herman Melville

36. Don't dive there! The water is too *shallow*! Do you want to fracture your skull?

37. The detectives continued their search of the apartment, believing that the missing letter was *concealed* somewhere in it.

38. There are no clothing shops in the *vicinity* of the school; the nearest one is about a mile away.

39. To halt the *pilfering* of construction materials, the builder has decided to hire security guards.

40. "Then he advanced to the stockade, threw over his crutch, got a leg up, and with great vigor and skill succeeded in *surmounting* the fence and dropping safely to the other side."—Robert Louis Stevenson

Study Your Lesson Words, Group 6

WORD	MEANING AND TYPICAL USE
accommodate (*v.*) ə′käm-ə,dāt	1. hold or contain without crowding or inconvenience; have room for The new restaurant will *accommodate* 128 persons. 2. oblige; do a favor for; furnish with something desired I'm sorry I have no pen to lend you. Ask Norman. Perhaps he can *accommodate* you.
apprehend (*v.*) ,a-prə′hend	1. anticipate (foresee) with fear; dread Now I see how foolish I was to *apprehend* the outcome of the test. I passed easily. 2. arrest The escaped prisoners were *apprehended* as they tried to cross the border.
apprehension (*n.*)	alarm; uneasiness
apprehensive (*adj.*)	fearful; afraid
cleave (*v.*) ′klēv	stick; adhere; cling; be faithful Some of the residents are hostile to new ways; they *cleave* to the customs and traditions of the past.
conceal (*v.*) kən′sēl	keep secret; withdraw from observation; hide; secrete I answered all questions truthfully, for I had nothing to *conceal*.
content (*adj.*) kən′tent	satisfied; pleased If you are not *content* with the merchandise, you may return it for an exchange or a refund.

culprit (*n.*)
'kəl-prət

one guilty of a fault or crime; offender; wrong-doer
The last time we were late for the party, I was the *culprit*. I wasn't ready when you called for me.

eliminate (*v.*)
ə'lim-ə,nāt

drop; exclude; remove; get rid of; rule out
The new director hopes to reduce expenses by *eliminating* unnecessary jobs.

facetious (*adj.*)
fə'sē-shəs

given to joking; not to be taken seriously; witty; funny
Bea meant it when she said she was quitting the team. She was not being *facetious*.

fatigue (*v.*)
fə'tēg

tire; exhaust; weary
Why not take the elevator? Climbing the stairs will *fatigue* you.

fatigue (*n.*)

exhaustion; weariness

infallible (*adj.*)
in'fa-lə-bəl

incapable of being in error; sure; certain; absolutely reliable
When Phil disputes my answer or I question his, we take it to our math teacher. We consider her judgment *infallible*.

pilfer (*v.*)
'pil-fə(r)

steal (in small amounts); purloin
The shoplifter was apprehended after *pilfering* several small articles.

province (*n.*)
'prä-vəns

1. proper business or duty; sphere; jurisdiction
If your brother misbehaves, you have no right to punish him; that is not your *province*.

2. territory; region; domain

reflect (*v.*)
rə'flekt

think carefully; meditate; contemplate
I could have given a much better answer if I had had the time to *reflect*.

reverse (*v.*)
rə'vərs

turn completely about; change to the opposite position; revoke; annul
If found guilty, a person may appeal to a higher court in the hope that it will *reverse* the verdict.

reverse (*n.*)

setback; defeat; reversal
In 1805, Napoleon's fleet met with a serious *reverse* at the Battle of Trafalgar.

reversible (*adj.*)

able to be worn with either side out

shallow (*adj.*)
'sha-lō

1. not deep
   Nonswimmers must use the *shallow* part of the pool.

2. lacking intellectual depth; superficial; uncritical

superfluous (*adj.*)
sü'pər-flə-wəs

beyond what is necessary or desirable; surplus; needless
   We already have enough volunteers; additional help would be *superfluous*.

surmount (*v.*)
sər'maúnt

conquer; overcome; climb over
   At the end of the third quarter, the visitors were ahead by 18 points, a lead that our team was unable to *surmount*.

urban (*adj.*)
'ər-bən

having to do with cities or towns
   In the United States today, the *urban* population far outnumbers the farm population.

vicinity (*n.*)
və'sin-ə-tē

neighborhood; locality; region about or near a place
   Lost: Tan cat answering to ''Tiger.'' *Vicinity* of Main Street and First Avenue. Reward. 912-0146.

vocation (*n.*)
vō'kā-shən

occupation; calling; business; trade; profession
   Ruth will be studying to be an engineer. Bob plans to enter teaching. I, however, have not yet chosen a *vocation*.

Apply What You Have Learned

EXERCISE 1.31: SENTENCE COMPLETION

Write the lesson word that best fits the meaning of the sentence.

1. Most __?__ residents are __?__ to live in the city, despite its many problems.
2. The warden's staff carefully searched the __?__ of the zoo, hoping to __?__ the escaped tiger.
3. Only after practicing law for three years did Deirdre realize that medicine was her true __?__ .
4. If you want your writing to be concise, you must __?__ all __?__ words.
5. The new auditorium can __?__ three thousand people.
6. The police are empowered to arrest, but not to punish, an alleged __?__ because punishment is the __?__ of the courts.
7. The weary runner __?__ed her exhaustion with a final burst of speed to win the six-mile race.
8. If building supplies are left unattended at the construction site, someone may __?__ them.
9. After pausing to __?__, the speaker __?__d his position because he realized he had been completely wrong.
10. You shouldn't have taken me seriously when I boasted that my judgment is __?__ , for I was only being __?__ .

EXERCISE 1.32: SYNONYMS

Eliminate repetition by replacing the boldfaced word or words with a **synonym** from your lesson words.

1. Teaching children is not solely the **duty** of the schools; it is also a parental duty.
2. The new busses are roomier; they **have room for** thirty-six passengers.
3. There are no food shops in this neighborhood, but there are several in the **neighborhood** of the railroad station.
4. Even the experts are sometimes in error; no one is **absolutely incapable of error.**
5. A century ago, children generally followed the occupation of their elders, instead of choosing **an occupation** of their own.
6. It is not enough to get rid of spelling errors in your writing; you must also **get rid of** unnecessary words.

7. Prior to today's **defeat,** we were the only undefeated team in the league.
8. Physical exercise makes us very tired, though it does not seem to **tire** our gym instructor.
9. Progress is slow on the section of the highway near the city because of heavy **city** traffic.
10. The person initially blamed for the offense was not the real **offender.**

EXERCISE 1.33: ANTONYMS

On your answer paper, enter the lesson word that is most nearly the **opposite** of the boldfaced word.

1. Here, the water is __?__, but a few feet out it is quite **deep.**
2. Weather forecasters are sometimes **wrong;** they are not __?__.
3. Are more helpers **necessary,** or would they just be __?__?
4. I felt **refreshed** by our stroll along the beach, but my companion was __?__ed.
5. Some are __?__ with the outcome; others are **dissatisfied.**
6. The lawmakers decided to __?__ some of the jobs they had just voted to **create.**
7. If you say you are famished after that filling seven-course dinner, you cannot be **serious;** you are being __?__.
8. Let us __?__ to the principles of law and justice; we cannot **abandon** them.
9. Facts that for years were __?__ed from the public are now being **revealed.**
10. When the suspect was __?__ed, her attorneys petitioned a judge to **release** her.

EXERCISE 1.34: CONCISE WRITING

Express the thought of each sentence in **no more than four words.**

1. Are these coats able to be worn with either side out?
2. The opinions that he expresses are lacking in intellectual depth.
3. Most of the hotels have rooms for guests staying for only a short time.
4. The remarks that she made were not intended to be taken seriously.
5. We made a complete about-face and embraced the opposite point of view.

EXERCISE 1.35: SYNONYM SUMMARY

Each line, when completed, should have three words similar in meaning. The parentheses indicate the number of missing letters. On your answer paper, write the *complete* words. The answers to the first question are **tire, exhaust,** and **fatigue.**

1. t (1) re	ex (1) aust	fati (3)
2. conq (2) r	(4) come	(3) mount
3. (2) raid	appre (3) sive	fear (3)
4. occu (2) tion	(3) fession	(2) cation
5. satisf (2) d	pl (2) sed	con (2) nt
6. n (2) ghborhood	(2) cality	vi (3) ity
7. med (1) tate	con (3) plate	(2) flect
8. h (1) de	sec (2) te	con (1) eal
9. wit (2)	fun (1) y	face (3) us
10. (2) feat	(3) back	(2) verse
11. (2) move	ex (3) de	e (3) inate
12. st (2) l	(3) loin	pilf (2)
13. need (4)	surp (2) s	su (3) fluous
14. cl (1) ng	(2) here	cl (2) ve
15. h (1) ld	cont (2) n	accom (2) date
16. (2) critical	superfi (3) l	shal (3)
17. s (1) re	cert (2) n	inf (3) ible
18. of (3) der	wrongd (2) r	(3) prit
19. d (1) ty	b (1) s (1) ness	prov (4)
20. (1) larm	(2) easiness	ap (3) hension

EXERCISE 1.36: ANALOGIES

Which lettered pair of words—*a, b, c, d,* or *e*—most nearly expresses the same relationship as the capitalized pair?

1. SHALLOW : DEEP
   - (a) remote : distant
   - (c) scarce : abundant
   - (e) depressing : sad
   - (b) frigid : cold
   - (d) transient : brief

2. PROVINCE : COUNTRY
   - (a) story : edifice
   - (c) month : day
   - (e) flock : bird
   - (b) island : sea
   - (d) hand : finger

3. OBLIGING : ACCOMMODATE
   - (a) timorous : complain
   - (b) reticent : gossip
   - (c) industrious : loaf
   - (d) contentious : argue
   - (e) obstinate : yield

4. CULPRIT : REPRIMAND
   - (a) victim : suffer
   - (b) hostage : release
   - (c) tutor : instruct
   - (d) donor : give
   - (e) tenant : rent

5. SHOPLIFTER : PILFER
   - (a) dissenter : concur
   - (b) scofflaw : obey
   - (c) transient : remain
   - (d) perjurer : lie
   - (e) vagrant : reside

6. APPREHENSIVE : CONFIDENCE
   - (a) appreciative : gratitude
   - (b) cordial : warmth
   - (c) diplomatic : tact
   - (d) polite : manners
   - (e) spineless : determination

7. CONTENT : DISSATISFIED
   - (a) normal : atypical
   - (b) lukewarm : tepid
   - (c) rare : extraordinary
   - (d) enthusiastic : zealous
   - (e) despotic : authoritarian

8. URBAN : CITY
   - (a) metropolitan : town
   - (b) suburban : nation
   - (c) global : world
   - (d) national : region
   - (e) municipal : state

9. MEDITATE : MIND
   - (a) grope : eyes
   - (b) kneel : ground
   - (c) swelter : perspiration
   - (d) speak : tongue
   - (e) yell : din

10. REFLECT : CONTEMPLATION
    - (a) confront : timidity
    - (b) plan : confusion
    - (c) confess : guilt
    - (d) swerve : collision
    - (e) intimidate : coercion

    Hint: When we **reflect,** we engage in **contemplation.**

Part 4

Mixed Contexts

This section deals with *all* types of contexts studied so far—those containing a contrasting word, a similar word, or a commonsense clue.

Pretest 7

---

1. "You shall hear how Hiawatha/Prayed and fasted in the forest,/Not for greater skill in hunting,/Not for greater *craft* in fishing. . . ." —Henry Wadsworth Longfellow

2. If you lose the key to your apartment, go to the superintendent. He has a *duplicate* of every key in our building.

3. Geri didn't notice me in the crowd, but she spotted my brother, who is *conspicuous* because of his red hair.

4. Children who do not want their cereal should not be required to finish it against their *volition*.

5. "Daring burglaries by armed men, and highway robberies, took place in the capital itself every night; families were publicly cautioned not to go out of town without removing their furniture to upholsterers' warehouses for *security*."—Charles Dickens

6. The team's uniforms were *immaculate* at the start of play, but by the end of the first quarter they were dirty with mud.

7. Let's wait. It's raining too hard now. As soon as it *abates*, we'll make a dash for the car.

8. Cows, pigs, and chickens are familiar sights to a *rural* youngster, but they are rarely seen by an urban child.

9. A pound of *miniature* chocolates contains many more pieces than a pound of the ordinary size.

10. "Stubb was the second mate. He was a native of Cape Cod; and hence, according to local usage, was called a Cape-Codman. A happy-go-lucky; neither *craven* nor valiant. . . ."—Herman Melville

11. I expected the medicine to alleviate my cough, but it seems to have *aggravated* it.

12. After their quarrel, Cynthia and Warren didn't talk to each other until Ann succeeded in *reconciling* them.

13. "The Man Without a Country," by Edward Everett Hale, is not a true story; the incidents and characters are entirely *fictitious*.

14. When traveling in Canada, you may exchange American money for Canadian *currency* at any bank.

15. Some students would probably collapse if they had to run two miles; they don't have the *stamina*.

16. Donald was defeated in last year's election, but that won't *deter* him from running again.

17. Several neutral countries are trying to get the *belligerent* nations to stop fighting.

18. Company and union officials have been in conference around the clock in an attempt to reach an *accord* on wages.

19. The fight might have been serious if a passerby had not *intervened* and sent the participants on their way.

20. Our band now has four players and, if you join, it will become a *quintet*.

Study Your Lesson Words, Group 7

WORD	MEANING AND TYPICAL USE
abate (*v.*) ə'bāt	1. become less; decrease; diminish; let up The water shortage is *abating*, but it is still a matter of some concern. 2. make less; reduce; moderate Helen's close defeat in the tennis tournament has not *abated* her zeal for the game.
abatement (*n.*)	slackening; letup
accord (*n.*) ə'kȯ(r)d	agreement; understanding If both sides to the dispute can be brought to the conference table, perhaps they can come to an *accord*.
accord (*v.*)	agree; correspond Check to see if your definition *accords* with the one in the dictionary.
aggravate (*v.*) 'a-grə,vāt	make worse; worsen; intensify If your sunburn itches, don't scratch; that will only *aggravate* it.
belligerent (*adj.*) bə'li-jə-rənt	fond of fighting; warlike; combative Bert still has a tendency to settle his arguments with his fists. When will he learn that it's childish to be so *belligerent*?

conspicuous (*adj.*)
kən'spik-yə-wəs

noticeable; easily seen; prominent; striking
Among Manhattan's skyscrapers, the World Trade Center is *conspicuous* for its superior height.

craft (*n.*)
'kraft

1. skill; art; trade
The weavers of Oriental rugs are famous for their remarkable *craft*.

2. skill or art in a bad sense; guile
The Greeks took Troy by *craft*; they used the trick of the wooden horse.

crafty (*adj.*)

sly; cunning

craven (*adj.*)
'krā-vən

cowardly; dastardly; pusillanimous; gutless
Henry Fleming thought he would be a hero, but as the fighting began he fled from the field in *craven* fear.

craven (*n.*)

coward; dastard

currency (*n.*)
'kə-rən-sē

something in circulation as a medium of exchange; money; coin; bank notes
Some New England tribes used beads as *currency*.

deter (*v.*)
də'tə(r)

turn aside through fear; discourage; hinder; keep back
The heavy rain did not *deter* people from coming to the play. Nearly every seat was occupied.

duplicate (*n.*)
'd(y)ü-plə-kət

one of two things exactly alike; copy; reproduction
If I had had carbon paper, I could have made a *duplicate* of my history notes for my friend who was absent.

fictitious (*adj.*)
fik'ti-shəs

1. made up; imaginary; not real
In JOHNNY TREMAIN, there are *fictitious* characters like Johnny and Rab, as well as real ones, like Samuel Adams and Paul Revere.

2. false; pretended; assumed for the purpose of deceiving
The suspect said she lived at 423 Green Street, but she later admitted it was a *fictitious* address.

immaculate (*adj.*)
ə'mak-yə-lət

spotless; without a stain; absolutely clean; unblemished
The curtains were spotless; the tablecloth was *immaculate*, too.

intervene (*v.*)
,in-tə(r)'vēn

1. occur between; be between; come between
More than two months *intervene* between a President's election and the day he takes office.

2. come between to help settle a quarrel; intercede; interfere
Ralph is unhappy that I stepped into the dispute between him and his brother. He did not want me to *intervene*.

intervention (*n.*)

interference; interposition

miniature (*adj.*)
'min-ē-ə,chu̇(ə)r

small; tiny
Joan has a *miniature* stapler in her knapsack. It takes up very little room.

quintet (*n.*)
kwin'tet

group of five
A basketball team, because it has five players, is often called a *quintet*.

reconcile (*v.*)
'rek-ən-sīl

1. cause to be friends again; restore to friendship or harmony
Surprisingly, Alison and Jerry are friends again. I wonder who *reconciled* them.

2. settle; resolve
We are friends again; we have *reconciled* our differences.

rural (*adj.*)
'ru̇r-əl

having to do with the country (as distinguished from the city or town)
Six inches of snow fell in the city and up to fourteen inches in the *rural* areas upstate.

security (*n.*)
sə'kyu̇-rə-tē

1. safety; protection
Guests are advised to deposit their valuables in the hotel's vault for greater *security*.

2. measures taken to assure protection against attack, crime, sabotage, etc.
Security has been tightened at airports.

stamina (*n.*)
'sta-mə-nə

strength; vigor; endurance
Swimming the English Channel is a feat that requires considerable *stamina*.

volition (*n.*)
vō'li-shən

act of willing or choosing; will; choice
Did the employer dismiss him, or did he leave of his own *volition*?

Apply What You Have Learned

EXERCISE 1.37: SENTENCE COMPLETION

On your answer paper, write the lesson word that best fits the meaning of the sentence.

1. Only when the United Nations __?__d did the two __?__ nations agree to stop fighting.
2. It is almost certain that the bitter rivals would not have reached a(n) __?__ of their own __?__.
3. Geraldine still lacks the __?__ to go on a ski trip; her miserable cold has not __?__d.
4. Since the assassination attempt, the __?__ surrounding the prime minister has been particularly __?__.
5. The two singers should __?__ their differences; they made much better music together than they now do apart.
6. The jazz __?__ has a drummer, a saxophonist, a bassist, a trumpeter, and a pianist.
7. At auction, the 1856 British Guiana one-penny postage stamp will command a huge price because it has no __?__.
8. The __?__ of stained glass painting flourished during the thirteenth century.
9. I fear that my intervention will only __?__ an already difficult situation.
10. Residents of the farming county insist that the construction of a large airport will not __?__ with the __?__ life they are determined to preserve.

EXERCISE 1.38: SYNONYMS

Eliminate repetition by replacing the boldfaced word or words with a **synonym** from your lesson words.

1. We can settle our dispute without interference; please do not **interfere.**
2. Some urban residents who move to the country find it hard to adjust to **country** life.
3. A few of the strikers do not agree with the **agreement** tentatively reached with their employer.
4. Insert the original into the copier, and in seconds you will have a clear **copy.**
5. Anti-theft devices that discourage an amateur thief may not **discourage** a professional burglar.

6. I could barely notice the moon an hour ago, but now it is much more **noticeable.**

7. The dining room is a model of cleanliness; the tablecloths and the curtains are **spotlessly clean.**

8. Since his recent excuses have been shown to be false, we suspect his earlier ones may have been **false,** too.

9. What can be done to **make** these two ex-friends **friendly again?**

10. The Armed Forces protect us. Without them we would have no **protection** against aggression.

EXERCISE 1.39: ANTONYMS

Enter the lesson word that is most nearly the **opposite** of the boldfaced word or words.

1. By no stretch of the imagination can a(n) __?__ withdrawal be viewed as a **valorous** deed.

2. No __?__ was reached; the meeting ended in **dissension.**

3. With a worrier, __?__ problems sometimes assume **mammoth** proportions.

4. It is hard to understand why a **friendly** neighbor like Alicia should suddenly turn __?__ .

5. By reducing the occupants' exposure to **danger,** buckled seatbelts provide a measure of __?__ .

6. Employers began to **augment** their staffs as the recession __?__d.

7. The stop sign was not __?__ ; an overhanging tree limb made the warning sign **hard to see.**

8. At mealtime, an infant's __?__ bib soon becomes **full of stains.**

9. Weak security does not __?__ attack but tends to **encourage** it.

10. Intervention by outsiders may __?__ , rather than **alleviate,** the tension between the foes.

EXERCISE 1.40: CONCISE WRITING

Express the thought of each sentence in **no more than four words.**

1. The paper money that they have been using as a medium of exchange is not worth anything.

2. Hostile engagements are continuing to take place without any sign of letting up.

3. Living in the country does not cost a great deal of money.

4. The reputation that she has achieved with people in general does not have a single stain or blemish.

5. Are the measures that we have taken to protect ourselves against attack adequate to do the job?

EXERCISE 1.41: SYNONYM SUMMARY

Each line, when completed, should have three words similar in meaning. The parentheses indicate the number of missing letters. On your answer paper, write the *complete* words.

1. saf (1) ty	(3) tection	(2) curity
2. notic (2) ble	prom (1) nent	conspic (4)
3. stain (4)	(2) blemished	im (4) late
4. sett (2)	rec (3) ile	(2) solve
5. disc (2) rage	hind (2)	d (1) t (1) r
6. str (3) th	vig (2)	stam (3)
7. combat (3)	(3) like	bel (3) erent
8. let (1) p	slack (2) ing	(1) bat (1) ment
9. interf (3)	in (3) vene	(2) terc (3)
10. cr (2) ty	cun (4)	(1) ly
11. (1) gree	(3) respond	(2) cord
12. fal (2)	(3) ginary	ficti (5)
13. (1) ill	choi (2)	(2) lition
14. gutl (3)	(3) illanimous	(1) rave (1)
15. wors (2)	intens (3)	(2) grav (3)
16. min (2) ture	(2) ny	sm (3)
17. mon (2)	(1) oi (1)	curr (4)
18. (1) opy	(2) prod (2) tion	(4) icate
19. dast (3)	cow (3)	(3) ven
20. in (3) ference	(5) vention	(2) terpo (2) tion

EXERCISE 1.42: ANALOGIES

Which lettered pair of words—*a, b, c, d,* or *e*—most nearly expresses the same relationship as the capitalized pair?

1. QUINTET : FIVE
- *(a)* decade : year
- *(c)* score : twenty
- *(e)* ounce : pound
- *(b)* dozen : gross
- *(d)* liter : quart

2. RURAL : COUNTRY
- *(a)* urban : population
- *(c)* initial : conclusion
- *(e)* parallel : line
- *(b)* local : vicinity
- *(d)* terminal : beginning

3. IMMACULATE : SPOT
- *(a)* infinite : end
- *(c)* erroneous : fault
- *(e)* mute : silence
- *(b)* significant : meaning
- *(d)* unanimous : support

4. SENTINEL : SECURITY
- *(a)* child : supervision
- *(c)* coach : competition
- *(e)* companion : company
- *(b)* motorist : insurance
- *(d)* proprietor : risk

5. PROMINENT : SEE
- *(a)* cumbersome : carry
- *(c)* fragile : break
- *(e)* faint : hear
- *(b)* complex : understand
- *(d)* inconspicuous : notice

6. AGGRAVATE : WORSE
- *(a)* facilitate : difficult
- *(c)* nullify : valid
- *(e)* complicate : simple
- *(b)* rectify : correct
- *(d)* elucidate : obscure

7. WRITING : CRAFT
- *(a)* skill : reading
- *(c)* patience : virtue
- *(e)* sobriety : fault
- *(b)* science : biology
- *(d)* education : ignorance

8. BELLIGERENT : CONTENTION
- *(a)* craven : valor
- *(c)* frank : concealment
- *(e)* honest : fraud
- *(b)* underhanded : deception
- *(d)* reserved : conversation

9. RECONCILE : ESTRANGE
   (a) succeed : precede   (b) vanquish : surmount
   (c) abandon : neglect   (d) abate : moderate
   (e) accommodate : oblige

10. CHICKEN : PUSILLANIMOUS
   (a) hawk : timid   (b) tortoise : speedy
   (c) swan : awkward   (d) dove : warlike
   (e) bat : blind

Pretest 8

Write the meaning of the italicized word.

21. "... I doubted not that I might one day, by taking a voyage, see with my own eyes the little fields, houses, and trees, the *diminutive* people, the tiny cows. ..."—Charlotte Brontë

22. Walter left, saying he would return *presently*, but he was gone for a long time.

23. If you miss the bus, you have the choice of walking or waiting an hour for the next bus. There is no other *alternative*.

24. My aim for this weekend is to finish my history and English assignments. I shall be disappointed if I cannot achieve this *objective*.

25. "In most books, the *I*, or first person, is omitted; in this it will be *retained*. ..."—Henry Thoreau

26. The Goodmans don't mind leaving their children in your *custody* because you are an excellent babysitter.

27. Is it fair for the partner who made the smaller investment to receive the *major* share of the profits?

28. Most people will change their minds when shown they are wrong, but not Timothy. He is too *opinionated*.

29. Last year, I shared a gym locker with another student. Now I have one *exclusively* for myself.

30. "Perceiving myself in a *blunder*, I attempted to correct it."—Emily Brontë

31. Some volcanoes have erupted in recent times; others have been *dormant* for many years.

32. Frequent absence will make you fall behind in your work and *imperil* your chances of passing.

33. There were no soft drinks. The only *beverages* on the menu were milk, coffee, tea, and hot chocolate.

34. Two girls at the next table started quarreling, but I couldn't learn what their *controversy* was about.

35. "As the news of my arrival spread through the kingdom, it brought *prodigious* numbers of rich, idle, and curious people to see me; so that the villages were almost emptied. . . ."—Jonathan Swift

36. Everyone in the class must take the final examination to pass the course. No student is *exempt*.

37. Don't put off what you should do today to "tomorrow," or "next week," or simply "later." Stop *procrastinating*.

38. My fears of the dentist were *dispelled* when I had a relatively painless first visit.

39. Dad fell behind in his work at the office because of a *protracted* illness lasting several weeks.

40. "For though Lorna's father was a nobleman of high and goodly *lineage*, her mother was of yet more ancient and renowned descent. . . ."—Richard D. Blackmore

---

Study Your Lesson Words, Group 8

WORD	MEANING AND TYPICAL USE
alternative (*n.*) ȯl'tər-nə-tiv	1. choice; one of two or more things offered for choice If given the choice of making either an oral or a written report, I would pick the second *alternative*. 2. other or remaining choice
beverage (*n.*) 'be-və-rij	drink; liquid for drinking Orange juice is a healthful *beverage*.
blunder (*n.*) 'blən-də(r)	mistake or error caused by stupidity or carelessness Have you ever committed the *blunder* of mailing a letter without a postage stamp?
controversy (*n.*) 'kän-trə-vər-sē	dispute; quarrel; debate; strife The Republicans and the Democrats have been engaged in a *controversy* over which party is responsible for the increased taxes.
controversial (*adj.*)	arousing controversy; contentious; disputatious
custody (*n.*) 'kəs-tə-dē	care; safekeeping; guardianship The treasurer has *custody* of our club's financial records.

diminutive (*adj.*)
də'min-yə,tiv

below average size; small; tiny
    To an observer in an airplane high over the city, even the largest buildings seem *diminutive*.

dispel (*v.*)
də'spel

drive away by scattering; scatter; disperse
    The two officers were commended for their skill in *dispelling* the mob and preventing violence.

dormant (*adj.*)
'do(r)-mənt

inactive, as if asleep; sleeping; quiet; sluggish; resting
    In early spring, new buds begin to appear on trees and shrubs that have been *dormant* all winter.

exclusively (*adv.*)
ik'sklü-səv-lē

solely; without sharing with others; undividedly
    Mrs. Lopez had bought the encyclopedia for all of her children, but the oldest behaved as if it were *exclusively* his.

exclusive (*adj.*)

sole; single; unshared

exempt (*adj.*)
ig'zempt

freed or released from a duty, liability, or rule to which others are subject
    A certain portion of each person's income is legally *exempt* from taxation.

exemption (*n.*)

immunity; impunity

imperil (*v.*)
əm'per-əl

endanger; jeopardize
    The fishing vessel was *imperiled* by high winds, but it managed to reach port safely.

lineage (*n.*)
'lin-ē-ij

descent (in a direct line from a common ancestor); ancestry; family; extraction
    A study of Franklin D. Roosevelt's *lineage* shows that he was descended from a Dutch ancestor who settled in America about 1638.

major (*adj.*)
'mā-jə(r)

greater; larger; more important; principal
    When the *major* companies in an industry raise prices, the smaller ones usually follow suit.

objective (*n.*)
əb'jek-tiv

aim or end (of an action); goal
    Our fund has already raised $650; its *objective* is $1000.

objective (*adj.*)

involving facts, rather than personal feelings or opinions
    College admissions committees consider two kinds of data: subjective evidence, such as letters

of recommendation; and *objective* evidence, such as your scores on college-entrance tests.

opinionated (*adj.*)
ə'pin-yən-ā-təd

unduly attached to one's own opinion; obstinate; stubborn

If you keep arguing that you are right, in the face of overwhelming objective evidence that you are wrong, you are *opinionated*.

presently (*adv.*)
'pre-zənt-lē

in a little time; shortly; soon; before long

We won't have to wait long for our bus. It will be here *presently*.

procrastinate (*v.*)
prō'kras-tə,nāt

put things off; delay; postpone; defer; dawdle

When a book is due, return it to the library promptly. Otherwise you will be fined 10¢ for every day you *procrastinate*.

prodigious (*adj.*)
prə'di-jəs

extraordinary in size, quantity, or extent; vast; enormous; huge; amazing

The average American city requires a *prodigious* amount of fresh milk daily.

prodigy (*n.*)

something extraordinary; wonder; phenomenon

protract (*v.*)
prō'trakt

draw out; lengthen in time; prolong; extend

The visitors had planned to stay for a few hours only, but they were persuaded to *protract* their visit.

retain (*v.*)
rə'tān

keep; continue to have, hold, or use

The department store is closing down its restaurant but *retaining* its lunch counter.

retentive (*adj.*)

having the power to retain or remember; tenacious

Dora has a *retentive* memory.

Apply What You Have Learned

EXERCISE 1.43: SENTENCE COMPLETION

Write the lesson word that best fits the meaning of the sentence.

1. When Reuben learned Friday that the library would close for the weekend, he realized what a(n) __?__ it was to have __?__d with his research paper.
2. We must stop quarreling. If this committee spends another hour in __?__, it will be unable to achieve its __?__.
3. To __?__ the workers' apprehensions of losing their jobs, the new employer promised to __?__ all of them.
4. Most of the time, Pam has to share a swimming lane with others, but today she had one __?__ for herself.
5. Though many of the secondary roads are impassable, the __?__ highways have all been plowed.
6. Replacing the old bridge will cost a(n) __?__ amount of money, but there is no practical __?__.
7. Neither side is inclined to __?__ the dispute much longer; a settlement is expected __?__.
8. In the days of special privilege, individuals of royal __?__ were generally __?__ from taxation.
9. We stopped for a(n) __?__ to quench our thirst.
10. When the parents are at work, the children are in the __?__ of their grandparents.

EXERCISE 1.44: SYNONYMS

Eliminate repetition by replacing the boldfaced word or words with a **synonym** from your lesson words.

1. You can leave the dogs in Antoine's **care;** he will take excellent care of them.
2. Elections with only one choice are a farce because the voters have no **other choice.**
3. Grace cannot be held solely responsible if the accident was not **solely** her fault.
4. People make the common **mistake** of mistaking one of the twins for the other.
5. Two quarrelsome members are responsible for most of the **quarreling** in the club.

6. We decided not to **prolong** our conversation since we had been on the telephone long enough.
7. When asked what I wanted to drink, I asked for a cold **drink.**
8. You may have the original, and we will **keep** the copy.
9. She traces her ancestors back several generations, but I know little about my own **ancestry.**
10. People with an enormous appetite for knowledge usually do **an enormous** amount of reading.

EXERCISE 1.45: ANTONYMS

Enter the lesson word that is most nearly the **opposite** of the boldfaced word or words.

1. In spring, many living things that have been __?__ all winter gradually become **active** again.
2. Unfortunately, __?__ has developed; there had been a period of total **absence of strife.**
3. The residents __?__ed by the flood are now **out of danger.**
4. When her term expires, she will **give up** the presidency but __?__ her seat on the executive board.
5. We were planning to __?__ our stay, when an unforeseen shortage of funds caused us instead to **curtail** it.
6. Some **minor** issues remain to be settled, but the __?__ ones have all been resolved.
7. When that __?__ blue spruce was planted a score of years ago, it was a(n) **tiny** seedling.
8. Everything you buy is not necessarily **subject** to the sales tax; food purchases, for example, may be __?__ .
9. In the search for truth, __?__ considerations are more reliable than those **based on feelings or opinions.**
10. For every person who does **not put off today's work to some other time,** there are many who __?__ .

EXERCISE 1.46: CONCISE WRITING

Express the thought of each sentence in **no more than four words.**

1. Does this belong to you alone and to no one else?
2. They will bring the meeting to a close in a little while.
3. What are the choices that are being offered to us?

4. The individuals on both sides are unduly attached to their own opinions.

5. We presented evidence that is based on fact, rather than on what people think or feel.

EXERCISE 1.47: SYNONYM SUMMARY

Each line, when completed, should have three words similar in meaning. The parentheses indicate the number of missing letters. On your answer paper, write the *complete* words.

1. d (1) scent	an (1) estry	lin (2) ge
2. prol (1) ng	(2) tend	(3) tract
3. err (2)	(3) take	(2) under
4. s (2) n	(2) ortly	(3) sently
5. dr (1) nk	liq (2) d	(1) ever (3)
6. go (1) l	(2) m	(2) jective
7. s (1) le	(2) shared	ex (3) sive
8. c (1) re	(2) ardianship	(1) us (4)
9. d (1) lay	d (2) dle	(7) tinate
10. d (1) sp (1) rse	(1) cat (3)	(2) spel
11. (2) danger	(3) pardize	(2) peril
12. extr (2) rdinary	(1) norm (3)	(3) dig (2) us
13. (1) mall	t (1) ny	(2) min (1) tive
14. h (1) ld	k (2) p	(2) tain
15. (2) munity	imp (1) nity	(3) mption
16. stub (4)	(2) stin (1) te	opin (2) nated
17. r (1) sting	slug (2) sh	dorm (3)
18. content (4)	dis (2) tatious	(3) troversial
19. l (1) rger	princip (2)	(2) jor
20. w (1) nder	(2) enomenon	(3) digy

EXERCISE 1.48: ANALOGIES

Which lettered pair of words—*a, b, c, d,* or *e*—most nearly expresses the same relationship as the capitalized pair?

1. MILK : BEVERAGE
   - (*a*) utensil : fork
   - (*b*) spider : web
   - (*c*) distance : mile
   - (*d*) moccasin : shoe
   - (*e*) metal : aluminum

2. CONTROVERSY : HARMONY
- *(a)* expertise : experience
- *(b)* shallowness : depth
- *(c)* wealth : means
- *(d)* tact : judgment
- *(e)* inundation : precipitation

3. OPINIONATED : LISTEN
- *(a)* docile : obey
- *(b)* extravagant : squander
- *(c)* alert : observe
- *(d)* submissive : yield
- *(e)* suspicious : trust

4. PRODIGIOUS : AMAZEMENT
- *(a)* irrational : admiration
- *(b)* subjective : infallibility
- *(c)* controversial : accord
- *(d)* inconspicuous : attention
- *(e)* outrageous : indignation

5. SCATTER : DISPEL
- *(a)* adjourn : convene
- *(b)* divulge : secrete
- *(c)* expel : admit
- *(d)* meddle : intervene
- *(e)* disoblige : accommodate

6. TENACIOUS : HOLD
- *(a)* belligerent : contend
- *(b)* permissive : ban
- *(c)* persistent : relinquish
- *(d)* disputatious : assent
- *(e)* reticent : inform

7. BLUNDER : IGNORANCE
- *(a)* infection : fever
- *(b)* flu : virus
- *(c)* needle : perforation
- *(d)* rumor : panic
- *(e)* explosion : din

8. EXEMPTION : PRIVILEGE
- *(a)* exclamation : sigh
- *(b)* asset : liability
- *(c)* interval : fortnight
- *(d)* reading : skill
- *(e)* vehicle : van

9. INDOLENT : PROCRASTINATE
- *(a)* implacable : forgive
- *(b)* conservative : change
- *(c)* curious : inquire
- *(d)* timid : protest
- *(e)* indifferent : care

10. SHIFTLESS : OBJECTIVE
- *(a)* crafty : cunning
- *(b)* wary : caution
- *(c)* disgruntled : complaint
- *(d)* partial : prejudice
- *(e)* callous : sympathy

CHAPTER 2

Enlarging Vocabulary Through Central Ideas

What is a central idea?

Examine these words: *devour, edible, glutton, luscious, palatable, voracious.* What do they have in common?

As you may have guessed, these words revolve around the idea of *eating*. We may therefore call *EATING* the central idea of this word group.

Every central idea discussed in this book has several words that we can associate with it. For example, under *DISAGREEMENT* we may include *antagonize, discord, discrepancy, dissent, irreconcilable,* and *wrangle*. Similarly, we may group *bulwark, dynamic, impregnable, invigorate, robust,* and *vigor* under the central idea *STRENGTH*.

In this unit you will enlarge your vocabulary by learning words grouped under twenty central ideas like *EATING, DISAGREEMENT,* and *STRENGTH*.

Why study words through central ideas?

When you study vocabulary by the central-ideas method, you are dealing with groups of *related* words. Each word you learn helps you with some other word, or words, in the group. Consider, for example, the words *frugal* and *economize* that you will meet under *POVERTY*. *Frugal* means "thrifty," or "avoiding waste." To *economize* is to "cut down expenses" or to "be frugal." Notice that *economize* can strengthen your grasp of *frugal*, and vice versa. As a result, you should be better able to understand, as well as use, both *frugal* and *economize*. By the interesting central-ideas method, you can effectively learn many words in a short time.

How to use this vocabulary unit

To get the most out of this unit, follow these suggestions:

1. Notice the spelling. Then pronounce the word, using the pronunciation indicated below it.

2. Learn all the definitions in the MEANING column.

3. Pay particular attention to the TYPICAL USE feature. Each sentence has been constructed to help you fix in mind the meaning and use of a new word. Follow up by constructing, at least in your mind, a similar sentence using your own context.

4. Do the exercises thoughtfully, not mechanically. Then review each word you have missed.

5. Make a point of *using* newly learned words whenever appropriate: in class discussions, informal conversations, compositions, and letters. A new word does not become a part of your vocabulary until you have *used* it a few times.

CENTRAL IDEAS 1–5

Pretest 1

Write the *letter* of the best answer.

1. If you are *versatile*, you __?__ .
   (A) like sports (B) are easily angered (C) can do many things well

2. You have no reason to be *apprehensive*. Stop __?__ .
   (A) boasting (B) worrying (C) arguing

3. When you are *rash*, you are __?__ .
   (A) taking risks (B) not in a hurry (C) too cautious

4. *Affluent* people are __?__ .
   (A) polite (B) poor (C) very wealthy

5. Since we have __?__ , we don't have to be *frugal*.
   (A) no means (B) more than enough (C) very little

> THE ANSWERS ARE
>
> 1. C 2. B 3. A 4. C 5. B

As you work through Central Ideas 1–5, you will become familiar with several interesting and useful words, including the italicized words on which you have just been tested.

1. Skill

WORD	MEANING AND TYPICAL USE
adroit (*adj.*) ə'dròit	expert in using the hands or mind; skillful; clever; deft; dexterous Our *adroit* passing enabled us to score four touchdowns.
ambidextrous (*adj.*) ,am-bə'dek-strəs	able to use both hands equally well Ruth is an *ambidextrous* hitter; she can bat right-handed or left-handed.

apprentice (*n.*) ə'pren-təs	person learning an art or trade under a skilled worker; learner; beginner; novice; tyro Young Ben Franklin learned the printing trade by serving as an *apprentice* to his half-brother James.
aptitude (*n.*) 'ap-tə,tüd	natural tendency to learn or understand; bent; talent Cindy is not clumsy with tools; she has mechanical *aptitude*.
craftsperson (*n.*) 'krafts-pərs-ᵊn	skilled worker; artisan To build a house, you need the services of carpenters, bricklayers, plumbers, electricians, and several other *craftspersons*.
dexterity (*n.*) dek'ste-rə-tē	skill in using the hands or mind; deftness; adroitness; expertise You can't expect an apprentice to have the same *dexterity* as a skilled worker.
maladroit (*adj.*) ,mal-ə'droit	clumsy; inept; awkward A *maladroit* worker banged his thumb with a hammer.
versatile (*adj.*) 'vər-sə-təl	capable of doing many things well; many-sided; all-around Leonardo da Vinci was remarkably *versatile*. He was a painter, sculptor, architect, musician, engineer, and scientist.

EXERCISE 2.1: *SKILL* WORDS

Complete the partially spelled skill word. The parentheses indicate the number of missing letters.

1. If you have musical (3) it (3), you ought to learn to play an instrument.
2. A century ago, one learned a trade by serving as an (3) rent (3).
3. Janet is a (3) sat (3) athlete with letters in swimming, tennis, and volleyball.
4. When I injured my right hand, I realized what an advantage it must be to be (2) bid (4) ous.
5. A (1) raftspe (4)'s dexterity with tools is the result of years of experience.

2. Poverty

destitute (*adj.*)
'des-tə,tüt

not possessing the necessities of life such as food, shelter, and clothing; needy; indigent
The severe earthquake killed hundreds of persons and left thousands *destitute*.

economize (*v.*)
e'kä-nə,mīz

reduce expenses; be frugal
Consumers can *economize* by buying their milk in gallon containers.

frugal (*adj.*)
'frü-gəl

1. barely enough; scanty
The old man had nothing to eat but bread and cheese; yet he offered to share this *frugal* meal with his visitor.

2. avoiding waste; economical; sparing; saving; thrifty
My weekly allowance for lunches and fares isn't much, but I can get by on it if I am *frugal*.

impoverish (*v.*)
əm'pä-və-rish

make very poor; reduce to poverty; bankrupt; ruin; pauperize
The increase in dues of only a dollar a year will not *impoverish* anyone.

indigence (*n.*)
'in-də-jəns

poverty; penury
By hard work, countless thousands of Americans have raised themselves from *indigence* to wealth.

3. Wealth

affluent (*adj.*)
'a-flü-ənt

very wealthy; rich; opulent
The new wing to the hospital is a gift from an *affluent* humanitarian.

avarice (*n.*)
'a-və-rəs

excessive desire for wealth; greediness; cupidity
If manufacturers were to raise prices without justification, they could be accused of *avarice*.

avaricious (*adj.*)
,av-ə'rish-əs

greedy; grasping; covetous
An *avaricious* person likes to get and keep, but not to give or share.

covet (*v.*)
'kə-vət

desire; long for; crave, especially something belonging to another
Chicot *coveted* his neighbor's farm but could not get her to sell it.

dowry (*n.*)
'dau̇-rē

money, property, etc., that a bride brings to her husband

The *dowry* that his wife brought him enabled the Italian engraver Piranesi to devote himself completely to art.

financial (*adj.*)
fə'nan-chəl

having to do with money matters; monetary; pecuniary; fiscal

People who keep spending more than they earn usually get into *financial* difficulties.

fleece (*v.*)
'flēs

(literally, to remove the wool from a sheep or a similar animal) deprive or strip of money or belongings by fraud; charge excessively for goods or services; rob; cheat; swindle

If your sister paid $3000 for that car, she was *fleeced*. The mechanic says it is worth $800.

hoard (*v.*)
'hȯ(ə)rd

save and conceal; accumulate; amass

Mother Magloire had a reputation as a miser who *hoarded* every penny she could get her hands on.

lavish (*adj.*)
'la-vish

1. too free in giving, using, or spending; profuse; prodigal

The young heir was warned that he would soon have nothing left if he continued to be *lavish* with money.

2. given or spent too freely; very abundant; extravagant; profuse

Vera's composition is good, but it doesn't deserve the *lavish* praise that Linda gave it.

lucrative (*adj.*)
'lü-krə-tiv

profitable; moneymaking

Because the gift shop did not produce a sufficient profit, the owner decided to go into a more *lucrative* business.

means (*n. pl.*)
'mēnz

wealth; property; resources

To own an expensive home, a yacht, and a limousine, you have to be a person of *means*.

opulence (*n.*)
'äp-yə-ləns

wealth; riches; affluence

Dickens contrasts the *opulence* of France's nobility with the indigence of her peasants.

sumptuous (*adj.*)
'səmp-chə-wəs

involving large expense; luxurious; costly

The car with the leather upholstery and thick rugs is beautiful but a bit *sumptuous* for my simple tastes.

EXERCISE 2.2: *POVERTY* AND *WEALTH* WORDS

Complete the partially spelled poverty or wealth word. The parentheses indicate the number of missing letters.

1. As an (2) flu (3) nation, the United States has given billions to aid the world's needy.
2. 18th-century France was impoverished by the (4) use spending of her royal family.
3. It is not surprising that needy people (2) vet the possessions of prosperous neighbors.
4. The bride is bringing her husband a large dowry, as her parents are people of (2) an (1).
5. If it does not begin to (1) con (5), the nation will be in serious financial trouble.

---

4. Fear

---

apprehensive (*adj.*)
,a-prə'hen-siv

expecting something unfavorable; afraid; anxious
   Apprehensive parents telephoned the school when the class was late in getting home from the museum.

cower (*v.*)
'kaủ-ə(r)

draw back tremblingly; shrink or crouch in fear; cringe; recoil
   If you stand up to your bullying sister instead of *cowering* before her, she may back down.

dastardly (*adj.*)
'das-tə(r)d-lē

cowardly and mean
   It was *dastardly* of the captain to desert the sinking vessel and leave the passengers to fend for themselves.

intimidate (*v.*)
ən'tim-ə-dāt

make fearful or timid; frighten; force by fear; cow; bully
   The younger children would not have given up the playing field so quickly if the older ones hadn't *intimidated* them.

poltroon (*n.*)
päl'trün

thorough coward; dastard; craven
   Like the *poltroon* that he was, Tonseten hid under a bed when he saw a fight coming.

timid (*adj.*)
'tim-əd

lacking courage or self-confidence; fearful; timorous; shy
   If the other team challenges us, we should accept. Let's not be so *timid!*

trepidation (*n.*)
,tre-pə'dā-shən

nervous agitation; fear; fright; trembling
    I thought Carol would be nervous when she made her speech, but she delivered it without *trepidation*.

---

5. Courage

---

audacious (*adj.*)
ȯ'dā-shəs

1. bold; fearlessly daring
    Risking serious injury, the outfielder made an *audacious* leap against the concrete wall and caught the powerfully hit ball.

2. too bold; insolent; impudent
    After we had waited for about twenty minutes, an *audacious* latecomer strolled up and tried to get in at the head of our line.

audacity (*n.*)
ȯ-'das-ət-ē

nerve; rashness; temerity
    Oliver Twist, nine-year-old poorhouse inmate, was put into solitary confinement when he had the *audacity* to ask for a second helping of porridge.

dauntless (*adj.*)
'dȯnt-ləs

fearless; intrepid; very brave; valiant
    The frightened sailors wanted to turn back, but their *dauntless* captain urged them to sail on.

exploit (*n.*)
'eks,plȯit

heroic act; daring deed; feat
    Amelia Earhart won worldwide fame for her *exploits* as an aviator.

fortitude (*n.*)
'fȯ(r)-tə,tüd

courage in facing danger, hardship, or pain; endurance; bravery; pluck; backbone; valor
    The officer showed remarkable *fortitude* in remaining on duty despite a painful wound.

indomitable (*adj.*)
ən'dä-mə-tə-bəl

incapable of being subdued; unconquerable; invincible
    The bronco that would not be broken threw all its riders. It had an *indomitable* will to be free.

plucky (*adj.*)
'plə-kē

courageous; brave; valiant; valorous
    After two days on a life raft, the *plucky* survivors were rescued by a helicopter.

rash (*adj.*)
'rash

overhasty; foolhardy; reckless; impetuous; taking too much risk
    When you lose your temper, you may say or do something *rash* and regret it afterward.

EXERCISE 2.3: *FEAR* AND *COURAGE* WORDS

Complete the partially spelled fear or courage word.

1. Don't think you can (6) date us by shaking your fists at us!
2. Queen Elizabeth I knighted Francis Drake for his (5) its at sea.
3. The champions looked (6) tab (2) when they took the field, but we beat them.
4. Who would have thought that a (2) mid sophomore like Sophie would have had the courage to address so large an audience?
5. It would be (1) as (1) to drop out of school because of failure in a single test.

Review Exercises

REVIEW 1: SENTENCE COMPLETION

On your answer paper write the word from the list below that best fits the context. Use each word only once.

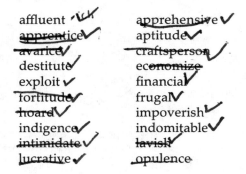

affluent	apprehensive
apprentice	aptitude
avarice	craftsperson
destitute	economize
exploit	financial
fortitude	frugal
hoard	impoverish
indigence	indomitable
intimidate	lavish
lucrative	opulence

1. Many unprofitable businesses have been made __?__ by immigrants who were __?__ when they first arrived in this country.

2. Sir Edmund Hillary and Tenzing Norkay showed amazing __?__ in 1953 when they climbed Mt. Everest, a peak that had been __?__ .

3. Why are some people inclined to __?__ even when they have accumulated more than enough? Can it be __?__ ?

4. No one would expect a(n) __?__ to have the expertise of a(n) __?__ .

5. Gertrude Ederle's early _?_ for swimming marked her for future greatness. When she swam the English Channel—the first woman to do so—she broke the men's speed record for that swim. What a(n) _?_!

6. The Wall Street crash of 1929 reduced countless investors from _?_ to _?_.

7. When _?_ spenders suddenly lose their jobs, they may wish that they had been more _?_ in managing their money.

8. The violent storm did not seem to _?_ the crew, but it made the passengers _?_.

9. Soaring outlays for employee pension and medical benefits can bring a(n) _?_ corporation to the brink of _?_ ruin.

10. If we do not _?_ in the use of our precious natural resources, we will _?_ our country.

REVIEW 2: SYNONYMS

Avoid repetition by replacing the boldfaced word with a **synonym** from the following list. The answer to question 1 is **bent**.

anxious	~~bent~~
~~indigent~~	fleece
~~pluck~~	~~pauperize~~
~~invincible~~	~~cow~~
~~lucrative~~	~~affluence~~

1. Cheryl is talented in many areas but she has no **talent** for dramatics.
2. In a time of need, the **needy** look to the government for help.
3. Wealthy people tend to associate with people of **wealth.**
4. Conquerors often commit the blunder of believing they are **unconquerable.**
5. Don't let that bully **bully** you.
6. A sales tax is no way to fight poverty because it will more deeply **impoverish** those who are already impoverished.
7. It has not been a **profitable** year. Profits are way down.
8. Don't be **afraid.** There is nothing to be afraid of.
9. The press lauded the courageous rescuers for their **courage.**
10. Know with whom you are dealing if you do not want to be cheated. A reputable firm will not **cheat** you.

REVIEW 3: ANTONYMS

Write the word from the following list that is most nearly the **opposite** of the boldfaced word or words. The first answer is **enric**

~~adroit~~	dastardly
~~destitute~~	~~economize~~
~~undercharge~~	~~frugal~~
~~enrich~~	~~unprofitable~~
~~rash~~	~~sumptuous~~

1. Dictators __?__ themselves but **impoverish** their subjects.
2. An **inept** person cannot provide the __?__ leadership that we need.
3. This is a time to __?__, rather than to **increase expenses.**
4. When funds are low, one must be __?__ to survive; **wasteful** spending cannot be tolerated.
5. Under questioning, the accused tend to be **cautious**, knowing that __?__ answers can make problems for them.
6. Attacking unarmed civilians is a(n) __?__ deed, but the aggressor considered it a **daring** act.
7. At first the thief claimed he stole from the **opulent** only to aid the __?__.
8. The purchase of Alaska, which many had regarded as __?__, turned out to be quite **lucrative.**
9. Investigation showed that the customers who thought they had been **fleeced** were in fact __?__d.
10. Most gift shoppers look for items **that involve little expense;** they cannot afford __?__ merchandise.

REVIEW 4: CONCISE WRITING

Express the thought of each sentence below in **no more than four words.**

1. There are millions of people who lack the basic necessities of life, such as food, shelter, and clothing.
2. Employees who are in the process of learning a trade under the guidance of a skilled worker do not receive very high salaries.
3. Those who practice the art of swindling charge their victims excessively for goods and services.
4. There are occasions when people are inclined to do things that entail altogether too much risk.
5. Those who have no confidence in themselves lack the courage to face danger, hardship, or pain.

REVIEW 5: SYNONYM SUMMARY

Each line, when completed, should have three words similar in meaning. The parentheses indicate the number of missing letters. Write the *complete* words. Answers to the first line are **pauperize, bankrupt,** and **impoverish.**

1. p (2) perize	bankr (1) pt	(2) poverish
2. f (2) lhardy	impet (1) ous	(1) ash
3. mon (1) tary	pec (1) niary	finan (2) al
4. n (1) vice	t (1) ro	apprent (1) ce
5. n (1) rve	tem (1) rity	(2) dacity
6. pr (1) f (1) se	prod (1) gal	lav (3)
7. (2) kward	in (1) pt	maladr (2) t
8. (1) mass	accum (1) late	h (2) rd
9. val (2) nt	(2) trepid	d (2) ntless
10. pov (1) rty	pen (1) ry	ind (1) gence
11. cr (1) ve	d (1) sire	c (1) v (1) t
12. cr (1) nge	(2) coil	cow (2)
13. t (1) lent	b (1) nt	(2) titude
14. gr (2) diness	cup (1) dity	av (1) r (1) ce
15. trem (1) ling	(1) right	tr (1) p (1) dation
16. l (1) x (1) rious	cost (2)	sum (2) uous
17. unconq (2) rable	invin (2) ble	ind (1) mit (1) ble
18. gr (1) sping	covet (2) s	ava (2) cious
19. (2) rifty	(3) nomical	fr (1) g (1) l
20. adr (2) tness	exp (1) rtise	dex (2) rity

REVIEW 6: ANALOGIES

Which lettered pair of words—*a, b, c, d,* or *e*—most nearly expresses the same relationship as the capitalized pair?

1. PECUNIARY : MONEY
- (*a*) lunar : sun
- (*b*) meteorological : weather
- (*c*) toxic : waste
- (*d*) urban : nation
- (*e*) vocational : leisure

2. BUNGLER : MALADROIT
- (*a*) scapegoat : blameworthy
- (*b*) windbag : silent
- (*c*) flatterer : sincere
- (*d*) maverick : submissive
- (*e*) jack-of-all-trades : versatile

3. INTIMIDATE : COW
   - (a) ignore : badger
   - (b) harass : hound
   - (c) offend : please
   - (c) praise : nag
   - (d) outfox : help

4. ASTRONAUT : INTREPID
   - (a) fact finder : objective
   - (c) chauffeur : intoxicated
   - (e) mediator : partial
   - (b) apprentice : inattentive
   - (d) custodian : unwary

5. AUDACIOUS : MANNERS
   - (a) dauntless : courage
   - (c) indigent : means
   - (e) competent : skill
   - (b) vigorous : stamina
   - (d) ambitious : goal

6. EXPLOIT : ADMIRATION
   - (a) blunder : self-esteem
   - (c) felony : crime
   - (e) calamity : dismay
   - (b) setback : prestige
   - (d) repetition : interest

   Hint: An **exploit** arouses **admiration**.

7. ECONOMIZE : THRIFTY
   - (a) annoy : helpful
   - (c) worry : apprehensive
   - (e) tarry : punctual
   - (b) sympathize : lukewarm
   - (d) bully : cordial

8. DEXTERITY : TRAIT
   - (a) whale : fish
   - (c) utensil : shovel
   - (e) bird : sparrow
   - (b) arrow : missile
   - (d) beverage : thirst

9. AVARICE : PRODIGALITY
   - (a) enmity : hostility
   - (c) confidence : trust
   - (e) yearning : desire
   - (b) reluctance : unwillingness
   - (d) security : anxiety

10. PALACE : OPULENCE
    - (a) prison : liberty
    - (c) paradise : discord
    - (e) sweatshop : drudgery
    - (b) hovel : comfort
    - (d) dove : belligerence

CENTRAL IDEAS 6–10

Pretest 2

Write the *letter* of the best answer.

1. An *estranged* friend is a friend __?__.
   (A) you hardly know   (B) with whom you have quarreled
   (C) who has moved away

2. If a criminal's name is *divulged*, it is __?__.
   (A) made public   (B) kept secret   (C) legally changed

3. The two nations are old __?__ because their goals almost always *correspond*.
   (A) allies   (B) rivals   (C) enemies

4. __?__ is not a *condiment*.
   (A) Pepper   (B) Lettuce   (C) Mustard

5. Anything that is *latent* cannot be __?__.
   (A) present   (B) hidden   (C) visible

THE ANSWERS ARE

1. B   2. A   3. A   4. B   5. C

The italicized words on which you were tested are a sample of the new vocabulary you are about to meet in Central Ideas 6–10.

---

6. Concealment

---

alias (*n.*) ′ā-lē-əs	assumed name Inspector Javert discovered that Monsieur Madeleine was not the mayor's real name but an *alias* for Jean Valjean, the ex-convict.
alias (*adv.*)	otherwise called; otherwise known as Jean Valjean, *alias* Monsieur Madeleine, was arrested by Inspector Javert.

clandestine (*adj.*)
klan'des-tən

carried on in secrecy and concealment; secret; covert; underhand; undercover

    Before the Revolutionary War, a patriot underground organization used to hold *clandestine* meetings in Boston.

enigma (*n.*)
ə'nig-mə

puzzling statement; riddle; mystery; puzzling problem or person

    I have read the sentence several times but cannot understand it. Maybe you can help me with this *enigma*.

    enigmatic (*adj.*)
    ,en-ig'mat-ik

mysterious; puzzling; obscure

    Her statement is *enigmatic*; we cannot make head or tail of it.

latent (*adj.*)
'lā-tənt

present but not showing itself; hidden but capable of being brought to light; dormant; potential

    A good education will help you discover and develop your *latent* talents.

lurk (*v.*)
'lərk

1. be hidden; lie in ambush

    Katherine called the police when she noticed a stranger *lurking* behind her neighbor's garage.

2. move stealthily; sneak; slink

seclude (*v.*)
sə'klüd

shut up apart from others; confine in a place hard to reach; hide; cloister; sequester

    To find a quiet place to study, Amy had to *seclude* herself in the attic.

stealthy (*adj.*)
'stel-thē

secret in action or character; catlike; sly; furtive

    The burglar had to be very *stealthy* to get past the two guards without being noticed.

---

7. Disclosure

---

apprise (*v.*)
ə'prīz

inform; notify; advise

    The magazine has *apprised* its readers of an increase in rates beginning May 1.

avowal (*n.*)
ə'vaủ-əl

open acknowledgment; frank declaration; admission; confession

    The white flag of surrender is an *avowal* of defeat.

divulge (*v.*) make public; disclose; reveal; tell
də'vəlj I told my secret only to Margaret because I knew she would not *divulge* it.

elicit (*v.*) draw forth; bring out; evoke; extract
ē'lis-ət By questioning the witness, the attorney *elicited* that it was raining at the time of the accident.

enlighten (*v.*) shed the light of truth and knowledge upon; free from
ən'lī-tən ignorance; inform; instruct
  The newcomer was going in the wrong direction until someone *enlightened* him that his room was at the other end of the hall.

manifest (*v.*) show; reveal; display; evidence
'ma-nə,fest I am surprised that Harriet is taking an art course because she has never, to my knowledge, *manifested* any interest in the subject.

manifest (*adj.*) plain; clear; evident; not obscure; obvious
  It is now *manifest* that the family across the street intends to move.

overt (*adj.*) open to view; not covert or hidden; public; manifest
ō'vərt The concealed camera recorded the *overt* acceptance of the bribe.

EXERCISE 2.4: *CONCEALMENT* AND *DISCLOSURE* WORDS

Complete the partially spelled concealment or disclosure word.

1. Price fluctuations are often (4) mat (2); we cannot tell why they occur.
2. Can I call without (5) gin (1) my identity?
3. He is confused. Will you please (2) light (2) him?
4. Two large companies were suspected of having made a cove (2) agreement to fix prices.
5. It takes time for (2) tent talents to show themselves.

8. Agreement

accede (*v.*) (usually followed by *to*) agree; assent; consent; ac-
ak'sēd quiesce
  When I asked my teacher if I might change my topic, he readily *acceded* to my request.

accord (*n.*)
ə'kȯ(r)d

agreement; harmony
Though we are in *accord* on what our goals should be, we differ on the means for achieving them.

compact (*n.*)
'käm-pakt

agreement; understanding; accord; covenant
The states bordering on the Delaware River have entered into a *compact* for the sharing of its water.

compatible (*adj.*)
kəm'pa-tə-bəl

able to exist together harmoniously; in harmony; agreeable; congenial
Arthur and I can't be on the same committee. We're not *compatible*.

compromise (*n.*)
'käm-prə,mīz

settlement reached by a partial yielding on both sides
At first, the union and management were far apart on wages, but they finally came to a *compromise*.

conform (*v.*)
kən'fȯ(r)m

be in agreement or harmony with; act in accordance with accepted standards or customs; comply; obey
When a new style in clothes appears, do you hasten to *conform*?

consistent (*adj.*)
kən'sis-tənt

keeping to the same principles throughout; showing no contradiction; in accord; compatible; consonant
By bringing up an unrelated matter you are not being *consistent* with your previous statement that we should stick to the topic.

correspond (*v.*)
,kä-rə'spänd

be in harmony; match; fit; agree; be similar
The rank of second lieutenant in the Army *corresponds* to that of ensign in the Navy.

dovetail (*v.*)
'dəv,tāl

to fit together with, so as to form a harmonious whole; interlock with
Gilbert's skill as a writer *dovetailed* Sullivan's talent as a composer, resulting in the famous Gilbert and Sullivan operettas.

reconcile (*v.*)
're-kən,sīl

cause to be friendly again; bring back to harmony
After their quarrel, Althea and Pat refused to talk to each other until I *reconciled* them.

relent (*v.*)
rə'lent

become less harsh, severe, or strict; soften in temper; yield
The Mayor had banned all lawn sprinkling because of the water shortage. However, after the heavy rains, he *relented* somewhat.

9. Disagreement

altercation (*n.*)
,ȯl-tə(r)'kā-shən

noisy, angry dispute; quarrel, wrangle
We halted the *altercation* by separating the two opponents before they could come to blows.

antagonize (*v.*)
an'ta-gə,nīz

make an enemy of; arouse the hostility of
The official *antagonized* the leader of her own party by not campaigning for him.

cleavage (*n.*)
'klē-vij

split; division; schism; chasm
We hope compromise will repair the *cleavage* in our ranks.

discord (*n.*)
'di-skȯrd

disagreement; dissension; strife
Billy Budd put an end to the *discord* aboard the *Rights-of-Man*. He was an excellent peacemaker.

discrepancy (*n.*)
də'skre-pən-sē

difference; disagreement; variation; inconsistency
Eighty people were at the dance but only seventy-four tickets were collected at the door. What accounts for this *discrepancy*?

dissent (*v.*)
də'sent

differ in opinion; disagree; object
The vote approving the amendment was far from unanimous; six members *dissented*.

embroil (*v.*)
əm'brȯil

draw into a conflict
My enthusiastic support for Linda's candidacy has *embroiled* me with her opponents.

estrange (*v.*)
ə'strānj

turn (someone) from affection to dislike or enmity; make unfriendly; separate; alienate
A quarrel over an inheritance *estranged* the brothers for many years.

friction (*n.*)
'frik-shən

conflict of ideas between persons or parties of opposing views; disagreement
At the budget hearing, there was considerable *friction* between the supporters and the opponents of higher taxes.

irreconcilable (*adj.*)
,i-re-kən'sī-lə-bəl

unable to be brought into friendly accord or understanding; hostile beyond the possibility of reconciliation; not reconcilable; incompatible
It is doubtful whether anyone can make peace between the estranged partners; they have become *irreconcilable*.

litigation (*n.*)
,li-tə'gā-shən

lawsuit; act or process of carrying on a lawsuit
Some business disputes can be settled out of court; others require *litigation*.

at variance
,at've-rē-əns

in disagreement; at odds
Cynthia is an independent thinker. Her opinions are often *at variance* with those of the rest of our group.

wrangle (*v.*)
'raŋ-gəl

quarrel noisily; dispute angrily; brawl; bicker
When I left, our two neighbors were quarreling noisily. When I returned an hour later, they were still *wrangling*.

EXERCISE 2.5: *AGREEMENT* AND *DISAGREEMENT* WORDS

Complete the partially spelled agreement or disagreement word.

1. We tried to (2) con (4) the two friends who had quarreled, but we failed.
2. If our bus and train schedules (4) tail, we won't have to sit around in the waiting rooms.
3. Both sides must give in a little if there is to be a (4) act.
4. Our dog and cat are (3) pat (4); they get along well.
5. There is no reason for you to (4) oil yourself in their altercation.

---

10. Eating

---

condiment (*n.*)
'kän-də-mənt

something (such as pepper or spices) added to or served with food to enhance its flavor; seasoning
There is a shelf in our kitchen for pepper, salt, mustard, catsup, and other *condiments*.

devour (*v.*)
də'vau̇-ə(r)

eat up greedily; feast upon like an animal or a glutton; dispatch
The hikers were so hungry that they *devoured* the food as fast as it was served.

edible (*adj.*)
'e-də-bəl

fit for human consumption; eatable; comestible; non-poisonous
Never eat wild mushrooms, even though they look *edible*. They may be poisonous.

glutton (*n.*)
'glə-tən

1. greedy eater; person in the habit of eating too much
Andrea had a second helping and would have taken a third except that she didn't want to be considered a *glutton*.

2. person with a great capacity for enduring or doing something
He is a *glutton* for punishment.

luscious (*adj.*)
'lə-shəs

delicious; juicy and sweet; delectable
Ripe watermelon is *luscious*. Everyone will want a second slice.

palatable (*adj.*)
'pa-lə-tə-bəl

agreeable to the taste; pleasing; savory
The main dish had little flavor, but I made it more *palatable* by adding condiments.

slake (*v.*)
'slāk

(with reference to thirst) bring to an end through refreshing drink; satisfy; quench
On a sultry afternoon, there is a long line of people at the drinking fountain, waiting to *slake* their thirst.

succulent (*adj.*)
'sək-yə-lənt

full of juice; juicy
The steak will be dry if you leave it in the oven longer. Take it out now if you want it to be *succulent*.

voracious (*adj.*)
vȯ'rā-shəs

having a huge appetite; greedy in eating; gluttonous; ravenous
If Chester skips breakfast, he is *voracious* by lunchtime.

EXERCISE 2.6: *EATING* WORDS

Complete the partially spelled eating word.

1. There will be a choice of beverages for (3) king your thirst.
2. Please leave some of that pie for us; don't be (4) ton (3).
3. These oranges have too much pulp; they are not (5) lent.
4. We have plenty of food on hand when our relatives come for dinner because they have (1) or (6) appetites.
5. Some prefer their food served unseasoned so that they themselves may add the (3) dim (3).

Review Exercises

REVIEW 7: SENTENCE COMPLETION

On your answer paper, write the word from the list below that best fits the context. Use each word only once.

accord	antagonize
apprise	at variance
clandestine	compatible
condiment	devour
divulge	elicit
embroil	enigma
estrange	glutton
litigation	palatable
reconcile	relent
slake	succulent

1. When the water in her canteen was consumed, the hiker __?__d her thirst on some __?__ berries that she found along the trail.

2. The reason for the treasurer's resignation was never __?__d. To this day, it remains a(n) __?__ .

3. Gulliver was __?__d of the king's plot to kill him by a daring friend who visited him __?__ly.

4. Neither party could afford the high cost of __?__ , so they reached a(n) __?__ out of court.

5. By intense questioning, the lawyer __?__ed from the witness that her testimony was __?__ with what she had told the police.

6. Though I sprinkled a heavy dose of __?__s on the food I was served, I could not make it __?__ .

7. Several of us tried to __?__ the two __?__d cronies, but we succeeded only in making them more hostile to each other.

8. Mark __?__d so many of his coworkers that the boss had to lecture him on the importance of being __?__ .

9. If she had not had to skip lunch, Sara would not have __?__ed her dinner. Ordinarily, she is no __?__ .

10. The two neighboring countries have been __?__ed with each other for centuries, and it is unlikely they will soon __?__ in their hatreds.

REVIEW 8: SYNONYMS

Avoid repetition by replacing the boldfaced word or expression with a **synonym** from the list.

compact	correspond
covert	discrepancy
dovetail	edible
enlighten	luscious
manifest	wrangle

1. It was a delicious meal; the food was **delicious.**
2. Can you **inform** us about how the Johnsons are doing? We have had no information from them since they moved.
3. The truth is now **obvious** to everyone but Jack, who is obviously still confused.
4. It was no secret to our military experts that the ruthless dictator was making **secret** preparations for war.
5. Both sides agree to the truce and are ready to sign a(n) **agreement** to respect its conditions.
6. It takes an expert to distinguish poisonous mushrooms from those that are **nonpoisonous.**
7. They **quarrel noisily** all the time. They are unusually quarrelsome.
8. Here are two pieces of the picture puzzle that I cannot **fit together.** Can you help me make them fit?
9. We agree on most matters, but there are times when our views do not **agree.**
10. There is a difference between the price we paid and the price we should have paid, but fortunately it is only a slight **difference.**

REVIEW 9: ANTONYMS

Write the word from the list below that is most nearly the **opposite** of the boldfaced word or words.

acquiesce	alienate
altercation	avoid
fit	inedible
latent	lurk
overt	unpalatable

1. Some of the catch was **fit for human consumption;** the rest was __?__ .
2. We had hoped for an **accord,** but the session ended in __?__ .
3. No sooner were they **reconciled** than they became __?__d again.
4. Many now __?__ fatty foods that they used to **devour.**
5. With condiments, this dish is **agreeable to my taste;** otherwise it is __?__ .
6. Nobody **objected** to the proposal; all of us __?__d.
7. Counter-intelligence operations are **closed to public scrutiny;** they cannot be __?__ .
8. Some details telephoned by civilians about strangers in their vicinity **dovetail** with the description of the escapee; others do not __?__ .
9. There is more to be feared from foes who __?__ in the shadows than from those who **are in open view.**
10. Some of the child's talents are already **visible;** others are __?__ and may emerge later.

REVIEW 10: CONCISE WRITING

Express the thought of each sentence below in no more than four words.

1. The process of carrying on a lawsuit may cost a great deal of money.
2. Lack of flexibility prevented a settlement from being reached in which each side would have yielded a little in its demands.
3. The negotiations that had been carried on in secrecy failed to get anywhere.
4. A conflict of ideas between parties of opposing views threatens to break up the alliance.
5. The practice of lying can turn friends from affection to dislike for each other.

REVIEW 11: SYNONYM SUMMARY

Each line, when completed, should have three words similar in meaning.

1. f (1) t	m (1) tch	(6) pond
2. sep (1) rate	al (2) nate	(3) range
3. sat (2) fy	q (2) nch	(1) lake
4. y (2) ld	sof (1) en	(2) lent
5. (5) cover	c (1) vert	clan (7)
6. sl (1)	f (1) rtive	st (2) lthy

7. inconsisten (1) y	var (2) tion	(3) crepancy
8. glut (2) nous	raven (3)	(2) racious
9. dorm (1) nt	potent (2) l	late (2)
10. str (1) fe	(3) sension	(3) cord
11. sh (1) w	(3) play	m (1) n (1) fest
12. delic (3) s	(2) lectable	l (1) s (1) ious
13. sn (2) k	(2) ink	l (1) rk
14. agr (3) ble	congen (2) l	comp (1) t (1) ble
15. ass (1) nt	(2) quiesce	a (1) cede
16. extr (2) t	(1) voke	el (1) c (1) t
17. seq (2) ster	cl (2) ster	(2) clude
18. c (1) mply	ob (1) y	(3) form
19. a (1) c (1) rd	coven (1) nt	(3) pact
20. spl (1) t	s (1) hism	cl (2) v (1) ge

REVIEW 12: ANALOGIES

Which lettered pair of words—*a, b, c, d,* or *e*—most nearly expresses the same relationship as the capitalized pair?

1. ENIGMA : BEWILDERMENT
   - (*a*) pain : swelling
   - (*b*) irritability : fatigue
   - (*c*) conservation : scarcity
   - (*d*) blunder : embarrassment
   - (*e*) skid : icing

2. GLUTTON : FOOD
   - (*a*) alcoholic : beverages
   - (*b*) miser : hoarding
   - (*c*) aggressor : restraint
   - (*d*) workaholic : whiskey
   - (*e*) gossip : secrecy

3. CLANDESTINE : SECRET
   - (*a*) gutless : dastardly
   - (*b*) equitable : oppressive
   - (*c*) initial : terminal
   - (*d*) evasive : frank
   - (*e*) atypical : customary

4. STEALTHY : CAT
   - (*a*) gentle : mule
   - (*b*) deliberate : hare
   - (*c*) timid : panther
   - (*d*) lumbering : elephant
   - (*e*) blind : eagle

5. COMESTIBLE : CONSUME
   - (*a*) unforgivable : condone
   - (*b*) permissible : allow
   - (*c*) enigmatic : understand
   - (*d*) transient : remain
   - (*e*) intolerable : endure

6. MUSTARD : CONDIMENT
   (a) cinnamon : appetite   (b) bulb : socket
   (c) oak : evergreen   (d) saw : tool
   (e) shrub : tree

7. SLAKE : QUENCH
   (a) acquiesce : object   (b) deluge : inundate
   (c) impede : expedite   (d) ignite : extinguish
   (e) squander : conserve

8. SAVORY : TONGUE
   (a) distinct : voice   (b) wavy : hair
   (c) melodious : ear   (d) acute : vision
   (e) desirous : fingers

9. LATENT : INCONSPICUOUS
   (a) manifest : invisible   (b) toxic : nonpoisonous
   (c) final : unalterable   (d) rational : illogical
   (e) tasty : unpalatable

10. ALIAS : NAME
   (a) wig : hair   (b) arrow : direction
   (c) razor : beard   (d) detergent : dirt
   (e) reply : inquiry

CENTRAL IDEAS 11–15

Pretest 3

Write the *letter* of the best answer.

1. A wait of __?__ before being served is *inordinate*.
   (A) five minutes   (B) two hours   (C) thirty seconds

2. *Cogent* arguments are __?__.
   (A) illogical   (B) preventable   (C) convincing

3. A *scrupulous* person has a high regard for __?__.
   (A) what is right   (B) those in authority   (C) what is beautiful

4. If you feel *enervated*, you are not so __?__ as usual.
   (A) bored   (B) nervous   (C) strong

5. A team that *defaults* __?__ the game.
   (A) delays   (B) loses   (C) wins

THE ANSWERS ARE
1. B 2. C 3. A 4. C 5. B

How well did you do? Any questions that you may have missed or are uncertain about will be cleared up for you as you work through Central Ideas 11–15, which follow immediately.

11. Size, Quantity

colossal (*adj.*)
kə'lä-səl

huge; enormous; gigantic; mammoth; vast
The game was played in a *colossal* sports arena with a seating capacity of more than 60,000.

commodious (*adj.*)
kə'mō-dē-əs

spacious and comfortable; roomy; ample; not confining
It will be easy to move in the equipment because the halls and stairways are *commodious*.

gamut (*n.*)
'ga-mət

entire range of anything, as of musical notes, emotions, etc.
First I thought I had done very well, then well, and finally, poorly. I ran the *gamut* from confidence to despair.

infinite (*adj.*)
'in-fə-nət

without ends or limits; boundless; endless; inexhaustible
We do not know whether space is bounded or *infinite*.

infinitesimal (*adj.*)
,in,fi-nə'te-sə-məl

so small as to be almost nothing; immeasurably small; very minute
If there is any salt in this soup, it must be *infinitesimal*. I can't taste it.

inflate (*v.*)
ən'flāt

swell with air or gas; expand; puff up
Since one of the tires had lost air, we stopped at a gas station to *inflate* it.

inordinate (*adj.*)
ə'nȯ(r)-də-nət

much too great; not kept within reasonable bounds; excessive; immoderate
Alex kept my book for such an *inordinate* length of time that I shall never lend him anything again.

iota (*n.*)
i'ō-tə

(ninth and smallest letter of the Greek alphabet) very small quantity; infinitesimal amount; bit
If you make the same mistake again, despite all my warnings, I will not have one *iota* of sympathy for you.

magnitude (*n.*)
'mag-nə,tüd

size; greatness; largeness; importance
To supervise eight hundred employees is a responsibility of considerable *magnitude*.

picayune (*adj.*)
,pi-kə'yün

concerned with trifling matters; petty; small; of little value
In studying, don't spend too much time on *picayune* details. Concentrate on the really important matters.

pittance (*n.*)
'pi-təns

small amount; meager wage or allowance
At those low wages, few will apply for the job. Who wants to work for a *pittance*?

puny (*adj.*)
'pyü-nē

slight or inferior in size, power, or importance; weak; insignificant
The skyscraper dwarfs the surrounding buildings. By comparison to it, they seem *puny*.

superabundance (*n.*) ,sü-pə(r)-ə'bən-dəns	great abundance; surplus; excess Ronald's committee doesn't need any more assistance. He has a *superabundance* of helpers.

EXERCISE 2.7: *SIZE* AND *QUANTITY* WORDS

Complete the partially spelled size or quantity word.

1. The homes from which students come run the (1) am (2) from afflu-ence to indigence.
2. This (3) mod (4) sofa can accommodate four people comfortably.
3. There was a (3) era (8) of food. We could have had several more guests for dinner.
4. The spare tire needs to be (3) late (1); it has too much air.
5. Management regards the demand for an immediate twenty percent increase in wages as (4) din (3).

---

12. Weakness

---

debilitate (*v.*) də'bi-lə,tāt	impair the strength of; enfeeble; weaken The fever had so *debilitated* the patient that she lacked the strength to sit up.
decadent (*adj.*) 'de-kə-dənt	marked by decay or decline; falling off; declining; de-teriorating When industry moves away, a flourishing town may quickly become *decadent*.
decrepit (*adj.*) də'kre-pət	broken down or weakened by old age or use; worn out Billy Dawes rode past the redcoats on a horse that looked *decrepit* and about to collapse.
dilapidated (*adj.*) də'la-pə,dā-təd	falling to pieces; decayed; partly ruined or decayed through neglect Up the road was an abandoned farmhouse, par-tially in ruins, and near it a barn, even more *dilapi-dated*.
enervate (*v.*) 'e-nə(r),vāt	lessen the vigor or strength of; weaken; enfeeble The extreme heat had *enervated* us. We had to rest under a shady tree until our strength was restored.

flimsy (*adj.*)   lacking strength or solidity; frail; unsubstantial
'flim-zē   Judy understands algebra well, but I have only a
             flimsy grasp of the subject.

frail (*adj.*)   not very strong; weak; fragile
'frāl   Mountain climbing is for the robust, not the *frail*.

incapacitate (*v.*)   render incapable or unfit; disable; paralyze
,in-kə'pa-sə,tāt   Ruth will be absent today. A sore throat has *inca-
             pacitated* her.

infirmity (*n.*)   weakness; feebleness; frailty
ən'fər-mə-tē   On leaving the hospital, John felt almost too weak
             to walk, but he soon overcame this *infirmity*.

---

13. Strength

bulwark (*n.*)   wall-like defensive structure; rampart; defense; pro-
'bul-wə(r)k   tection; safeguard
             For centuries the British regarded their Navy as
             their principal *bulwark* against invasion.

citadel (*n.*)   fortress; stronghold
'si-tə-dəl   The fortified city of Singapore was once consid-
             ered unconquerable. In 1942, however, this *citadel* fell
             to the Japanese.

cogent (*adj.*)   forcible; compelling; powerful; convincing
'kō-jənt   A request for a raise is more likely to succeed if
             supported with *cogent* reasons.

dynamic (*adj.*)   forceful; energetic; active
dī'na-mik   Audrey represents us forcefully and energetically.
             She is a *dynamic* speaker.

formidable (*adj.*) exciting fear by reason of strength, size, difficulty,
'fo(r)-mə-də-bəl   etc.; hard to overcome; to be dreaded
             The climbers gasped when they caught sight of the
             formidable peak.

forte (*n.*)   strong point; that which one does with excellence
'fo(r)t   I am better than Jack in writing but not in math;
             that is his *forte*.

impregnable (*adj.*) im'preg-nə-bəl	incapable of being taken by assault; unconquerable; invincible Before World War II, the French regarded their Maginot Line fortifications as an *impregnable* bulwark against a German invasion.
invigorate (*v.*) ən'vi-gə,rāt	give vigor to; fill with life and energy; strengthen; enliven If you feel enervated by the heat, try a swim in the cool ocean. It will *invigorate* you.
robust (*adj.*) rō'bəst	strong and healthy; vigorous; sturdy; sound The lifeguard was in excellent physical condition. I had never seen anyone more *robust*.
tenacious (*adj.*) tə'nā-shəs	holding fast or tending to hold fast; unyielding; stubborn; strong After the dog got the ball, I tried to dislodge it from her *tenacious* jaws, but I couldn't.
vehement (*adj.*) 'vē-ə-mənt	showing strong feeling; forceful; violent; furious Your protest was too mild. If it had been more *vehement*, the supervisor might have paid attention to it.
vigor (*n.*) 'vi-gə(r)	active strength or force; energy The robust young pitcher performed with extraordinary *vigor* for seven innings, but weakened in the eighth and was removed from the game.

EXERCISE 2.8: *WEAKNESS* AND *STRENGTH* WORDS

Complete the partially spelled weakness or strength word.

1. It will be difficult to defeat the faculty players; they certainly do not look (5) pit.
2. Ed was quite (2) ail until the age of twelve, but then he developed into a robust youth.
3. I doubt you can beat Ann in tennis. It happens to be her (1) or (2).
4. A sprained ankle may sideline you for several weeks, but a fractured ankle will (2) cap (7) you for months.
5. Laziness, luxury, and a lack of initiative are some of the characteristics of a (2) cad (3) society.

14. Neglect

default (*n.*)
də'fólt
 failure to do something required; neglect; negligence; failure to meet a financial obligation
  The Royals must be on the playing field by 4 p.m. If they do not appear, they will lose the game by *default.*

default (*v.*)
 fail to pay or appear when due
  The finance company took away Mr. Lee's car when he *defaulted* on the payments.

heedless (*adj.*)
'hēd-ləs
 not taking heed; inattentive; careless; thoughtless; unmindful; reckless
  If you drive in a blizzard, *heedless* of the weather bureau's warnings, you may not reach your destination.

ignore (*v.*)
ig'nȯə(r)
 refuse to take notice of; disregard; overlook
  The motorist was given a ticket for *ignoring* a stop sign.

inadvertent (*adj.*)
,in-əd'vər-tənt
 (used to describe blunders, mistakes, etc., rather than people) heedless; thoughtless; careless
  Unfortunately, I made an *inadvertent* remark in Irma's presence about her losing the election.

neglect (*v.*)
nə'glekt
 give little or no attention to; leave undone; disregard
  Most members of the cast *neglected* their studies during rehearsals, but after the performance they caught up quickly.

neglect (*n.*)
 lack of proper care or attention; disregard; negligence
  For leaving his post, the guard was charged with *neglect* of duty.

remiss (*adj.*)
rə'mis
 negligent; careless; lax
  The owner of the stolen car was *remiss* in having left the keys in the vehicle.

sloven (*n.*)
'sləv-ən
 untidy person
  Cleanup is easy at our lunch table if there are no *slovens.*

slovenly (*adj.*)
'slə-vən-lē
 negligent of neatness or order in one's dress, habits, work, etc.; slipshod; sloppy
  You would not expect anyone so neat in personal appearance to be *slovenly* in housekeeping.

15. Care

discreet (*adj.*)
də'skrēt
showing good judgment in speech and action; wisely cautious
　　You were *discreet* not to say anything about our plans when Harry was here. He can't keep a secret.

heed (*v.*)
'hēd
take notice of; give careful attention to; mind
　　I didn't *heed* the warning that the pavements were icy. That's why I slipped.

meticulous (*adj.*)
mə'tik-yə-ləs
extremely or excessively careful about small details; fussy
　　Before signing a contract, read it carefully, including the fine print. This is one case where it pays to be *meticulous*.

scrupulous (*adj.*)
'skrü-pyə-ləs
having painstaking regard for what is right; conscientious; honest; strict; precise
　　My instructor refuses to be a judge because two of her former students are contestants. She is very *scrupulous*.

scrutinize (*v.*)
'skrü-tə,nīz
examine closely; inspect
　　The gatekeeper *scrutinized* Harvey's pass before letting him in, but he just glanced at mine.

solicitude (*n.*)
sə'li-sə,tüd
anxious or excessive care; concern; anxiety
　　My sister's *solicitude* over getting into college ended when she received word that she had been accepted.

vigilance (*n.*)
'vi-jə-ləns
alert watchfulness to discover and avoid danger; alertness; caution; watchfulness
　　The security guard who apprehended the thief was praised for *vigilance*.

wary (*adj.*)
'we(ə)-rē
on one's guard against danger, deception, etc.; cautious; vigilant
　　General Braddock might not have been defeated if he had been *wary* of an ambush.

EXERCISE 2.9: *NEGLECT* AND *CARE* WORDS

Complete the partially spelled neglect or care word.

1. Before handing in my paper, I (2) rut (5) d it to see if there were any errors.
2. When Mom scolded Jeffrey for the (2) oven (2) appearance of his room, he promised to make it more tidy.
3. If you (2) nor (1) the warning, you may have to suffer the consequences.
4. My aunt would have lost her case by (2) fault if she had failed to appear in court.
5. Deborah is (3) up (5) about returning books to the library on time. She has never had to pay a fine.

Review Exercises

REVIEW 13: SENTENCE COMPLETION

On your answer paper, write the word from the list below that best fits the context. Use each word only once.

colossal	debilitate
decrepit	default
discreet	formidable
forte	frail
heed	ignore
impregnable	inadvertent
invigorate	iota
puny	remiss
scrupulous	vehement
vigilance	vigor

1. Milly regrets that she __?__d your directions. She could have saved a great deal of time and trouble if she had __?__ed them.
2. Undercover detectives must be exceptionally __?__. If they make one __?__ remark, they may risk death.
3. Although Nathan, our __?__ linebacker, is only of average size, he is so quick and strong that he has made our defense __?__. Not one team has scored a touchdown against us.
4. In Lilliput, where people were six inches tall, Gulliver was __?__, but in Brobdingnag, the land of the giants, he looked __?__.
5. There is not one __?__ of truth in the rumor that Barbara has misused club funds. She is the most __?__ person I have ever met.
6. Her brother's __?__ is carpentry. He can rebuild a(n) __?__ house in a few weeks.
7. Despite their __?__ protests, the farmer and his family were forced to vacate their property because they had __?__ed on their mortgage.
8. Bart's long illness has left him so __?__ that he has to postpone his return to the team to regain his __?__.
9. The convict got away because his guards were __?__. If they had exercised proper __?__, he would not have escaped.
10. Pam felt __?__d on Friday, after working fourteen hours at her office, but she hoped that the relaxation of the weekend would __?__ her.

REVIEW 14: SYNONYMS

Avoid repetition by replacing the boldfaced word or expression with a synonym from the following words.

bulwark	cogent
commodious	dynamic
flimsy	incapacitate
magnitude	robust
slovenly	solicitude

1. The Armed Forces protect our freedom. They are our principal **protection** against foreign aggression.
2. Arthritis is his most important ailment. He has other problems, too, but they are of lesser **importance.**
3. We are concerned about my sister's health, and when we don't hear from her our **concern** increases.
4. You seem to lack energy today. Usually, you are much more **energetic.**
5. The locker I was assigned to had been used by an untidy person; it was very **untidy.**
6. Injuries sustained in practice often **disable** athletes and put them on the disability list.
7. There is not too much room in this closet; that one is more **roomy.**
8. I am convinced you are in error, unless you can offer **convincing** proof to the contrary.
9. Eileen was not very strong before her appendectomy, but she will soon be **strong and healthy** again.
10. Most of the excuses that were given had almost no substance whatsoever; they were very **unsubstantial.**

REVIEW 15: ANTONYMS

Write the word from the list below that is most nearly the opposite of the boldfaced word or words.

confining	heedless
ignore	infinite
inflate	meticulous
picayune	scrutinize
sloven	wary

1. Most of the salesclerks were not **fussy about small details,** but one was truly __?__ .

2. Thoughtless consumers behave as if our water supplies were __?__ , when in fact they are quite **limited.**

3. It is unlikely that a(n) __?__ will quickly acquire the habits of a **neat person.**

4. The __?__ motorist slows down and looks in all directions before crossing an intersection; the **foolhardy** one speeds right through.

5. Hardly anyone **took notice of** the latecomers; most of the audience __?__d them.

6. People used to **commodious** accommodations may find the ship's cabins too __?__ .

7. Customs guards do not **closely examine** every piece of a traveler's luggage, but they may select one valise and __?__ its contents.

8. Smoking by visitors in a patient's room is a **major** violation of hospital rules; it is not a(n) __?__ matter.

9. The driver was __?__ of the altercation at the back of the bus because she had to be **attentive** to the road.

10. Try to have an even temper. Do not let one victory __?__ , or one defeat **deflate,** your self-esteem.

REVIEW 16: CONCISE WRITING

Express the thought of each sentence below in no more than four words.

1. The expenses that we had were so small that they came to almost nothing.

2. Addicts are subject to cravings that they are unable to keep within reasonable bounds.

3. Those who do proofreading have to be extremely careful about small details.

4. Many people pay little or no attention to the responsibilities that they are supposed to carry out.

5. There is no fortress in the whole wide world that is not capable of being taken by assault.

REVIEW 17: SYNONYM SUMMARY

Each line, when completed, should have three words similar in meaning.

1. stren (1) then	(2) liven	invig (1) r (1) te
2. l (1) x	car (1) less	(2) miss
3. con (1) ern	(2) xiety	soli (1) itude
4. (1) well	exp (1) nd	(2) flate
5. dis (1) ble	paral (1) ze	inca (2) citate
6. f (1) rceful	(2) ergetic	(2) namic
7. st (1) rdy	(2) gorous	(2) bust
8. decl (1) ning	(2) teriorating	dec (1) dent
9. (3) regard	(4) look	(2) nore
10. (2) gantic	mamm (1) th	c (1) l (1) ss (1) l
11. (2) nest	consc (2) nt (1) ous	scr (1) p (1) lous
12. w (2) k	insigni (2) cant	p (1) ny
13. (2) fense	r (1) mpart	bulw (2) k
14. fr (2) l	(2) substantial	flim (1) y
15. (2) cessive	(2) moderate	in (1) rd (1) nate
16. (2) attentive	c (3) less	heed (4)
17. s (1) rpl (1) s	(2) cess	(5) abundance
18. r (2) my	(1) mple	(3) modious
19. strongh (2) d	fort (4)	c (1) t (1) del
20. (2) feeble	weak (2)	(1) nervate

REVIEW 18: ANALOGIES

Which lettered pair of words—*a, b, c, d,* or *e*—most nearly expresses the same relationship as the capitalized pair?

1. DEBILITATE : VIGOR
   - (*a*) pauperize : penury
   - (*b*) jeopardize : danger
   - (*c*) incarcerate : liberty
   - (*d*) economize : conservation
   - (*e*) fortify : courage

2. INFINITE : END
   - (*a*) vital : life
   - (*b*) significant : meaning
   - (*c*) immortal : existence
   - (*d*) commodious : room
   - (*e*) anonymous : name

3. PITTANCE : ABUNDANCE
   (a) sprinkle : deluge   (b) smidgen : trace
   (c) conflagration : flame   (d) pity : compassion
   (e) mountain : hill

4. SLOVEN : IMMACULATE
   (a) glutton : voracious   (b) despot : domineering
   (c) craven : pusillanimous   (d) bigot : unprejudiced
   (e) buffoon : ridiculous

5. TENACIOUS : YIELD
   (a) remorseful : repent   (b) unforgiving : relent
   (c) wary : heed   (d) voracious : devour
   (e) contentious : fight

6. SCRUTINIZE : EXAMINE
   (a) saunter : walk   (b) skim : read
   (c) ape : copy   (d) mumble : talk
   (e) doze : sleep

7. IGNORE : OVERLOOK
   (a) hoard : squander   (b) learn : instruct
   (c) abate : intensify   (d) initiate : terminate
   (e) acknowledge : avow

8. COLOSSAL : ELEPHANT
   (a) puny : whale   (b) gentle : lamb
   (c) microscopic : ameba   (d) extinct : dinosaur
   (e) infectious : virus
   Hint: **Colossal** describes the size of an **elephant**.

9. DRUNKENNESS : FRAILTY
   (a) tomato : vegetable   (b) award : excellence
   (c) diploma : document   (d) gas : oxygen
   (e) condiment : appetite
   Hint: Note that **tomato** is not a **vegetable**.

10. DECADENT : FLOURISHING
   (a) picayune : invaluable   (b) avaricious : greedy
   (c) slipshod : untidy   (d) lax : remiss
   (e) scrupulous : precise

CENTRAL IDEAS 16–20

Pretest 4

Write the *letter* of the best answer.

1. When you *defer* to someone, you are __?__ .
   (A) wasting time   (B) being rude   (C) showing respect

2. Conditions were bad both __?__ and *abroad*.
   (A) on land   (B) at home   (C) below deck

3. A *perennial* danger is one that is __?__ .
   (A) constant   (B) avoidable   (C) temporary

4. __?__ is a serious *infraction*.
   (A) Losing your wallet   (B) Forgery   (C) Testifying under oath

5. Anything that is *incumbent* on you is __?__ .
   (A) unpleasant   (B) not your business   (C) your duty

THE ANSWERS ARE

1. C 2. B 3. A 4. B 5. C

Question 1 may have puzzled you, since *defer* was used in a way not yet studied. This is one of the vocabulary skills you will learn about in the final Central Ideas section, numbered 16–20.

16. Residence

abroad (*adv.*)
ə'bròd
    in or to a foreign land or lands
        After living *abroad* for a time, Robert Browning became homesick for his native England.

commute (*v.*)
kə'myüt
    travel back and forth daily, as from a home in the suburbs to a job in the city
        Large numbers of suburban residents regularly *commute* to the city.

commuter (*n.*)   person who commutes
Many a *commuter* spends as much as three hours a day in getting to and from work.

denizen (*n.*)   inhabitant; dweller; resident; occupant
'de-nə-zən   On their safari, the tourists photographed lions, tigers, and other ferocious *denizens* of the jungle.

domicile (*n.*)   house; home; dwelling; residence; abode
'dä-mə,sīl   Soon after they moved, the Coopers invited us to visit them at their new *domicile*.

inmate (*n.*)   person confined in an institution, prison, hospital, etc.
'in,māt   When the warden took charge, the prison had fewer than 100 *inmates*.

migrate (*v.*)   1. move from one place to settle in another
'mī,grāt   Because they were persecuted in England, the Puritans *migrated* to Holland.

2. move from one place to another with the change of season
In winter, many European birds *migrate* to the British Isles in search of a more temperate climate.

native (*n.*)   person born in a particular place
'nā-tiv   His entire family are *natives* of New Jersey except the grandparents, who were born abroad.

native (*adj.*)   born or originating in a particular place
Tobacco, potatoes, and tomatoes are *native* American plants that were introduced into Europe by explorers returning from the New World.

nomad (*n.*)   member of a tribe that has no fixed abode but wanders from place to place; wanderer
'nō,mad   *Nomads* have no fixed homes but move from region to region to secure their food supply.

nomadic (*adj.*)   roaming from place to place; wandering; roving
nō'ma-dik   Mobile homes appeal to people with *nomadic* inclinations.

sojourn (*n.*)   temporary stay
'sò-jərn   On her trip home, Geraldine will stop in St. Louis for a two-day *sojourn* with relatives.

EXERCISE 2.10: *RESIDENCE* WORDS

Complete the partially spelled residence word. The parentheses indicate the number of missing letters.

1. Many Northerners (2) grate to Florida in the winter.
2. Humans are vastly outnumbered by the other den (5) of this earth.
3. Most people are not affluent enough to have a summer residence in the country and a permanent (2) mi (4) in the city.
4. These are not native melons; they are shipped from (2) road.
5. The regulations permit (2) ma (3) to receive visitors on Sunday.

---

17. Disobedience

---

defiance (*n.*)
də'fī-əns

refusal to obey authority; disposition to resist; state of opposition
    The union showed *defiance* of the court order against a strike by calling the workers off their jobs.

infraction (*n.*)
ən'frak-shən

breaking (of a law, regulation, etc.); violation; breach
    Parking at the bus stop is illegal. Motorists committing this *infraction* are fined.

insubordinate (*adj.*)
‚in-sə'bȯ(r)-də-nət

not submitting to authority; disobedient; mutinous; rebellious
    Had the cabinet officer ignored the President's instructions, he would have been *insubordinate* and would have been asked to resign.

insurgent (*n.*)
ən'sər-jənt

person who rises in revolt; rebel
    When the revolt broke out, the government ordered its troops to arrest the *insurgents*.

insurrection (*n.*)
in-sə'rek-shən

uprising against established authority; rebellion; revolt
    Troops had to be used in 1794 to put down an *insurrection* in Pennsylvania known as the Whisky Rebellion.

malcontent (*n.*)
'mal-kən-tent

discontented person; rebel
    The work stoppage was caused by a few *malcontents* who felt they had been ignored when promotions were made.

perverse (*adj.*)
pə(r)'vərs

obstinate (in opposing what is right or reasonable); willful; wayward

Though I had carefully explained the shorter route to him, the *perverse* youngster came by the longer way.

sedition (*n.*)
sə'di-shən

speech, writing, or action seeking to overthrow the government; treason

During World War I, about 1500 persons who spoke or wrote against our form of government or the war effort were arrested for *sedition*.

transgress (*v.*)
trans'gres

go beyond set limits of; violate, break, or overstep a command or law

Mrs. Joe Gargery imposed strict regulations on her husband and her young brother, and she punished them whenever they *transgressed*.

trespass (*v.*)
'tres-pəs

encroach on another's rights, privileges, property, etc.

The owner erected a "Keep Off" sign to discourage people from *trespassing* on her land.

18. Obedience

acquiesce (*v.*)
,ak-wē'es

accept by keeping silent; submit quietly; comply

When Tom suggested that we go to the movies, I *acquiesced* because there seemed nothing else to do.

allegiance (*n.*)
ə'lē-jəns

loyalty; devotion; faithfulness; fidelity

When aliens become American citizens, they must pledge *allegiance* to the United States.

defer (*v.*)
də'fə(r)

yield to another out of respect, authority, or courtesy; submit politely

I thought my answer was correct, but I *deferred* to the teacher's opinion because of her superior knowledge.

discipline (*v.*)
'di-sə-plin

train in obedience; bring under control

The Walkers should not complain that their son does not obey because they never tried to *discipline* him.

docile (*adj.*)
'dä-səl

easily taught; obedient; tractable; submissive

Diane listens when you explain something to her, but her sister is much less *docile*.

meek (*adj.*)
'mēk

submissive; yielding without resentment when ordered about or hurt by others; acquiescent
    About a third of the commuters protested the fare hike. The rest were too *meek* to complain.

pliable (*adj.*)
'plī-ə-bəl

easily bent or influenced; yielding; adaptable
    We tried to get Joe to change his mind, but he was not *pliable*. Perhaps you can influence him.

submit (*v.*)
səb'mit

yield to another's will, authority, or power; yield; surrender
    Though he had boasted he would never be taken alive, the fugitive *submitted* without a struggle when the police arrived.

tractable (*adj.*)
'trak-tə-bəl

easily controlled, led, or taught; docile
    George III wanted the Thirteen Colonies to be *tractable*.

EXERCISE 2.11: *DISOBEDIENCE* AND *OBEDIENCE* WORDS

Complete the partially spelled disobedience or obedience word.

1. Dictators want their subjects to be me (2).
2. Mrs. Farrell often leaves her children in our care because they are very do (4) with us.
3. The insurgents were ordered to yield, but they will never (4) it.
4. When I asked my brother to turn down his radio, he made it even louder. I couldn't understand why he was so (3) verse.
5. If the neighbors complain about your playing your saxophone after 10 p.m., you should, as a matter of courtesy, de (3) to their wishes.

19. Time

chronic (*adj.*)
'krä-nik

1. marked by long duration or frequent recurrence
    Carl's sore arm is not a new development but the return of a *chronic* ailment.

2. having a characteristic, habit, disease, etc., for a long time; confirmed; habitual
    Some people are *chronic* complainers. They are always dissatisfied.

concurrent (*adj.*)
kən'kər-ənt

occurring at the same time; simultaneous; contemporary

When the strike is settled, there will probably be an increase in wages and a *concurrent* increase in prices.

dawdle (*v.*)
'dȯ-dəl

waste time; loiter; idle

Let's get going. If we *dawdle* we'll be late for dinner.

imminent (*adj.*)
'i-mə-nənt

about to happen; threatening to occur soon; near at hand

The sudden darkening of the skies and the thunder in the distance apprised us that rain was *imminent*.

incipient (*adj.*)
in'si-pē-ənt

beginning to show itself; commencing; in an early stage; initial

Certain serious diseases can be successfully treated if detected in an *incipient* stage.

intermittent (*adj.*)
,in-tə(r)'mi-tənt

coming and going at intervals; stopping and beginning again; recurrent; periodic

The showers were *intermittent*; there were intervals when the sun broke through the clouds.

perennial (*adj.*)
pə're-nē-əl

1. lasting indefinitely; incessant; enduring; permanent; constant; perpetual; everlasting

Don't think that war has plagued only modern times. It has been a *perennial* curse.

2. (of plants) continuing to live from year to year

Some grasses last only a year. Others are *perennial*.

procrastinate (*v.*)
prō'kras-tə,nāt

put off things that should be done until later; defer; postpone

Most of the picnickers took cover when rain seemed imminent. The few that *procrastinated* got drenched.

protract (*v.*)
prō'trakt

draw out; lengthen in time; prolong; continue; extend

We had planned to stay only for lunch but, at our host's insistence, we *protracted* our visit until after dinner.

sporadic (*adj.*)
spə'ra-dik

occurring occasionally or in scattered instances; isolated; infrequent

Though polio has been practically wiped out, there have been *sporadic* cases of the disease.

EXERCISE 2.12: *TIME* WORDS

Complete the partially spelled time word.

1. My sister is perverse. If I ask her when she will be through with the phone, she will deliberately (1) rot (4) her conversation.
2. There are two excellent TV programs tonight but, unfortunately, they are (3) cur (4).
3. If public utilities provided (2) term (6) service, consumers would not stand for it.
4. Hay fever is a (3) on (2) sickness that affects millions, particularly in the spring and fall.
5. The complaints, (2) or (4) at first, have become quite frequent.

---

20. Necessity

---

compulsory (*adj.*)
kəm'pəl-sə-rē

required by authority; obligatory
   State law makes attendance at school *compulsory* for children of certain ages.

entail (*v.*)
ən'tāl

involve as a necessary consequence; impose; require
   A larger apartment will of course *entail* greater expense.

essence (*n.*)
'e-səns

most necessary or significant part, aspect, or feature; fundamental nature; core
   The union and management held a lengthy meeting without getting to the *essence* of the dispute—wages.

gratuitous (*adj.*)
grə'-tyü-ə-təs

uncalled for; unwarranted
   Were it not for her *gratuitous* interference, the opposing sides would have quickly settled their dispute.

imperative (*adj.*)
əm'pe-rə-tiv

not to be avoided; urgent; necessary; obligatory; compulsory
   To maintain a good credit rating, it is *imperative* that you pay your bills on time.

incumbent (*adj.*)
ən'kəm-bənt

(with *on* or *upon*) imposed as a duty; obligatory
   Arlo felt it *incumbent* on him to pay for the window, since he had hit the ball that broke it.

indispensable (*adj.*)
,in-də'spen-sə-bəl

absolutely necessary; essential
　　If we have to, we can do without luxuries and entertainment. However, food, shelter, and clothing are *indispensable*.

necessitate (*v.*)
nə'se-sə,tāt

make necessary; require; demand
　　The sharp increase in the cost of fuel *necessitated* a rise in the bus fare.

oblige (*v.*)
ə'blīj

compel; force; put under a duty or obligation
　　The law *obliges* the police to secure a warrant before making a search.

obviate (*v.*)
'äb-vē,āt

make unnecessary; preclude
　　Karen has agreed to lend me the book I need. This *obviates* my trip to the library.

prerequisite (*n.*)
prē'rek-wə-zət

something required beforehand
　　A satisfactory grade in Basic Art is a *prerequisite* for Advanced Art.

pressing (*adj.*)
'pre-siŋ

requiring immediate attention; urgent
　　Before rearranging my furniture, I have some more *pressing* matters to attend to, such as finishing my research paper.

superfluous (*adj.*)
sü'pə(r)-flə-wəs

more than what is enough or necessary; surplus; excessive; unnecessary
　　Our town already has enough gas stations; an additional one would be *superfluous*.

EXERCISE 2.13: *NECESSITY* WORDS

Complete the partially spelled necessity word.

1. Since our trunk is rather small, we can take along only things that are (5) pens (4).
2. Since they are your guests, isn't it (4) mbent on you to make them feel at home?
3. Automation, if adopted by the company, may (2) via (2) the hiring of additional employees.
4. The ess (4) of the Bill of Rights is that it protects us against tyranny.
5. I was surprised to hear the team needs me because I had thought I was super (6).

Review Exercises

REVIEW 19: SENTENCE COMPLETION

On your answer paper, write the word from the list below that best fits the context. Use each word only once.

abroad	chronic
commute	defer
denizen	docile
domicile	entail
imperative	incumbent
insubordinate	insurrection
migrate	nomad
oblige	obviate
prerequisite	pressing
procrastinate	protract

1. If the __?__s of this community want better street lighting, it is __?__ on them to contribute to the expense of additional lampposts.
2. When her fans applauded so enthusiastically, the fatigued singer felt __?__d to __?__ her concert for an additional thirty minutes.
3. Because Andrea's job commands a high salary, she is willing to __?__ three hours a day between her __?__ and the company's headquarters.
4. Being a professional basketball player __?__s living the life of a(n) __?__, as pro teams have to travel from city to city across the country.
5. Unlike his predecessor, who was usually __?__, Major obeys my every command. I am lucky to have such a(n) __?__ dog.
6. Your research paper is due in three days, so it is __?__ that you start working on it. Why do you always __?__?
7. Renata has decided to __?__ to a drier climate because of her __?__ asthma.
8. A(n) __?__ in his country required the president of the new democracy to end his travels __?__ and return home immediately.
9. The reporter had to __?__ her story on the museum exhibit when she was given a more __?__ assignment.
10. Herman was told that his year of study in France will __?__ his taking Introductory French, the __?__ for Second-Year French.

REVIEW 20: SYNONYMS

Avoid repetition by replacing the boldfaced word or expression with a synonym from the following words.

acquiesce	allegiance
dawdle	discipline(d)
indispensable	insurgent(s)
pliable	perennial
sojourn	trespass

1. Some youngsters fail to obey regulations because they have never been **trained in obedience.**
2. The **rebels** refuse to end their rebellion unless their terms are met.
3. They stupidly took along unnecessary equipment, but forgot a few small items that were **absolutely necessary.**
4. Anyone who complains constantly about trivial matters is bound to be regarded as a **constant** nuisance.
5. We enjoyed our **temporary stay** with you; we regret we could not stay longer.
6. When unreasonable demands were made, we did not **submit quietly.** Why were you quiet?
7. The military leaders say they are loyal to the central government, but questions nevertheless remain about their **loyalty.**
8. We never encroached on their property. Why did they **encroach** on ours?
9. Let's not **waste time.** Time is precious.
10. The mayors have considerable influence with the governor, but sometimes he is not **easily influenced.**

REVIEW 21: ANTONYMS

Enter the word from the list below that is most nearly the opposite of the boldfaced word or words.

alien	indispensable
intermittent	meek
native	perennial
pliable	protract
submit	tractable

1. Some of the fruits and vegetables we buy are **imported.** Others are of __?__ origin.
2. **Curtail** your introductory remarks. If you __?__ them, you may bore the audience.
3. __?__ individuals consider themselves dispensable; they would never be so **arrogant** as to say they are irreplaceable.
4. There would have been no room for compromise if the negotiators were **obstinate;** fortunately, they were __?__ .
5. Freedom-loving people would rather **resist** injustice than __?__ to it.
6. The rain was **continuous.** If it were __?__ , I could have been outdoors briefly without getting drenched.
7. **Native** Americans usually do not understand the conversations they often hear that are conducted in __?__ languages.
8. With adequate security, a large crowd is __?__ ; otherwise it may become **unruly.**
9. **Annual** plants die at the end of the growing season, but __?__ ones flower year after year.
10. Americans consume some foods that are __?__ for nutrition, and some that definitely are **not essential.**

REVIEW 22: CONCISE WRITING

Express the thought of each sentence below in no more than four words.

1. Every workday, Beverly travels from her home in the suburbs to the city.
2. The noise would stop for a while, and then it would start up all over again.
3. Going to court either to sue someone or to resolve a dispute involves a great deal of expense as a necessary consequence.
4. Tribes that used to roam from province to province were a threat to the continued existence of Rome.
5. Europe was plagued by wars that went on and on for long periods of time.

REVIEW 23: SYNONYM SUMMARY

Each line, when completed, should have three words similar in meaning. Supply the missing letters.

1. pr (1) l (1) ng	(2) tend	(3) tract
2. w (2) dering	(2) ving	(2) madic
3. f (1) rce	c (1) mp (1) l	(2) lige
4. y (2) lding	ad (1) pt (1) ble	pl (2) ble
5. rev (1) lt	(2) rising	in (3) rection
6. (1) weller	(2) habitant	den (4)
7. nec (3) ary	obl (1) g (1) tory	(2) per (1) tive
8. hab (1) t (1) al	(3) firmed	(2) ronic
9. v (2) lation	br (2) ch	(2) fraction
10. (2) frequent	is (1) l (1) ted	sp (1) r (1) dic
11. loyal (2)	(2) votion	alleg (2) nce
12. const (1) nt	(2) during	(3) ennial
13. obst (1) n (1) te	w (2) lful	p (1) rv (1) rse
14. (3) ecessary	s (1) rpl (1) s	s (1) p (1) rfl (1) ous
15. (2) quiescent	s (2) missive	m (2) k
16. rebe (2) ious	m (1) t (1) nous	(2) sub (1) rd (1) nate
17. commen (1) ing	in (1) t (2) l	incip (2) nt
18. per (2) dic	rec (2) ring	in (3) mittent
19. sim (1) ltan (1) ous	con (2) mporary	(3) current
20. ab (1) de	(2) sidence	(3) icile

REVIEW 24: ANALOGIES

Which lettered pair of words—*a*, *b*, *c*, *d*, or *e*—most nearly expresses the same relationship as the capitalized pair?

1. INDISPENSABLE : REPLACE
   - *(a)* insignificant : ignore
   - *(b)* edible : devour
   - *(c)* foreseeable : avoid
   - *(d)* incomprehensible : grasp
   - *(e)* inconsequential : disregard

   Hint: Something that is **indispensable** cannot be **replaced**.

2. NOMAD : ROVE
   - *(a)* nonconformist : acquiesce
   - *(b)* hoarder : consume
   - *(c)* drudge : toil
   - *(d)* obstructionist : cooperate
   - *(e)* transient : remain

3. JAYWALKING : INFRACTION
- *(a)* opinion : fact
- *(b)* silk : fiber
- *(c)* homicide : misdemeanor
- *(d)* sole : shoe
- *(e)* moon : planet

4. DOCILE : DEFIANCE
- *(a)* intelligent : curiosity
- *(b)* apprehensive : alarm
- *(c)* discreet : caution
- *(d)* fair-minded : partiality
- *(e)* appreciative : gratitude

  Hint: A **docile** person does not show **defiance**.

5. PROTRACT : CURTAIL
- *(a)* obviate : preclude
- *(b)* extend : abbreviate
- *(c)* lengthen : broaden
- *(d)* resist : withstand
- *(e)* dawdle : procrastinate

6. SOJOURN : STAY
- *(a)* lull : cessation
- *(b)* monument : reminder
- *(c)* superabundance : supply
- *(d)* age : time
- *(e)* odyssey : trip

7. SPORADIC : FREQUENT
- *(a)* distant : remote
- *(b)* ordinary : commonplace
- *(c)* frugal : economical
- *(d)* scrupulous : honest
- *(e)* initial : terminal

8. INSUBORDINATE : OBEY
- *(a)* cooperative : hinder
- *(b)* flexible : adapt
- *(c)* shy : withdraw
- *(d)* meek : conform
- *(e)* extravagant : waste

9. MALCONTENT : COMPLAINER
- *(a)* acquaintance : crony
- *(b)* defendant : plaintiff
- *(c)* competitor : rival
- *(d)* adversary : ally
- *(e)* alien : citizen

10. MANSION : DOMICILE
- *(a)* vehicle : limousine
- *(b)* cottage : castle
- *(c)* banquet : meal
- *(d)* warehouse : storage
- *(e)* hobby : vocation

CHAPTER 3

Enlarging Vocabulary Through Anglo-Saxon Prefixes

What is a prefix?

A *prefix* is a sound (or combination of sounds) placed before and connected to a word or root to form a new word. Examples:

PREFIX	WORD OR ROOT	NEW WORD
FORE (Anglo-Saxon prefix meaning "beforehand")	+ SEE	= FORESEE (meaning "see beforehand")
DIS (Latin prefix meaning "apart")	+ SECT (root meaning "cut")	= DISSECT (meaning "cut apart")
HYPER (Greek prefix meaning "over")	+ CRITICAL	= HYPERCRITICAL (meaning "overcritical")

Why study prefixes?

A knowledge of prefixes and their meanings can help you enlarge your vocabulary. The number of English words beginning with prefixes is considerable, and it keeps increasing. Once you know what a particular prefix means, you have a clue to the meaning of every word beginning with that prefix. For example, when you learn that the Latin prefix *bi* means "two," you will understand—and remember—the meaning of *bi-*

partisan ("representing two political parties"), *bilingual* ("speaking two languages"), *bisect* ("cut in two"), etc.

Our prefixes come mainly from Anglo-Saxon (Old English), Latin, and Ancient Greek.

Purpose of this unit

This unit has a double purpose: (1) to acquaint you with important Anglo-Saxon prefixes, and (2) to help you add to your vocabulary a number of useful words beginning with these prefixes.

ANGLO-SAXON PREFIXES 1–4

Pretest 1

Write the *letter* of the best answer.

1. An *outspoken* person is not likely to be __?__ .
   (A) bold   (B) frank   (C) shy

2. When you have a *foreboding,* you feel that something __?__ is going to happen.
   (A) unimportant   (B) unfortunate   (C) good

3. *Misgivings* result from __?__ .
   (A) doubts and suspicions   (B) selfishness   (C) increased output

4. *Forebears* are associated mainly with the __?__ .
   (A) present   (B) past   (C) future

5. If you __?__ , you are being *overconfident.*
   (A) strike while the iron is hot   (B) count your chickens before they are hatched   (C) lock the barn after the horses are stolen

```
             THE ANSWERS ARE
     1. C  2. B  3. A  4. B  5. B
```

In the following pages you will learn many more words formed with the prefixes you have just met, namely, *fore-, mis-, out-,* and *over-.*

1. FORE-: "beforehand," "front," "before"

WORD	MEANING AND TYPICAL USE
forearm (*n.*) 'fȯ(r),ä(r)m	(literally, "front part of the arm") part of the arm from the wrist to the elbow A weightlifter has well-developed *forearms*.
forebear (*n.*) 'fȯ(r),be(r)	(literally, "one who has been or existed before") ancestor; forefather Do you know from whom you are descended? Who were your *forebears*?
foreboding (*n.*) fȯ(r)'bōd-iŋ	feeling beforehand of coming trouble; misgiving; presentiment; omen The day before the accident, I had a *foreboding* that something would go wrong.
forecast (*n.*) 'fȯ(r),kast	estimate beforehand of a future happening; prediction; prophecy Have you listened to the weather *forecast* for the weekend?
forefront (*n.*) 'fȯ(r),frәnt	(literally, "front part of the front") foremost place or part; vanguard The Mayor is at the *forefront* of the drive to attract new industry to the city.
foregoing (*adj.*) 'fȯ(r),gō-iŋ	going before; preceding; previous Carefully review the *foregoing* chapter before reading any further.
foremost (*adj.*) 'fȯ(r),mōst	standing at the front; first; most advanced; leading; principal; chief Marie Curie was one of the *foremost* scientists of the twentieth century.
foreshadow (*v.*) fȯ(r)'sha-dō	indicate beforehand; augur; portend Our defeat in the championship game was *foreshadowed* by injuries to two of our star players.
foresight (*n.*) 'fȯ(r),sīt	act of looking forward; prudence; power of seeing beforehand what is likely to happen *Foresight* is better than hindsight.
foreword (*n.*) 'fȯ(r),wәrd	front matter preceding the text of a book; preface; introduction; prologue Before Chapter I, there is a brief *foreword* in which the author explains the aims of the book.

EXERCISE 3.1: *FORE-* WORDS

Fill each blank with the most appropriate *fore-* word.

1. When asked if she thought we would win, the coach refused to make a __?__ .
2. Instead of cramming for a test the night before, be sensible and spread your review over several of the __?__ days.
3. These plastic gloves cover the hand, the wrist, and part of the __?__ .
4. I should have had the __?__ to buy a sweater before it got too cold; now all the best ones have been sold.
5. As he set out on his last mission, Per Hansa had a __?__ that he might not return.

---

2. MIS-: "bad," "badly," "wrong," "wrongly"

---

misbelief (*n.*)
,mis-bə'lēf

wrong or erroneous belief
    People generally believed the earth was flat until Columbus' momentous voyage corrected that *misbelief*.

misdeed (*n.*)
mis'dēd

bad act; wicked deed; crime; offense
    The criminals were punished for their *misdeeds* by fines and prison terms.

misfire (*v.*)
mis'fīr

(literally, "fire wrongly") fail to be fired or exploded properly
    The intended victim escaped when the assailant's weapon *misfired*.

misgiving (*n.*)
mis'giv-iŋ

uneasy feeling; feeling of doubt or suspicion; foreboding; lack of confidence
    With excellent weather and a fine driver, we had no *misgivings* about the trip.

mishap (*n.*)
'mis-hap

bad happening; misfortune; unlucky accident; mischance
    Right after the collision, each driver blamed the other for the *mishap*.

mislay (*v.*)
mis'lā

put or lay in an unremembered place; lose
    Yesterday I *mislaid* my keys, and it took me about a half-hour to find them.

mislead (*v.*) mis'lēd	lead astray (in the wrong direction); deceive; delude; beguile Some labels are so confusing that they *mislead* shoppers.
misstep (*n.*) mi'step	wrong step; slip in conduct or judgment; blunder Quitting school is a *misstep* that you may regret for the rest of your life.

EXERCISE 3.2: *MIS-* WORDS

Fill each blank with the most appropriate *mis-* word.

1. Luckily, no one was seriously hurt in the __?__ .
2. Where is your pen? Did you lose it or __?__ it?
3. I hated to lend Marie my notes because of a __?__ that she might not return them in time.
4. There is always the likelihood that a rifle may __?__ .
5. Consumer groups have been attacking advertisements that __?__ the public.

---

3. OUT-: "beyond," "out," "more than," "longer (faster, better) than"

---

outgrow (*v.*) aut'grō	grow beyond or too large for The jacket I got last year is too small. I have *outgrown* it.
outlandish (*adj.*) aut'land-ish	looking or sounding as if it belongs to a (foreign) land beyond ours; strange; fantastic A masquerade is always interesting because people come in such *outlandish* costumes.
outlast (*v.*) aut'last	last longer than; outlive; survive The table is more solidly constructed than the chairs and will probably *outlast* them.
outlook (*n.*) 'aut-luk	looking ahead or beyond; prospect for the future The *outlook* for unskilled laborers is not bright.
output (*n.*) 'aut,put	(literally, what is "put out") yield or product; amount produced The *output* of the average American factory increases as new equipment is introduced.

outrun (*v.*)   run faster than
aút'rən   The thief thought he could *outrun* his pursuers.

outspoken (*adj.*)   speaking out freely or boldly; frank; vocal; not re-
,aút'spō-kən   served
            Alma sometimes hurts others when she criticizes
            their work because she is too *outspoken*.

outwit (*v.*)   get the better of by being more clever; outsmart; outfox
aút'wit   The fictional detective Sherlock Holmes manages to
            outwit the cleverest criminals.

EXERCISE 3.3: *OUT-* WORDS

Fill each blank with the most appropriate *out-* word.

1. I know I shall get the truth when I ask Alice because she is very __?__ .
2. Where did you get that __?__ hat? I never saw anything like it.
3. My little brother suffers from shyness, but Mom hopes he will __?__ it.
4. These sneakers are the best I have ever had. They will __?__ any other brand.
5. Our prospects of avoiding a deficit are good, but the __?__ may change if we have unforeseen expenses.

---

4. OVER-: "too," "excessively," "over," "beyond"

---

overbearing (*adj.*)   domineering; bossy; inclined to dictate
,ō-və(r)'be(ə)-riŋ   Once Jason was given a little authority, he began
                to issue orders in an *overbearing* manner.

overburden (*v.*)   place too heavy a load on; burden excessively;
,ō-və(r)'bər-dən   overtax; overload
                It would *overburden* me to go shopping Thursday
                because I have so much homework that day.

overconfident (*adj.*)   too sure of oneself; excessively confident
,ō-və(r)'kän-fə-dənt   I was so sure of passing that I wasn't going to
                    study, but Dave advised me not to be *overconfident*.

overdose (*n.*)   quantity of medicine beyond what is to be taken at
'ō-və(r),dōs   one time or in a given period; too big a dose
                Do not take more of the medicine than the doctor
                ordered; an *overdose* may be dangerous.

overestimate (*v.*)
,ō-və(r)′es-tə-māt

make too high an estimate (rough calculation) of the worth or size of something or someone; overvalue; overrate

Joe *overestimated* the capacity of the bus. He thought it could hold 60; it has room for only 48.

overgenerous (*adj.*)
,ō-və(r)′jen-ə-rəs

too liberal in giving; excessively openhanded

Because the service was poor, Gina thought I was *overgenerous* in leaving a 15% tip.

overshadow (*v.*)
,ō-və(r)′sha-dō

1. cast a shadow over; overcloud; obscure

Gary's errors in the field *overshadowed* his good work at the plate.

2. be more important than; outweigh

Don's game-saving catch *overshadowed* his previous errors in the outfield.

oversupply (*n.*)
,ō-və(r)-sə′plī

too great a supply; an excessive supply

There is a shortage of skilled technicians but an *oversupply* of unskilled workers.

overwhelm (*v.*)
,ō-və(r)′hwelm

cover over completely; overpower; overthrow; crush

The security guards were nearly *overwhelmed* by the crowds of shoppers waiting for the sale to begin.

EXERCISE 3.4: *OVER-* WORDS

Fill each blank with the most appropriate *over-* word.

1. There will be little food left if you seriously __?__ the number who will attend the party.
2. Frances would have been our first choice, but she already has too many responsibilities and we did not want to __?__ her.
3. Why did you buy more ping-pong balls? Don't you know we have an __?__ ?
4. I think my English teacher was __?__ when he gave me 99 because I didn't deserve it.
5. At first the new supervisor was very domineering, but as she got to know the staff, she became less __?__ .

Review Exercises

REVIEW 1: WORDBUILDING WITH *FORE-*, *MIS-*, *OUT-*, AND *OVER-*

Change each of the following expressions to a single word. **Foreseen** is the answer to the first question.

1. seen beforehand
2. badly matched
3. grown to excess
4. use wrongly
5. cooked too much
6. person beyond the law
7. wrong interpretation
8. doom beforehand
9. ride faster than
10. inform incorrectly
11. too cautious
12. bad calculation
13. front feet (of a four-legged animal)
14. too simplified
15. swim better than
16. govern badly
17. stay too long
18. one who runs before
19. wrong statement
20. shout louder than

REVIEW 2: SENTENCE COMPLETION

Fill each blank with the word from the list below that best fits the context.

forearm	forecast
foremost	foreword
misgiving	mislaid
misled	misstep
outgrow	outlandish
output	outrun
outspoken	outwit
overbearing	overconfident
overdose	overestimate
oversupply	overwhelm

1. The __?__ of ''sunny with a high in the 70's'' __?__ me into scheduling the picnic for today. How was I to know it would rain?
2. Many of us, no matter how old we get, will never __?__ our love for circus clowns and their __?__ costumes.
3. Jim didn't practice because he thought he could easily __?__ his competitors. After the race, he realized he had been __?__ .

4. The master criminal __?_d his own cleverness when he thought he could __?_ Sherlock Holmes.

5. After the interview, Frank had few, if any, __?_s. He thought he had said all the correct things and could not recall a single __?_.

6. One reason our representative was reelected by a(n) __?_ing margin is that she has always been __?_ in her defense of the environment.

7. One thing that impressed me as I watched the __?_ tennis player in the world win his third straight championship was the huge size of his right __?_.

8. Ed did not read the book. He couldn't get beyond the first paragraph of the __?_ because he disliked the writer's __?_ attitude.

9. When she realized there was a(n) __?_ of shoes on the market, the company president ordered __?_ to be cut back at all her plants.

10. Andy wondered if he had lost his watch or just __?_ it. He had been sleepy all day, perhaps because of a(n) __?_ of his flu medicine.

REVIEW 3: SYNONYMS

Avoid repetition by replacing the boldfaced word or expression with a synonym from the following words.

forebear(s)	foreboding
forecast	misbelief
misdeed(s)	mishap
outlast(ed)	overburden(ed)
overgenerous	overshadow

1. When it comes to tipping for exceptional service, some people are **inclined to be exceptionally liberal.**

2. I had a **feeling beforehand** that we would lose. What did you feel the outcome would be?

3. Your recent successes are important. They **are more important than** your earlier mistakes.

4. Some criminals show no remorse for their **crimes.**

5. I thought the replacement soles would not last long, but they **lasted longer than** the original ones.

6. Unfortunately, they had one **misfortune** after another.

7. You are already **bearing too heavy a load.** We must not add to your load.

8. A visit to the land of our **ancestors** can teach us much about our ancestry.

9. The pollsters are predicting that the governor will be reelected. Do you agree with that **prediction?**

10. I awoke on a holiday in the **mistaken belief** that it was a school day and was halfway to the bus stop before realizing my mistake.

REVIEW 4: ANTONYMS

Enter the word from the list below that is most nearly the opposite of the boldfaced word or words.

forebear   foregoing
foremost   foresight
foreword   misdeed
mislead   overcautious
overestimate undercook

1. Most of us are pretty good in **hindsight** but deficient in __?__ .

2. Some works have not only a(n) __?__, or prologue, but also a(n) **after-word,** or epilogue.

3. People who lack self-confidence **underestimate** themselves and __?__ their opponents.

4. If Adam and Eve were our __?__s, then all of us are their **descendants.**

5. In a eulogy, the speaker dwells on the **positive achievements,** rather than the __?__s, of the departed person.

6. Why is it that protection of the environment, which should be one of our __?__ concerns, so often gets the **least** attention?

7. In matters where your own judgment may __?__ you, seek out someone who can **enlighten** you.

8. Certain foods must not be served unless they have been **thoroughly cooked;** if __?__ed, they may cause food poisoning.

9. The character who appeared briefly in the __?__ scene will be seen again in one of the **subsequent** episodes.

10. After realizing that I had been **too careless,** I went to the extreme of becoming __?__ .

REVIEW 5: CONCISE WRITING

Express the thought of each sentence below in no more than four words.

1. Most people do not have the power of seeing beforehand what is likely to happen.

2. Doses of medicine that exceed the prescribed amount are capable of killing people.
3. Which spark plug is it that failed to fire in a proper way?
4. Grandma broke the part of her arm from her wrist to her elbow.
5. Percy managed to get the better of his enemies by being more clever than they were.

REVIEW 6: SYNONYM SUMMARY

Each line, when completed, should have three words similar in meaning. Supply the missing letters.

1. ch (2) f	princip (2)	(4) most
2. (2) fense	cr (1) me	(3) deed
3. (4) father	(2) cestor	(4) b (2) r
4. (3) fortune	(3) chance	mish (2)
5. str (1) nge	(3) tastic	(3) land (3)
6. fr (1) nk	v (1) c (1) l	(3) spoke (1)
7. (2) under	(1) lip	(3) step
8. boss (1)	(2) mineering	(4) bear (3)
9. cr (1) sh	(4) throw	(5) helm
10. (3) diction	prophe (1) y	(4) cast
11. overval (2)	(4) rate	(4) es (2) mate
12. (1) men	(3) sentiment	(4) boding
13. (4) mart	(3) fox	(2) twit
14. overt (2)	(4) load	(4) b (2) den
15. (3) face	in (3) duction	(4) word
16. pre (1) eding	prev (4)	fore (5)
17. (3) vive	(3) live	(3) last
18. overcl (2) d	(3) cure	(4) shad (2)
19. dec (2) ve	beg (2) le	(3) lead
20. a (1) g (1) r	p (1) rtend	(6) ado (1)

REVIEW 7: ANALOGIES

Which lettered pair of words—*a, b, c, d,* or *e*—most nearly expresses the same relationship as the capitalized pair?

1. OVERBEARING : DOMINEER
   (a) meek : complain
   (b) nomadic : rove
   (c) immaculate : litter
   (d) submissive : defy
   (e) scrupulous : deceive

2. GRANDPARENT : FOREBEAR
   (a) bowl : vessel
   (b) officer : lieutenant
   (c) civilian : combatant
   (d) ship : frigate
   (e) native : alien

3. FOREWORD : TEXT
   (a) dessert : dinner
   (b) book : encyclopedia
   (c) climax : play
   (d) dawn : sunrise
   (e) toll : tax

4. MISDEED : PENALIZE
   (a) infraction : overlook
   (b) offense : tolerate
   (c) obligation : forget
   (d) promise : break
   (e) feat : acclaim

5. FOREBODING : APPREHENSION
   (a) truce : hostility
   (b) confession : guilt
   (c) recovery : ecstasy
   (d) rumor : confidence
   (e) impasse : settlement

6. HOAX : MISLEAD
   (a) threat : intimidate
   (b) definition : confuse
   (c) duty : perform
   (d) enigma : resolve
   (e) fine : pay

7. OVERGENEROSITY : BANKRUPTCY
   (a) illiteracy : enlightenment
   (b) gluttony : indigestion
   (c) penury : riches
   (d) avarice : pity
   (e) impetuosity : patience

8. FOREARM : ELBOW
   (a) ankle : wrist
   (b) muscle : nerve
   (c) leg : knee
   (d) lip : mouth
   (e) knuckle : hand

9. OVERDOSE : FATALITY
   (a) mishap : blunder
   (b) covenant : disagreement
   (c) famine : drought
   (d) surplus : scarcity
   (e) thaw : avalanche

ANGLO-SAXON PREFIXES 5–8

Pretest 2

Write the *letter* of the best answer.

1. An *understudy* is not a __?__ performer.
   (A) prepared   (B) substitute   (C) regular
2. Cars with a high *upkeep* __?__ .
   (A) use less costly fuels   (B) are often in the repair shop   (C) pick up speed rapidly
3. A *withdrawal* is the same as __?__ .
   (A) a retreat   (B) a deposit   (C) an attack
4. When you wish to __?__ something in a sentence, *underscore* it.
   (A) stress   (B) correct   (C) erase
5. An *unabridged* dictionary __?__ .
   (A) is not complete   (B) has no illustrations   (C) has not been shortened

```
            THE ANSWERS ARE

     1. C   2. B   3. A   4. A   5. C
```

The material that follows will introduce you to many additional words formed with the prefixes *un-*, *under-*, *up-*, and *with-*.

5. UN-: "not," "lack of," "do the opposite of," "remove or release from"

unabridged (*adj.*)	not abridged; not made shorter; uncut; complete
ˌən-ə'brijd	Though an abridged dictionary is convenient to use, it contains far fewer definitions than an *unabridged* dictionary.

unbiased (*adj.*)
,ən'bī-əst

not biased; not prejudiced in favor of or against; fair

Don't ask the mother of a contestant to serve as a judge because it may be hard for her to remain *unbiased*.

unconcern (*n.*)
,ən-kən'sərn

lack of concern, anxiety, or interest; indifference; apathy

The audience was breathless with anxiety during the daring tightrope act, though the acrobats themselves performed with seeming *unconcern* for their own safety.

undeceive (*v.*)
,ən-də'sēv

free from deception or mistaken ideas; set straight; disabuse

If you think I can get Mrs. Owens to hire you because she is my cousin, let me *undeceive* you. I have no influence with her.

ungag (*v.*)
,ən'gag

remove a gag from; release from censorship

With the dictator's downfall, the censorship decrees were abolished and the press was *ungagged*.

unnerve (*v.*)
,ən'nərv

deprive of nerve or courage; cause to lose self-control; upset; enervate

The harassing noises of hostile fans so *unnerved* our star player that he missed two foul shots in a row.

unquenchable (*adj.*)
,ən'kwen-chə-bəl

not quenchable; not capable of being satisfied; insatiable; inextinguishable

As a teenager, Jules had an *unquenchable* thirst for adventure stories; he read one after another.

unscramble (*v.*)
,ən'skram-bəl

do the opposite of scramble; restore to intelligible form

The previous secretary had mixed up the files so badly that it took me a week to *unscramble* them.

unshackle (*v.*)
,ən'shak-əl

release from a shackle (anything that confines the legs or arms); set free; liberate

When a captain put mutinous sailors in irons in the olden days, nobody was allowed to *unshackle* them.

unwary (*adj.*)
,ən'wa(ə)-rē

not wary; not alert; heedless; rash

An *unwary* pedestrian is much more likely to be struck by a car than one who looks both ways and crosses with the light.

EXERCISE 3.5: *UN-* WORDS

Fill each blank with the most appropriate *un-* word.

1. Some baseball fans never miss a home game; they have an __?__ appetite for the sport.
2. The guards were warned that their prisoner was desperate and would try to escape if they were the least bit __?__ .
3. I visited Grandma every day she was in the hospital. I can't understand why you accuse me of __?__ about her health.
4. For a reliable definition of a technical word, consult an __?__ dictionary.
5. Both the strikers and their employers want the Mayor to arbitrate their dispute because they consider him __?__ .

---

6. UNDER-: "beneath," "lower," "insufficient(ly)"

---

underbrush (*n.*)
'ən-də(r),brəsh

shrubs, bushes, etc., growing beneath large trees in a wood; undergrowth
    On its way through the dense jungle, the patrol had to be constantly wary of enemy soldiers who might be lurking in the *underbrush.*

underdeveloped (*adj.*)
,ən-də(r)-də'vel-əpt

insufficiently developed because of a lack of capital and trained personnel for exploiting natural resources; backward; behindhand
    The United States has spent billions to help the *underdeveloped* nations improve their standard of living.

undergraduate (*n.*)
,ən-də(r)'graj-ə-wət

(literally, "lower than a graduate") a student in a college or university who has not yet earned a bachelor's degree
    Full-time *undergraduates* can earn a bachelor's degree in four years.

underpayment (*n.*)
'ən-de(r),pā-mənt

insufficient payment
    If too little is deducted from your weekly wages for income tax, the result is an *underpayment* at the end of the year.

underprivileged (*adj.*)
'ən-də(r)'priv-ə-ləjd

insufficiently privileged; deprived through social or economic oppression of some fundamental rights supposed to belong to all; disadvantaged; deprived

The goal of the fund is to give as many *under-privileged* children as possible an opportunity for a vacation away from the city next summer.

underscore (*v.*)
'ən-də(r)-skȯ(r)

draw a line beneath; emphasize; stress
When you take notes, *underscore* items that are especially important.

undersell (*v.*)
,ən-də(r)'sel

sell at a lower price than
The expression "You can't get it anywhere else for less" means about the same as "We will not be *undersold*."

undersigned (*n.*)
'ən-də(r),sīnd

person or persons who sign at the end of (literally, "under") a letter or document
Among the *undersigned* in the petition to the Governor were some of the most prominent persons in the state.

understatement (*n.*)
'ən-də(r),stāt-mənt

a statement below the truth; a restrained statement in mocking contrast to what might be said
Frank's remark that he was "slightly bruised" in the accident is an *understatement*; he suffered two fractured ribs.

understudy (*n.*)
'ən-də(r),stə-dē

one who "studies under" and learns the part of a regular performer so as to be a substitute if necessary
While Madeline is recuperating from her illness, her role will be played by an *understudy*.

EXERCISE 3.6: *UNDER-* WORDS

Fill each blank with the most appropriate *under-* word.

1. The advanced course is for students with a bachelor's degree, but a qualified __?__ may enroll if the instructor approves.
2. An __?__ must master long and difficult roles, yet has no assurance of ever being called on to perform.
3. Arline told me she "passed," but that's an __?__; she got the highest mark in the class.
4. Mike's tee shot disappeared after hitting one of the trees, and he had to hunt for the ball in the __?__.
5. Because they buy in larger quantities at lower prices, chain-store operators are usually able to __?__ small merchants.

7. UP-: "up," "upward"

upcoming (*adj.*)
'əp,kəm-iŋ

coming up; being in the near future; forthcoming; approaching

A monthly bulletin mailed to each customer gives news of *upcoming* sales.

update (*v.*)
'əp,dāt

bring up to date; modernize; renovate

New highway construction requires auto clubs to *update* their road maps annually.

upgrade (*v.*)
'əp,grād

raise the grade or quality of; improve

Many employees attend evening courses to *upgrade* their skills and improve their chances for promotion.

upheaval (*n.*)
,əp'hēv-əl

violent heaving up, as of the earth's crust; commotion; violent disturbance; outcry

The Prime Minister's proposal for new taxes created such an *upheaval* that his government fell.

upkeep (*n.*)
'əp,kēp

maintenance ("keeping up"); cost of operating and repairing

Susan traded in her old car because the *upkeep* had become too high.

uplift (*v.*)
əp-'lift

lift up; elevate; raise

The news that employers are rehiring has *uplifted* the hopes of many of the unemployed.

upright (*adj.*)
'əp,rīt

standing up straight on the feet; erect; honest; scrupulous

When knocked to the canvas, the boxer waited till the count of nine before resuming an *upright* position.

uproot (*v.*)
,əp'rüt

pull up by the roots; remove completely; eradicate; annihilate

The love of liberty is so firmly embedded in people's hearts that no tyrant can hope to *uproot* it.

upstart (*n.*)
'əp,stä(r)t

person who has suddenly risen to wealth and power, especially if he or she is conceited and unpleasant

When the new Representative entered the legislature, some older members regarded her as an *upstart*.

upturn (*n.*)
'əp,tərn

upward turn toward better conditions

Most merchants report a slowdown in sales for October, but confidently expect an *upturn* with the approach of Christmas.

EXERCISE 3.7: *UP-* WORDS

Fill each blank with the most appropriate *up-* word.

1. Perhaps today's victory, the first in four weeks, marks an __?__ in the team's fortunes.
2. To improve her book, the author will have to __?__ the last chapter, to include the events of the past ten years.
3. If practicable, __?__ weeds by hand, instead of destroying them with chemicals that might damage the environment.
4. What is the name of the city agency responsible for the __?__ of our roads?
5. To stay in business, manufacturers must improve the quality of their products whenever their competitors __?__ theirs.

---

8. WITH-: "back," "away," "against"

---

withdraw (*v.*)
wəth'drȯ

1. take or draw back or away; take out from a place of deposit
   The community association is her principal backer; if it *withdraws* its support, I don't see how she can be elected.

2. leave; retreat
   The invaders were ordered to *withdraw*.

withdrawal (*n.*)
wəth'drȯ(-ə)l

1. act of taking back or drawing out from a place of deposit
   When I am short of cash, I make a *withdrawal* from my bank account.

2. retreat; exit; departure
   The invaders made a hasty *withdrawal*.

withdrawn (*adj.*)
wəth'drȯn

drawn back or removed from easy approach; socially detached; unresponsive; introverted
   Lola's brother keeps to himself and hardly says anything, though we try to be friendly; he seems *withdrawn*.

withhold (*v.*)
wəth'hōld

hold back; keep from giving; restrain; curb
   I would appreciate it if you would please *withhold* your comment until I have finished speaking.

withholding tax (*n.*) wəth'hōl-diŋ 'taks	sum withheld or deducted from wages for tax purposes Your employer is required to deduct a certain amount from your salary as a *withholding tax* payable to the federal government.
withstand (*v.*) wəth'stand	stand up against; hold out; resist; endure The walls of a dam must be strong enough to *withstand* tremendous water pressure.
notwithstanding (*prep.*) ,nät-wəth'stand-iŋ	(literally, "not standing against") in spite of; despite *Notwithstanding* their advantage of height, the visitors were unable to beat our basketball team.

EXERCISE 3.8: *WITH-* WORDS

Fill each blank with the most appropriate *with-* word.

1. You can make a deposit or a __?__ by mail, without going to the bank.
2. Whenever you get a raise, your __?__ goes up.
3. Construction of the new roadway has been approved, __?__ the protests from residents of the area.
4. Because of a disagreement with her partners, the lawyer announced that she would __?__ from the firm and open an office of her own.
5. The training that astronauts receive equips them to __?__ the hazards of space exploration.

Review Exercises

REVIEW 8: WORDBUILDING WITH *UN-*, *UNDER-*, *UP-*, AND *WITH-*

Change each of the following expressions to a single word. The first answer is **underlying**.

1. lying beneath
2. not able to be avoided
3. holds back
4. insufficiently paid
5. act or instance of rising up
6. do the opposite of *lock*
7. lower (criminal) part of the world
8. standing up against
9. one who holds up, supports, or defends
10. sum taken (drawn) back from a bank account

11. not sociable
12. upward stroke
13. charged lower than the proper price
14. drew back or away
15. lack of reality
16. lifted upward
17. one who holds back
18. released from a leash
19. beneath the surface of the sea
20. upward thrust

REVIEW 9: SENTENCE COMPLETION

On your answer paper, write the word from the list below that best fits the context.

notwithstanding	unabridged
unbiased	unconcern
undeceive	underbrush
underscore	undersell
undersigned	understudy
unnerve	unquenchable
unshackle	unwary
upcoming	upgrade
uplift	upright
withdrawn	withhold

1. The parents of the __?__ youngster took him to the circus, hoping that it might help to __?__ his spirits.
2. If you expect to find this extremely technical word in that little dictionary of yours, let me __?__ you. Only a(n) __?__ dictionary will have it.
3. A(n) __?__ camper, walking barefoot in the __?__, was bitten by a snake.
4. The new electronics store is using heavy TV advertising to __?__ its claim that it will __?__ all competitors.
5. Spurred by their __?__ desire for liberty, the hostages managed gradually to __?__ their arms and legs.
6. Maxine's __?__ about the __?__ test contrasts sharply with my own anxiety over it.
7. The prospect of suddenly being called upon to be the star does not __?__ an experienced __?__ familiar with the role.
8. The petition reads: "We, the __?__ XYZ Club members, are willing to pay higher dues to __?__ the refreshments served after meetings."
9. __?__ rumors to the contrary, the candidate insists that she is __?__, and she pledges that she will be fair to everyone.
10. The dealer who sold us the used car was a(n) __?__ person. He did not __?__ information from us about the true condition of the vehicle.

REVIEW 10: ANTONYMS

Enter the word from the list below that is most nearly the opposite of the boldfaced word.

unabridged	unbiased
unconcern	underdeveloped
undergraduate	underpayment
understatement	unscrambled
unwary	upgraded

1. Be **cautious** this morning. You may slip on the ice if you are __?__ .
2. Once you receive your bachelor's degree, you are no longer an __?__ but a **graduate.**
3. Only __?__ persons should be on the jury. No one **prejudiced** in favor of or against the defendant should be chosen to serve.
4. Be accurate in describing your injuries when you file an accident report. Avoid both **exaggeration** and __?__ .
5. It is a fact that **industrial** nations enjoy a higher standard of living than those that are __?__ .
6. Someone **jumbled** up the pieces of the picture puzzle after I had finally __?__ them.
7. If you have made an **overpayment,** you will receive a refund; but if you have made an __?__ , you still owe some money.
8. People who look with __?__ on the proposed legislation might show some **anxiety** if they knew how it might affect them.
9. An advantage an **abridged** dictionary has over one that is __?__ is that it is much less cumbersome.
10. If the winds diminish, the storm will be **downgraded** to a gale, but if they increase to 74 miles an hour, it will be __?__ to a hurricane.

REVIEW 11: SYNONYMS

Avoid repetition by replacing the boldfaced word or expression with a synonym from the following words.

eradicate	understudy
ungag	update(d)
upheaval	upkeep
upturn	withdraw
withdrawal	withstand

1. What caused the **disturbance?** Why were the people disturbed?

2. Though the new ruler has promised to **free** the press **from censorship,** he is now tightening censorship controls.

3. Jackie is learning the dispatcher's duties to qualify as his **substitute,** should substitution ever be necessary.

4. It is hard to **uproot** a weed that is deeply rooted.

5. The invaders were supposed to retreat to their own lines. What is delaying their **retreat?**

6. It cost $1400 to maintain our old car last year, and next year the **maintenance** may be even more expensive.

7. Our neighbors have **modernized** their kitchen. It now has a decidedly modern look.

8. Parents can hold their own against most complaints from children, but they cannot **hold out against** continual nagging.

9. It takes just a few seconds to **take out** money from your savings account when you use an automated teller machine.

10. Business is improving. There has been an encouraging **improvement** in retail sales.

REVIEW 12: CONCISE WRITING

Express the thought of each sentence below in no more than four words.

1. Houdini succeeded in getting out of the shackles that were restraining his arms and legs.
2. There are people who through no fault of their own are deprived of some of the fundamental rights that all human beings are supposed to have.
3. Conceited individuals who have suddenly come into wealth and power can be bossy and domineering over others.
4. Those who referee games must not show any favoritism to one side or the other.
5. Sally has learned the ins and outs of my job and can take over my duties in the event of an emergency.

REVIEW 13: SYNONYM SUMMARY

Each line, when completed, should have three words similar in meaning. Write the *complete* word.

1. end (1) re   res (1) st   (4) stand
2. r (1) sh   heed (4)   (2) wary
3. h (1) nest   scrup (1) lous   up (5)
4. st (1) ess   (2) phasize   under (5)
5. retr (2) t   l (2) ve   with (4)
6. f (2) r   unpre (2) diced   (2) biased
7. l (1) berate   fr (2)   (2) shack (2)
8. comm (1) tion   (3) cry   (2) heav (2)
9. inextin (2) ishable (2) satiable   (2) quench (1) ble
10. ex (1) t   depart (1) re   (4) draw (2)
11. compl (1) te   (2) cut   (3) bridged
12. m (1) dernize   (2) novate   (2) date
13. erad (1) cate   annihil (3)   (2) root
14. (3) advantaged   (2) prived   underpr (1) v (1) l (1) ged
15. (2) difference   ap (1) thy   (2) concern
16. appr (2) ching   f (1) rthcoming   up (6)
17. backw (1) rd   b (1) hindhand   (5) developed
18. restr (2) n   c (2) b   (4) hold
19. r (2) se   impr (1) ve   (2) grade
20. (2) set   en (1) rvate   (2) nerve

REVIEW 14: ANALOGIES

Which lettered pair of words—*a, b, c, d,* or *e*—most nearly expresses the same relationship as the capitalized pair?

1. UNGAG : CENSOR
   (a) overlook : neglect   (b) liberate : unshackle
   (c) abandon : retain   (d) inform : undeceive
   (e) hesitate : waver

2. WARY : HEED
   (a) acquiescent : rebel   (b) infallible : err
   (c) lavish : economize   (d) voracious : devour
   (e) opinionated : compromise

3. UNDERSTUDY : INSURANCE
   - (a) exercise : circulation
   - (b) privacy : door
   - (c) guest : hospitality
   - (d) bodyguard : security
   - (e) bore : excitement

4. SHACKLES : HANDCUFFS
   - (a) tree : birch
   - (b) legs : limbs
   - (c) measles : disease
   - (d) fence : barrier
   - (e) flavor : condiments

   Hint: **Shackles** is the category to which **handcuffs** belongs.

5. WITHDRAWN : SOCIABILITY
   - (a) arrogant : humility
   - (b) unassertive : timidity
   - (c) outgoing : warmth
   - (d) intrepid : valor
   - (e) immaculate : tidiness

6. UPDATE : MODERNIZE
   - (a) soothe : infuriate
   - (b) invalidate : approve
   - (c) yield : defer
   - (d) expedite : procrastinate
   - (e) bury : disinter

7. UPRIGHT : TRUST
   - (a) corrupt : contempt
   - (b) domineering : obedience
   - (c) indolent : promotion
   - (d) inhumane : sympathy
   - (e) gossipy : credence

   Hint: An **upright** person is worthy of **trust**.

8. UNDERSCORE : EMPHATIC
   - (a) simplify : complex
   - (b) overshadow : inconspicuous
   - (c) rectify : inequitable
   - (d) decontaminate : impure
   - (e) legalize : unlawful

9. UNCONCERN : INTEREST
   - (a) cordiality : friendliness
   - (b) perseverance : ambition
   - (c) fervor : enthusiasm
   - (d) honesty : virtue
   - (e) mediocrity : excellence

10. INTREPID : UNNERVE
    - (a) pliable : influence
    - (b) audible : hear
    - (c) timorous : scare
    - (d) outspoken : silence
    - (e) avaricious : share

    Hint: An **intrepid** person cannot be **unnerved**.

REVIEW 15: WORDBUILDING WITH EIGHT ANGLO-SAXON PREFIXES

Replace the italicized words with one word beginning with *fore-, mis-, out-, over-, un-, under-, up-,* or *with-*. **Foretell** is the answer to question 1.

1. If you study your opponent's habits, you may be able to *tell beforehand* what his or her next move will be.
2. We won because we *played better than* our opponents.
3. After the hike, we rested because we were *excessively tired*.
4. It is a mistake to exaggerate your abilities and talents, but it is just as bad to *set too low an estimate on* them.
5. The dispute has been *wrongly handled* from the very beginning.
6. Harry is usually *too critical* when he judges somebody else's work.
7. You will not get a good picture if the film is *exposed for less than the time needed*.
8. The will provided that all of the property was to go to the wife if she *lived longer than* her husband.
9. As a courteous guest, you should know when to leave; do not *stay beyond* your welcome.
10. The district attorney promised to *remove the mask of* the criminals posing as respectable citizens.
11. By stressing scholarship, our principal has succeeded in *lifting* the reputation of our school *up to a higher level*.
12. The early snowfall gave us a *taste beforehand* of the bitter winter to come.
13. A captain *has a higher rank than* a lieutenant.
14. We spoke in *lower tones* so as not to be overheard.
15. As I passed the kitchen, I caught a *glimpse beforehand* of what we are having for dinner.
16. Abe Lincoln had the *bad fortune* to lose his mother when he was only nine.
17. The hospital has beds for 90 patients; in addition, it provides daily treatment for hundreds of *patients who live beyond the hospital grounds*.
18. I have never heard you utter a single *statement lacking in accuracy*.
19. From the prisoners' outward appearance, it did not seem that they had been mistreated or *insufficiently fed*.
20. Martha wanted to take driving lessons, but Dad *held back* his consent, saying she was still too young.

CHAPTER 4

Enlarging Vocabulary Through Latin Prefixes

LATIN PREFIXES 1–6

Pretest 1

Write the *letter* of the best answer.

1. *Postscripts* are especially helpful to the letter writer who __?__ .
   (A) forgets to answer   (B) answers too late   (C) makes omissions

2. *Bicameral* legislatures __?__ .
   (A) serve for two years   (B) consist of two houses   (C) meet twice a year

3. There is more excitement over the *advent* of spring than over its __?__ .
   (A) departure   (B) onset   (C) arrival

4. You *antedate* me as a member because you joined the club __?__ me.
   (A) after   (B) with   (C) before

5. A *semidetached* building touches __?__ other building(s).
   (A) one   (B) no   (C) two

6. Was the story *absorbing* or __?__?
   (A) true to life   (B) interesting   (C) boring

In the following pages you will learn additional words formed with the six Latin prefixes involved in the pretest: *ab-*, *ad-*, *ante-*, *post-*, *bi-*, and *semi-*.

1. AB-, A-, ABS-: "from," "away," "off"

The prefix *ab* (sometimes written *a* or *abs*) means "from," "away," or "off." Examples:

PREFIX	ROOT
AB ("off")	+ RUPT ("broken")
A ("away")	+ VERT ("turn")
ABS ("from")	+ TAIN ("hold")

NEW WORD

= ABRUPT ("broken off; sudden")
= AVERT ("turn away")
= ABSTAIN ("hold from; refrain")

WORD	MEANING AND TYPICAL USE
abdicate (*v.*) 'ab-də,kāt	formally remove oneself from; give up; relinquish; renounce; resign The aging monarch *abdicated* the throne and went into retirement.
abduct (*v.*) ab'dəkt	carry off or lead away by force; kidnap The Greeks attacked Troy to recover Helen, who had been *abducted* by the Trojan prince Paris.
abhor (*v.*) ab'hȯ(r)	shrink from; detest; loathe; hate Janet is doing her best to pass the course because she *abhors* the thought of having to repeat it in summer school.

abnormal (*adj.*)
ab'nȯ(r)-məl

deviating from the normal; unusual; irregular
We had three absences today, which is *abnormal*. Usually, everyone is present.

abrasion (*n.*)
ə'brā-zhən

scraping or wearing away of the skin by friction; irritation
The automobile was a total wreck, but the driver, luckily, escaped with minor cuts and *abrasions*.

abrupt (*adj.*)
ə'brəpt

broken off; sudden; unexpected
Today's art lesson came to an *abrupt* end when the gongs sounded for a fire drill.

abscond (*v.*)
ab'skänd

steal off and hide; depart secretly; flee; escape
A wide search is under way for the manager who *absconded* with the company's funds.

absolve (*v.*)
ab'sälv

1. set free from some duty or responsibility; exempt; excuse
Ignorance of the law does not *absolve* a person from obeying it.

2. declare free from guilt or blame; exculpate; exonerate
Of the three suspects, two were found guilty, and the third was *absolved*.

absorbing (*adj.*)
əb'sȯ(r)-biŋ

fully taking away one's attention; extremely interesting; engrossing
That was an *absorbing* book. It held my interest from beginning to end.

abstain (*v.*)
ab'stān

withhold oneself deliberately from doing something; refrain; desist
My dentist said I would have fewer cavities if I *abstained* from sweets.

averse (*adj.*)
ə'vərs

literally, "turned from"; opposed; disinclined; unwilling
I am in favor of the dance, but I am *averse* to holding it on May 25.

avert (*v.*)
ə'vərt

turn away; ward off; prevent; forestall
The Mayor tried to *avert* a strike by municipal employees.

avocation (*n.*)
,a-və'kā-shən

occupation away from one's customary occupation; hobby
My aunt, a pediatrician, composes music as an *avocation*.

EXERCISE 4.1: *AB-, A-,* AND *ABS-* WORDS

Fill each blank with the most appropriate word from group 1.

1. Some love spinach; others __?__ it.
2. A snowstorm in late May is __?__ for Chicago.
3. My father plays golf. What is your father's __?__?
4. The dictator refused to __?__ and was eventually overthrown.
5. Gene said the movie was interesting, but I didn't find it too __?__ .
6. It was very decent of Marge to __?__ me of blame by admitting she was at fault.
7. The kidnapper was arrested when he tried to __?__ the executive.
8. I nominate Harriet for treasurer. She knows how to keep records and can be trusted not to __?__ with our dues.
9. The owner must raise $20,000 in cash at once if she is to __?__ bankruptcy.
10. We are __?__ to further increases in the sales tax. It is too high already.

---

2. AD-: "to," "toward," "near"

---

adapt (*v.*)
ə'dapt

1. (literally, "fit to") adjust; suit; fit
    People who work at night have to *adapt* themselves to sleeping in the daytime.

2. make suitable for a different use; modify
    Lorraine Hansberry's hit Broadway play, *A Raisin in the Sun*, was later *adapted* for the screen.

addicted (*adj.*)
ə'dik-təd

given over (to a habit); habituated; devoted
    You will not become *addicted* to smoking if you refuse cigarettes when they are offered.

adequate (*adj.*)
'a-də-kwət

equal to, or sufficient for, a specific need; enough; sufficient
    The student who arrived ten minutes late did not have *adequate* time to finish the test.

adherent (*n.*)
ad'hir-ənt

one who sticks to a leader, party, etc.; follower; faithful supporter
    You can count on Martha's support in your campaign for reelection. She is one of your most loyal *adherents*.

adjacent (*adj.*)   lying near; nearby; neighboring; bordering
ə'jās-ənt   The island of Cuba is *adjacent* to Florida.

adjoin (*v.*)   be next to; be in contact with; border; abut
ə'join   Mexico *adjoins* the United States.

adjourn (*v.*)   put off to another day; suspend a meeting to resume at
ə'jərn   a future time; defer; recess
              The judge *adjourned* the court to the following Mon-
              day.

advent (*n.*)   a "coming to"; arrival; approach
'ad,vent   The Weather Bureau gave adequate warning of the *ad-*
              vent of the hurricane.

adversary (*n.*)   person "turned toward" or facing another as an oppo-
'ad-və(r),se-rē   nent; foe; antagonist
              Before the contest began, the champion and her *ad-*
              versary shook hands.

adverse (*adj.*)   in opposition to one's interests; hostile; unfavorable
ad'vərs   Because of *adverse* reviews, the producer announced
              that the play will close with tonight's performance.

EXERCISE 4.2: *AD-* WORDS

Fill each blank with the most appropriate word from group 2.

1. With the __?__ of autumn, the days become shorter.
2. England was our __?__ in the War of 1812.
3. Is it very expensive to __?__ a summer home for year-round living?
4. We have sweets, but only occasionally. We are not __?__ to them.
5. The candidate has few supporters in the rural areas; most of his __?__s
   are in the cities.

---

3. ANTE-: "before"
4. POST-: "after"

---

antecedents (*n. pl.*)   ancestors; forebears; predecessors
,an-tə'sē-dənts   Ronald's *antecedents* came to this country more
                than a hundred years ago.

antedate (*v.*)   1. assign a date before the true date
'an-tə,dāt   If you used yesterday's date on a check written
                today, you have *antedated* the check.

2. come before in date; predate; precede

Alaska *antedates* Hawaii as a state, having gained statehood on January 3, 1959, seven months before Hawaii.

postdate (*v.*)   assign a date after the true date
'pōst'dāt   I *postdated* the check; it has tomorrow's date on it.

ante meridiem (*adj.*)   before noon
‚an-tē mə'rid-ē-əm   In *9 a.m., a.m.* stands for *ante meridiem,* meaning "*before* noon."

post meridiem   after noon
‚pōst mə'rid-ē-əm   In *9 p.m., p.m.* stands for *post meridiem,* meaning "*after* noon."

anteroom (*n.*)   room placed before and forming an entrance to another; antechamber; waiting room
'an-tē‚rüm   If the physician is busy when patients arrive, the nurse asks them to wait in the *anteroom.*

postgraduate (*adj.*)   having to do with study after graduation, especially after graduation from college
‚pōst'gra-jə-wət   After college, Nina hopes to do *postgraduate* work in law school.

postmortem (*n.*)   1. thorough examination of a body after death; autopsy
'pōst'mȯ(r)-təm   The purpose of a *postmortem* is to discover the cause of death.

2. detailed analysis or discussion of an event just ended

In a *postmortem* after a defeat, we discuss what went wrong and what we can do to improve.

postscript (*n.*)   note added to a letter after it has been written
'pōst‚skript   After signing the letter, I noticed I had omitted an important fact, and I had to add a *postscript.*

EXERCISE 4.3: *ANTE-* AND *POST-* WORDS

Fill each blank with the most appropriate word from groups 3 and 4.

1. After graduating from the College of the City of New York, Jonas Salk did __?__ study at New York University to earn an M.D. degree.
2. Mr. Sims told me to put tomorrow's date on the letter, but I forgot to __?__ it.

3. The ___?___ showed that the patient had died of natural causes.

4. In some areas, the peasants still use the same methods of farming as their ___?___ did centuries ago.

5. You will not need a(n) ___?___ if you plan your letter carefully.

---

5. BI-: "two"
6. SEMI-: "half," "partly"

---

bicameral (*adj.*)
bī′kam-ə-rəl

consisting of two chambers or legislative houses
Our legislature is *bicameral;* it consists of the House of Representatives and the Senate.

bicentennial (*n.*)
‚bī-sən′ten-ē-əl

two-hundredth anniversary
Our nation's *bicentennial* was celebrated in 1976.

biennial (*adj.*)
bī′en-ē-əl

occurring every two years
A defeated candidate for the House of Representatives can run again in two years because the elections are *biennial.*

semiannual (*adj.*)
‚se-mē′an-yə-wəl

occurring every half year, or twice a year; semi-yearly
Promotion in our school is *semiannual,* occurring in January and June.

bimonthly (*adj.*)
bī′mən-thlē

occurring every two months
We receive only six utility bills a year because we are billed on a *bimonthly* basis.

semimonthly (*adj.*)
‚se-mē′mən-thlē

occurring every half month, or twice a month
Employees paid on a *semimonthly* basis receive two salary checks per month.

bilateral (*adj.*)
bī′la-tə-rəl

having two sides
French forces joined the Americans in a *bilateral* action against the British at the Battle of Yorktown in 1781.

bilingual (*adj.*)
bī′liŋ-wəl

1. speaking two languages equally well
New York has a large number of *bilingual* citizens who speak English and a foreign language.

2. written in two languages
The instructions on the voting machine are *bilingual;* they are in English and Spanish.

bipartisan (*adj.*) ′bī′pä(r)-tə-zən	representing two political parties Congressional committees are *bipartisan;* they include Democratic and Republican members.
bisect (*v.*) ′bī,sekt	divide into two equal parts A diameter is a line that *bisects* a circle.
semicircle (*n.*) ′se-mē,sər-kəl	half of a circle At the end of the lesson, students gathered about the teacher in a *semicircle* to ask additional questions.
semiconscious (*adj.*) ′se-mē,kän-shəs	half conscious; not fully conscious In the morning, as you begin to awaken, you are in a *semiconscious* state.
semidetached (*adj.*) ,se-mē-də′tacht	partly detached; sharing a wall with an adjoining building on one side, but detached on the other All the houses on the block are attached, except the corner ones, which are *semidetached.*
semiskilled (*adj.*) ′se-mē,skild	partly skilled Workers in a *semiskilled* job usually do not require a long period of training.

EXERCISE 4.4: *BI-* AND *SEMI-* WORDS

Fill each blank with the most appropriate word from groups 5 and 6.

1. Everyone will benefit from the warmth of the fireplace if you arrange the chairs around it in a __?__ .
2. The inspections are __?__ ; there is one every six months.
3. A state that has both an assembly and a senate has a __?__ legislature.
4. America's foreign policy is __?__ ; it represents the views of both major political parties.
5. A __?__ house shares a common wall.

Review Exercises

REVIEW 1: LATIN PREFIXES 1–6

For each Latin prefix in column I, write the *letter* of its meaning from column II.

COLUMN I	COLUMN II
1. *ab-, a-,* or *abs-*	(A) half or partly
2. *semi-*	(B) two
3. *ante-*	(C) from, away, or off
4. *ad-*	(D) after
5. *post-*	(E) to, toward, or near
6. *bi-*	(F) before

REVIEW 2: WORDBUILDING

Fill in the prefix in column I and the complete word in column III. The answer to question 1 is AD + HERENT = ADHERENT.

I	II	III
1. __?__ *to*	+ HERENT *one who sticks*	= __?__ *one who sticks to; follower*
2. __?__ *two*	+ LINGUAL *pertaining to a tongue*	= __?__ *speaking two languages*
3. __?__ *after*	+ DATED	= __?__ *dated after (the true date)*
4. __?__ *away*	+ RASION *scraping*	= __?__ *scraping away (of the skin)*
5. __?__ *before*	+ CHAMBER *room*	= __?__ *room before another; waiting room*
6. __?__ *partly*	+ SKILLED	= __?__ *partly skilled*
7. __?__ *from*	+ HORS *shrinks*	= __?__ *shrinks from; loathes; detests*
8. __?__ *two*	+ LATERAL *pertaining to a side*	= __?__ *having two sides*
9. __?__ *half*	+ CIRCLE	= __?__ *half circle*

10. ?   + JACENT   =   ?
    near   *lying*   *lying near; neighboring*

11. ?   + RUPT   =   ?
    off   *broken*   *broken off; sudden; unexpected*

12. ?   + VERSE   =   ?
    away   *turned*   *turned away; opposed; unwilling*

13. ?   + PONING   =   ?
    after   *putting*   *putting after; deferring; delaying*

14. ?   + EQUATE   =   ?
    to   *equal*   *equal to; sufficient; enough*

15. ?   + CAMERAL   =   ?
    two   *pertaining to a chamber*   *consisting of two chambers*

16. ?   + CENTENNIAL   =   ?
    two   *hundredth anniversary*   *two hundredth anniversary*

17. ?   + APTED   =   ?
    to   *fitted*   *fitted to; adjusted*

18. ?   + TAINING   =   ?
    from   *holding*   *holding oneself from doing something; refraining*

19. ?   + SCRIPT   =   ?
    after   *written*   *note added after signature of a letter*

20. ?   + VERT   =   ?
    off   *turn; ward*   *ward off; turn away; prevent*

REVIEW 3: SENTENCE COMPLETION

Write the word from the list below that best fits the context.

abdicate	abhor
abrupt	abscond
absorbing	adapt
addicted	adequate
adjourn	advent
adversary	antecedents
anteroom	averse
avocation	bilingual
bipartisan	postmortem
postscript	semidetached

1. Ken, who plays golf eight hours a day, claims it is just his _?_, but he is quite obviously _?_ to it.
2. Though it is true that our _?_ were hunters, many of us _?_ the practice.
3. In the _?_ to her letter, Lucille indicated that she would not be _?_ to a phone call from her former friend.
4. Surprisingly enough, the _?_ committee reached agreement quickly and was able to _?_ in less than an hour.
5. Used to rural life, the family could not _?_ to their _?_ city home, where noises from their neighbor penetrated the common wall.
6. The book Alice was reading was so _?_ that she did not notice the _?_ of the storm.
7. In the coroner's _?_, the detective waited patiently for the results of the _?_ on the murder victim.
8. The game came to a(n) _?_ halt when a stranger dashed onto the court and _?_ed with the only basketball we had.
9. Believing his health was no longer _?_ for him to rule, the ailing monarch decided to _?_ his throne.
10. _?_ American officers who knew the language of our _?_ helped to negotiate the truce.

REVIEW 4: SYNONYMS

Avoid repetition by replacing the boldfaced word or expression with a synonym from the following words.

abnormal	absolve(d)
adjoin(s)	adversary
adverse	avert
bicentennial	bilateral
bisect	semiconscious

1. Two of the suspects were found guilty, and one was **declared free of guilt.**
2. **Cut** this six-foot board **in two** to give us two three-foot lengths.
3. It would be **unusual** if traffic were light at 5 p.m. because that is usually a busy hour.
4. Often, for the first minute or two after I awake, I am only **half awake.**
5. Was the accident unpreventable, or could you have done something to **prevent** it?
6. The weather yesterday was **unfavorable** for sailing, but today it is supposed to be favorable.
7. Who else is opposing you in the election? Is Olga your only **opponent?**

8. Both sides have joined in a **two-sided** effort to improve working conditions.

9. The post office is next to the railroad station, and the hardware store **is next to** the bakery.

10. The United States celebrated its one-hundredth anniversary as a nation in 1876, and its **two-hundredth anniversary** in 1976.

REVIEW 5: ANTONYMS

Enter the word from the list below that is most nearly the opposite of the boldfaced word or words.

abhor	abrupt
adequate	adherent
adjacent	adversary
adverse	antecedents
avocation	postgraduate

1. We __?__ villains but **admire** heroes and heroines.

2. Many a nation that was our __?__ in World War II is now our **ally.**

3. General Benedict Arnold was a loyal and courageous __?__ of the Revolutionary cause until 1780, when he turned **renegade.**

4. Though we were promised __?__ school funding, the money voted by the legislature is **insufficient.**

5. There was no parking space in the field __?__ to the building; we had to park in a **distant** lot.

6. The __?__ comments of the judges outweighed their **favorable** ones.

7. As __?__ of future generations, we must protect the resources of this planet. Otherwise, our **descendants** may not forgive us.

8. Growth in childhood is **gradual;** there are usually no __?__ changes.

9. The grades students earn in their __?__ courses are usually better than those they achieved in their **undergraduate** work.

10. From the knowledge Sarah has about gardening, one might think it is her **profession,** but it is just her __?__ .

REVIEW 6: CONCISE WRITING

Express the thought of each sentence below in no more than four words.

1. Wasn't Antony the one who stood in opposition to Brutus?

2. Skating is what she enjoys doing when she is not at work in her regular occupation.

3. The legislature that France has is made up of two houses.
4. What is the reason that made them depart in secret?
5. We met with circumstances that were not favorable to our interests.

REVIEW 7: SYNONYM SUMMARY

Each line, when completed, should have three words similar in meaning. Write the complete words.

1. n (2) ghboring	n (2) rby	(2) jacent
2. int (1) r (1) sting	(2) grossing	(2) sorbing
3. l (2) the	(2) test	abh (1) r
4. an (1) estors	foreb (2) rs	(4) cedents
5. f (1) t	su (1) t	(2) apt
6. host (1) le	(2) favorable	(2) verse
7. follow (2)	supp (2) ter	adh (1) r (1) nt
8. (2) expected	sudd (2)	(2) rupt
9. appr (2) ch	arriv (1) l	(2) vent
10. (2) nounce	resi (1) n	abdi (4)
11. d (1) f (1) r	r (1) cess	adj (2) rn
12. (1) scape	fl (2)	(2) scond
13. unus (2) l	(2) regular	(2) normal
14. b (1) rd (1) r	(1) but	(2) join
15. (2) topsy	anal (1) sis	post (3) tem
16. habit (1) ated	(2) voted	(2) dicted
17. prec (1) d (1)	(3) date	ante (4)
18. enou (2)	suffi (2) ent	(3) quate
19. opp (1) n (1) nt	(2) tagonist	(2) versary
20. ex (1) nerate	exc (1) lp (1) te	(2) solve

REVIEW 8: ANALOGIES

Which lettered pair of words—*a, b, c, d,* or *e*—most nearly expresses the same relationship as the capitalized pair?

1. AVERSE : OPPOSE
   - (*a*) devious : elucidate
   - (*b*) convinced : doubt
   - (*c*) cordial : alienate
   - (*d*) frank : disclose
   - (*e*) original : imitate

2. POSTSCRIPT : LETTER
- (a) postmark : envelope
- (b) headline : article
- (c) caboose : train
- (d) rain : rainbow
- (e) bookmark : place

3. UNPLIABLE : ADAPT
- (a) law-abiding : trespass
- (b) rational : think
- (c) literate : write
- (d) docile : heed
- (e) perceptive : foresee

    Hint: An **unpliable** person does not **adapt**.

4. ADHERENT : LOYALTY
- (a) beggar : resources
- (b) perjurer : credibility
- (c) fugitive : pursuit
- (d) bigot : tolerance
- (e) prodigy : talent

5. BILINGUAL : LANGUAGE
- (a) versatile : skill
- (b) outspoken : tongue
- (c) nimble : agility
- (d) observant : vision
- (e) ambidextrous : hand

6. ABSOLVE : GUILT
- (a) implicate : suspicion
- (b) enlighten : ignorance
- (c) incarcerate : penitentiary
- (d) upgrade : rank
- (e) illuminate : light

7. ADVERSARY : ALLY
- (a) fan : addict
- (b) spy : informer
- (c) radical : conservative
- (d) poltroon : craven
- (e) monarch : despot

8. SEMIANNUAL : YEARLY
- (a) half : whole
- (b) fragment : piece
- (c) month : year
- (d) core : exterior
- (e) crescent : moon

9. ABRASION : SKIN
- (a) fertility : soil
- (b) drought : precipitation
- (c) erosion : stone
- (d) propulsion : wind
- (e) conflagration : fire

10. ABSCOND : DEPART
- (a) state : proclaim
- (b) grant : withhold
- (c) conceal : reveal
- (d) conspire : agree
- (e) declare : announce

LATIN PREFIXES 7–12

Pretest 2

Write the *letter* of the best answer.

1. To take part in a school's *intramural* program, you must __?__.
   (A) be on the school team   (B) have approval for competing with students of other schools   (C) be a student at the school

2. A *countermanded* order should __?__.
   (A) be ignored   (B) receive preference   (C) be obeyed

3. When there is an *exclusive* showing of a film at a theater, __?__.
   (A) no other theater in town has it   (B) all seats are reserved
   (C) children unaccompanied by adults are excluded

4. People who *inhibit* their curiosity usually __?__.
   (A) open packages as soon as received   (B) mind their own business   (C) have little patience

5. The chairperson said Phil's suggestion was *extraneous,* but I thought it was __?__.
   (A) original   (B) relevant   (C) off the topic

6. A friend who *intercedes* for you __?__.
   (A) takes the blame for you   (B) takes your place   (C) pleads for you

THE ANSWERS ARE

1. C   2. A   3. A   4. B   5. B   6. C

The following pages will acquaint you with additional words formed with the six Latin prefixes involved in the pretest: *ex-, in-, extra-, intra-, contra-,* and *inter-.*

7. E-, EX-: "out," "from," "away"
8. IN-, IM-: "in," "into," "on," "against," "over"

WORD	MEANING AND TYPICAL USE
emigrate (*v.*) 'e-mə,grāt	move out of a country or region to settle in another At thirteen, Maria Callas *emigrated* from the United States.
immigrate (*v.*) 'i-mə,grāt	move into a foreign country or region as a permanent resident At thirteen, Maria Callas *immigrated* to Greece.
eminent (*adj.*) 'e-mə-nənt	standing or jutting out; conspicuous; famous; distinguished; noteworthy Maria Callas became an *eminent* opera singer.
imminent (*adj.*) 'i-mə-nənt	hanging over one's head; threatening; about to occur; impending At the first flash of lightning, the beach crowd scurried for shelter from the *imminent* storm.
enervate (*v.*) 'e-nə(r),vāt	(literally, "take out the nerves or strength") lessen the strength of; enfeeble; weaken I was so *enervated* by the broiling sun that I had to sit down.
erosion (*n.*) ə'rō-zhən	gradual wearing away; deterioration; depletion Running water is one of the principal causes of soil *erosion*.
evoke (*v.*) ə'vōk	bring out; call forth; elicit; produce The suggestion to lengthen the school year has *evoked* considerable opposition.
invoke (*v.*) ən'vōk	call on for help or protection; appeal to for support Refusing to answer the question, the witness *invoked* the Fifth Amendment, which protects persons from being compelled to testify against themselves.
excise (*v.*) ek'sīz	cut out; remove by cutting out With a penknife, he peeled the apple and *excised* the wormy part.
incise (*v.*) in'sīz	cut into; carve; engrave The letters on the cornerstone had been *incised* with a power drill.

exclusive (*adj.*)
eks'klü-siv

1. shutting out, or tending to shut out, others
An *exclusive* club does not readily accept newcomers.

2. not shared with others; single; sole
Before the game, each team had *exclusive* use of the field for a ten-minute practice period.

inclusive (*adj.*)
in'klü-siv

1. (literally, "shutting in") including the limits (dates, numbers, etc.) mentioned
The film will be shown from August 22 to 24, *inclusive*, for a total of three days.

2. broad in scope; comprehensive
An unabridged dictionary is much more *inclusive* than an ordinary desk dictionary.

exhibit (*v.*)
ig'zi-bət

(literally, "hold out") show; display
The museum is now *exhibiting* the art of the American Eskimo.

inhibit (*v.*)
ən'hi-bət

(literally, "hold in") hold in check; restrain; repress
Many could not *inhibit* their tears; they cried openly.

expel (*v.*)
iks'pel

drive out; force out; compel to leave; banish; eject
The student who was *expelled* from the university because of poor grades applied for readmission the following term.

impel (*v.*)
əm'pel

drive on; force; compel
We do not know what *impelled* the secretary to resign.

implicate (*v.*)
'im-plə,kāt

(literally, "fold in or involve") show to be part of or connected with; involve; entangle
One of the accused persons confessed and *implicated* two others in the crime.

impugn (*v.*)
əm'pyün

(literally, "fight against") call in question; assail by words or arguments; attack as false; contradict; attack; malign
The treasurer should not have been offended when asked for a financial report. No one was *impugning* his honesty.

incarcerate (*v.*)
ən'kä(r)-sə,rāt

put in prison; imprison; confine
After their escape and recapture, the convicts were *incarcerated* in a more secure prison.

inscribe (*v.*)
ən'skrīb

(literally, "write on") write, engrave, or print to create a lasting record; imprint; autograph
The name of the winner will be *inscribed* on the medal.

insurgent (*n.*)   one who rises in revolt against established authority;
ən'sər-jənt   rebel; mutineer
> The ruler promised to pardon any *insurgents* who
> would lay down their arms.

insurgent (*adj.*) rebellious; insubordinate; mutinous
> General Washington led the *insurgent* forces in the
> Revolutionary War.

EXERCISE 4.5: *E-*, *EX-*, *IN-*, AND *IM-* WORDS

Fill each blank with the most appropriate word from groups 7 and 8.

1. This afternoon the swimming team has __?__ use of the pool. No one
   else will be admitted.
2. No one can __?__ the settler's claim to the property, since he holds the
   deed to the land.
3. Over the centuries, the Colorado River has carved its bed out of solid
   rock by the process of __?__ .
4. A lack of opportunity compelled thousands to __?__ from their native
   land.
5. Proposals to increase taxes usually __?__ strong resistance.
6. The famine-stricken nation is expected to __?__ the help of its more
   fortunate neighbors.
7. On the front page, I am going to __?__ these words: "To Dad on his
   fortieth birthday. Love, Ruth."
8. Learning that their arrest was __?__ , the insurgent leaders went into
   hiding.
9. The judge asked the guards to __?__ the spectators who were creating
   a disturbance.
10. We just had to see what was in the package. We could not__?__ our
    curiosity.

---

9. EXTRA-: "outside"
10. INTRA-: "within"

---

extracurricular (*adj.*)   outside the regular curriculum, or course of study
,ek-strə-kə'rik-yə-lə(r)   Why don't you join an *extracurricular* activity,
such as a club, the school newspaper, or a team?

extraneous (*adj.*)   coming from or existing outside; foreign; not es-
ek'strā-nē-əs   sential; not pertinent; irrelevant

You said you would stick to the topic, but you keep introducing *extraneous* issues.

extravagant (*adj.*)
ik'stra-və-gənt

1. outside or beyond the bounds of reason; excessive
Reliable manufacturers do not make *extravagant* claims for their products.

2. spending lavishly; wasteful
In a few months, the *extravagant* heir spent the fortune of a lifetime.

intramural (*adj.*)
,in-trə'myü-rəl

within the walls or boundaries (of a school, college, etc.); confined to members (of a school, college, etc.)
At most schools, the students participating in *intramural* athletics vastly outnumber the students involved in interscholastic sports.

intraparty (*adj.*)
,in-trə'pä(r)-tē

within a party
The Democrats are trying to heal *intraparty* strife so as to present a united front in the coming election.

intrastate (*adj.*)
,in-trə'stāt

within a state
Commerce between the states is regulated by the Interstate Commerce Commission, but *intrastate* commerce is supervised by the states themselves.

intravenous (*adj.*)
,in-trə'vē-nəs

within or by way of the veins
Patients are nourished by *intravenous* feeding when too ill to take food by mouth.

EXERCISE 4.6: *EXTRA-* AND *INTRA-* WORDS

Fill each blank with the most appropriate word from groups 9 and 10.

1. Your claim that you would win by a landslide was certainly __?__, as you were nearly defeated.
2. An air conditioner cools a room and helps to shut out __?__ noises.
3. The theft must be regarded as an __?__ matter, unless the stolen goods have been transported across state lines.
4. Some educators want to concentrate on __?__ athletics and do away with interscholastic competition.
5. Though fencing is not in the curriculum, it is offered as an __?__ activity.

11. CONTRA-, CONTRO-, COUNTER-:
"against," "contrary"

con (*adv.*)
'kän

(short for *contra*) against; on the negative side
I abstained from casting my ballot because I could not decide whether to vote *pro* or *con*.

con (*n.*)

(used mainly in the plural) opposing argument; reason against
Before taking an important step, carefully study the *pros* and *cons* of the matter.

contraband (*n.*)
'kän-trə,band

merchandise imported or exported contrary to law; smuggled goods
Customs officials examined the luggage of the suspected smuggler but found no *contraband*.

contravene (*v.*)
,kän-trə'vēn

go or act contrary to; violate; disregard; infringe
By invading the neutral nation, the dictator *contravened* an earlier pledge to guarantee its independence.

controversy (*n.*)
'kän-trə,vər-sē

(literally, "a turning against") dispute; debate; quarrel
Our *controversy* with Great Britain over the Oregon Territory nearly led to war.

counter (*adv.*)
'kaün-tə(r)

(followed by *to*) contrary; in the opposite direction
The student's plan to drop out of school runs *counter* to his parents' wishes.

countermand (*v.*)
'kaün-tə(r),mand

cancel (an order) by issuing a contrary order; revoke
The health commissioner ordered the plant to close, but a judge *countermanded* the order.

incontrovertible (*adj.*)
,in-kän-trə'vər-tə-bəl

not able to be "turned against" or disputed; unquestionable; certain; indisputable
The suspect's fingerprints on the safe were considered *incontrovertible* evidence of participation in the robbery.

EXERCISE 4.7: *CONTRA-*, *CONTRO-*, AND *COUNTER-* WORDS

Fill each blank with the most appropriate word from group 11.

1. Until we became embroiled in __?__ , Peggy and I were the best of friends.
2. A birth certificate is __?__ proof of age.
3. Vessels carrying __?__ are subject to seizure.
4. A superior officer has the power to __?__ the orders of a subordinate.
5. I cannot support you in an activity that you undertook __?__ to my advice.

---

12. INTER-: "between"

---

intercede (*v.*)
,in-tə(r)'sēd
(literally, "go between") interfere to reconcile differences; mediate; plead in another's behalf; intervene

I would have lost my place on line if you hadn't *interceded* for me.

intercept (*v.*)
,in-tə(r)'sept
(literally, "catch between") stop or seize on the way from one place to another; interrupt; catch

We gained possession of the ball when Russ *intercepted* a forward pass.

interlinear (*adj.*)
,in-tə(r)'li-nē-ə(r)
inserted between lines already printed or written

It is difficult to make *interlinear* notes if the space between the lines is very small.

interlude (*n.*)
'in-tə(r),lüd
anything filling the time between two events; interval; break; intermission

Between World War I and II, there was a twenty-one-year *interlude* of peace.

intermediary (*n.*)
,in-tə(r)'mē-dē,e-rē
go-between; mediator

For his role as *intermediary* in helping to end the Russo-Japanese War, Theodore Roosevelt won the Nobel Peace Prize.

intermission (*n.*)
,in-tə(r)'mi-shən
pause between periods of activity; interval; interruption

During the *intermission* between the first and second acts, you will have a chance to purchase refreshments.

intersect (*v.*)
,in-tə(r)'sekt

(literally, "cut between") cut by passing through or across; divide; cross

Broadway *intersects* Seventh Avenue at Times Square.

interurban (*adj.*)
,in-tə(r)'ər-bən

between cities or towns

The only way to get to the next town is by automobile or taxi; there is no *interurban* bus.

intervene (*v.*)
,in-tə(r)'vēn

1. come between

The summer vacation *intervenes* between the close of one school year and the beginning of the next.

2. come in to settle a quarrel; intercede; mediate

Let the opponents settle the dispute by themselves; don't *intervene*.

EXERCISE 4.8: *INTER-* WORDS

Fill each blank with the most appropriate word from group 12.

1. A conspicuous warning signal must be posted wherever railroad tracks __?__ a highway.
2. Though asked repeatedly to be an __?__ in the labor dispute, the Mayor so far has refused to intercede.
3. Radio stations sometimes offer a brief __?__ of music between the end of one program and the start of another.
4. A special task force is trying to __?__ the invaders.
5. Construction funds have been voted for a four-lane __?__ highway linking the three cities.

Review Exercises

REVIEW 9: LATIN PREFIXES 7–12

For each Latin prefix in column I, write the *letter* of its meaning from column II.

COLUMN I	COLUMN II
1. *intra-*	(A) out, from, away
2. *inter-*	(B) against, contrary
3. *extra-*	(C) in, into, on, against, over
4. *e-, ex-*	(D) within
5. *contra-, contro-, counter-*	(E) between
6. *in-, im-*	(F) outside

REVIEW 10: WORDBUILDING

Fill in the prefix in column I and the complete word in column III.

I	II	III
1. __?__ *between*	+ VENE *come*	= __?__ *come between*
2. __?__ *in*	+ HIBIT *hold*	= __?__ *hold in; restrain*
3. __?__ *away*	+ ROSION *wearing*	= __?__ *gradual wearing away*
4. __?__ *against*	+ VERSY *turning*	= __?__ *a turning against; dispute*
5. __?__ *against*	+ SURGENT *rising*	= __?__ *rising against; rebellious*
6. __?__ *within*	+ VENOUS *pertaining to the veins*	= __?__ *within the veins*
7. __?__ *between*	+ LINEAR *pertaining to lines*	= __?__ *inserted between the lines*
8. __?__ *outside*	+ CURRICULAR *pertaining to the curriculum*	= __?__ *outside the curriculum*
9. __?__ *into*	+ MIGRATE *move*	= __?__ *move into a foreign country*

10. __?__   + CISE   = __?__
    out   *cut*   *cut out*

11. __?__   + MURAL   = __?__
    within   *pertaining to walls*   *within the walls or boundaries*

12. __?__   + MAND   = __?__
    against   *command*   *cancel by issuing a contrary order*

13. __?__   + URBAN   = __?__
    between   *pertaining to cities*   *between cities or towns*

14. __?__   + CISE   = __?__
    into   *cut*   *cut into; engrave*

15. __?__   + VAGANT   = __?__
    outside   *wandering*   *outside the bounds of reason; excessive*

16. __?__   + BAND   = __?__
    against   *ban; decree*   *goods imported contrary to law*

17. __?__   + PEL   = __?__
    on   *drive*   *drive on; force*

18. __?__   + HIBIT   = __?__
    out   *hold*   *hold out; show; display*

19. __?__   + CEDE   = __?__
    between   *go*   *go between to reconcile differences; mediate*

20. __?__   + MINENT   = __?__
    out   *projecting*   *projecting out; distinguished*

REVIEW 11: SENTENCE COMPLETION

Fill each blank with the word from the list below that best fits the context.

contraband	controversy
countermand	eminent
evoke	excise
exclusive	exhibit
extravagant	immigrate
imminent	impel
incarcerate	incontrovertible
inscribe	insurgent
intercept	intermission
intervene	intravenous

1. Acting on a tip from an informer, customs agents were able to __?__ a shipment of __?__.
2. The heir's spending has been so __?__ that his financial ruin is __?__.
3. When details of the proposed six-lane highway through the center of town are disclosed, they will surely __?__ considerable __?__.
4. Few had ever heard of Lynn until the Philadelphia Museum of Art __?__ed her work and transformed her into a(n) __?__ painter.
5. The thief would have been __?__d for ten years if a higher court had not __?__ed the sentence.
6. If the civil strife in that country continues much longer, it may __?__ many more of its inhabitants to __?__ to America.
7. The suit charges that the company has been unfairly __?__ in its hiring practices, and it asks the court to __?__.
8. After the tumor was __?__d, the patient required __?__ feeding for three days.
9. During the ten-minute __?__, several admirers approached the playwright and asked him to __?__ their programs.
10. The dictator's claim that the rebellion has failed is contradicted by __?__ evidence that the __?__s are gaining the upper hand.

REVIEW 12: SYNONYMS

Avoid repetition by replacing the boldfaced word or expression with a synonym.

contravene(s)	extracurricular
extraneous	extravagant
implicate(d)	impugn(ed)
intercede	intermediary
intersect	invoke

1. Not only did they call his ability into question, but they also **questioned** his character.
2. The law protects everyone. Even criminals **call upon** the Constitution **for protection.**
3. Sports are not a part of the curriculum; they are **outside the curriculum.**
4. Let us stick to the topic. We will get nowhere if we keep introducing matters that are **outside the topic of our discussion.**
5. The point where two roads **cross** is a dangerous crossing.

6. The accused falsely **involved** others who had no involvement what-soever with the plot.

7. We have little regard for anyone who **disregards** regulations that he or she wants others to observe.

8. How can you ask us to be reasonable when you yourself are making demands that are so **beyond the bounds of reason?**

9. Please do not **interfere;** we do not want any interference.

10. Communication between the two adversaries is being conducted through a(n) **go-between.**

REVIEW 13: ANTONYMS

Enter the word from the list below that is most nearly the opposite of the boldfaced word or words.

con	enervate
erosion	expel
extracurricular	extravagant
inhibit	interlinear
intraparty	intrastate

1. The tiresome shopping trip had __?__d my sister, but a short nap and a shower **reinvigorated** her.

2. Traffic usually moves faster on **interstate** highways than on __?__ roads.

3. After the severe beach __?__ caused by the storm, the town promised speedy **restoration** of the shoreline.

4. You made so many __?__ corrections that it was hard to read what you had written **on the lines.**

5. Why did he __?__ his resentment for so long before deciding to **express** it?

6. The club voted to __?__ a member for nonpayment of dues and to **admit** two new applicants.

7. Do they realize that they may have to be **frugal** later if they are __?__ now?

8. So far you have told us the **pros** of your plan, but how about the __?__s?

9. If the Independents continue their self-destructive __?__ sniping, they will be ill-equipped for the **interparty** contests that lie ahead.

10. Anyone who excels both in **curricular** work and __?__ activities is indeed an exceptional person.

REVIEW 14: CONCISE WRITING

Express the thought of each sentence below in no more than four words.

1. Who are the ones who have risen in revolt against established authority?
2. You made claims that are beyond the bounds of reason.
3. Shouldn't those who commit the crime of burglary be put behind prison bars?
4. Schools encourage sports activities that involve participation by their own students.
5. Rains are a cause of the gradual wearing away of the soil.

REVIEW 15: SYNONYM SUMMARY

Each line, when completed, should have three words similar in meaning. Write the *complete* words.

1. f (1) rce	comp (1) l	imp (2)
2. interv (1) l	(5) lude	inter (2) ssion
3. disting (2) shed	not (1) worthy	(1) minent
4. can (1) el	rev (1) ke	counter (2) nd
5. elic (1) t	prod (1) ce	(1) voke
6. q (2) rrel	(3) pute	contro (2) rsy
7. thr (2) tening	(2) pending	(2) minent
8. (2) prison	(3) fine	incar (2) rate
9. interf (1) r (1)	(5) vene	inter (2) de
10. compreh (2) sive	br (2) d	(2) clusive
11. restr (2) n	(2) press	(2) hibit
12. inv (1) lve	(2) tangle	(2) plicate
13. unsh (1) red	s (1) le	(2) clusive
14. weak (2)	(2) feeble	(1) nervate
15. cont (2) dict	mal (1) gn	imp (1) gn
16. v (1) olate	(3) regard	(3) travene
17. impr (1) nt	(2) grave	(2) scribe
18. (2) essential	irrel (1) v (1) nt	extran (1) ous
19. deter (2) ration	depl (1) tion	(1) r (1) sion
20. ej (1) ct	b (1) n (1) sh	(2) pel

REVIEW 16: ANALOGIES

Which lettered pair of words—*a, b, c, d,* or *e*—most nearly expresses the same relationship as the capitalized pair?

1. IMMINENT : ANXIETY
   - *(a)* reasonable : controversy
   - *(b)* uncomplicated : confusion
   - *(c)* abrupt : surprise
   - *(d)* objective : indignation
   - *(e)* commonplace : attention

   Hint: Something that is **imminent** causes **anxiety**.

2. INHIBIT : REPRESS
   - *(a)* grasp : release
   - *(b)* withhold : grant
   - *(c)* oblige : refuse
   - *(d)* conceal : display
   - *(e)* withstand : resist

3. INCONTROVERTIBLE : DISPUTE
   - *(a)* unimportant : ignore
   - *(b)* unique : replace
   - *(c)* accessible : approach
   - *(d)* vulnerable : injure
   - *(e)* excusable : forgive

4. INTERMEDIARY : UNBIASED
   - *(a)* interpreter : bilingual
   - *(b)* despot : glorified
   - *(c)* umpire : partisan
   - *(d)* infant : unsupervised
   - *(e)* ignoramus : heeded

5. CLIQUE : EXCLUSIVE
   - *(a)* benefactor : uncharitable
   - *(b)* mob : docile
   - *(c)* accomplice : irreproachable
   - *(d)* recluse : sociable
   - *(e)* conspiracy : clandestine

6. EMINENT : NOTE
   - *(a)* corrupt : trust
   - *(b)* admirable : contempt
   - *(c)* indolent : promotion
   - *(d)* culpable : blame
   - *(e)* helpless : ridicule

7. ENERVATE : FEEBLE
   - *(a)* misinform : knowledgeable
   - *(b)* pacify : tractable
   - *(c)* intimidate : intrepid
   - *(d)* accommodate : hostile
   - *(e)* convince : uncertain

8. EXTRANEOUS : PERTINENT
   - *(a)* outdated : fashionable
   - *(b)* rigid : inflexible
   - *(c)* foreign : alien
   - *(d)* enigmatic : mysterious
   - *(e)* improbable : unlikely

9. INTERMISSION : PAUSE

    (a) curtain : window   *(b)* commission : service

    (c) parsley : herb   *(d)* truce : combat

    (e) recess : energy

10. MINUTE : INTERLUDE

    (a) seed : plant   *(b)* whale : mammal

    (c) skyscraper : edifice   *(d)* tanker : vessel

    (e) pittance : amount

LATIN PREFIXES 13–18

Pretest 3

Write the *letter* of the best answer.

1. Inhabitants of a *secluded* dwelling have few __?__ .

    (A) windows   (B) expenses   (C) neighbors

2. *Malice* cannot exist between __?__ .

    (A) old rivals   (B) true friends   (C) close relatives

3. An *illegible* mark cannot be __?__ .

    (A) raised   (B) erased   (C) read

4. The opposite of a *benediction* is a __?__ .

    (A) curse   (B) contradiction   (C) blessing

5. A *dispassionate* witness is likely to be __?__ .

    (A) prejudiced   (B) calm   (C) easily upset

6. *Deciduous* trees __?__ .

    (A) shed their leaves   (B) resist disease   (C) are green all year

THE ANSWERS ARE

1. C 2. B 3. C 4. A 5. B 6. A

The following pages will introduce you to many more words formed with the six Latin prefixes involved in the pretest: *in-, bene-, mal-, de-, dis-,* and *se-.*

13. IN-, IL-, IM-, IR-: "not," "un-"

WORD	MEANING AND TYPICAL USE
illegible (*adj.*) i'le-jə-bəl	not legible; impossible or hard to read; undecipherable I could read most of the signatures, but a few were *illegible*.
illiterate (*adj.*) i'li-tə-rət	not literate; unable to read or write; uneducated The new nation undertook to teach its *illiterate* citizens to read and write.
illogical (*adj.*) i'lä-jə-kəl	not logical; not observing the rules of *logic* (correct reasoning); irrational; fallacious It is *illogical* to vote for a candidate whom you have no faith in.
immaculate (*adj.*) ə'mak-yə-lət	not spotted; absolutely clean; stainless Before dinner, the tablecloth was *immaculate*.
immature (*adj.*) ,i-mə'tyü-ə(r)	not mature; not fully grown or developed; young; childish Seniors often consider sophomores too *immature*.
impunity (*n.*) əm'pyü-nə-tē	state of being not punished; freedom from punishment, harm, loss, etc.; immunity As a result of stricter enforcement, speeders are no longer able to break the law with *impunity*.
inaccessible (*adj.*) ,in-ak'se-sə-bəl	not accessible; unreachable; hard to get to; unapproachable For most of the year, the Eskimo settlements in northern Quebec are *inaccessible*, except by air.
incessant (*adj.*) in'se-sənt	not ceasing; continuing without interruption; interminable; ceaseless It is almost impossible to cross the street during the rush hour because of the *incessant* flow of traffic.
inflexible (*adj.*) in'flek-sə-bəl	not flexible; not easily bent; firm; unyielding No compromise is possible when both sides remain *inflexible*.
ingratitude (*n.*) in'gra-tə,tüd	state of being not grateful; ungratefulness; lack of gratitude Valerie refuses to let me see her notes, though I have always lent her mine. What *ingratitude!*

inhospitable (*adj.*)
,in'häs-pi-tə-bəl

not hospitable; not showing kindness to guests and strangers; unfriendly

When the visitors come to our school, we should make them feel at home; otherwise they will think we are *inhospitable*.

insoluble (*adj.*)
in'säl-yə-bəl

1. not soluble; incapable of being solved; unsolvable; irresolvable

Scientists are finding solutions to many problems that formerly seemed *insoluble*.

2. not capable of being dissolved

Salt dissolves in water, but sand is *insoluble*.

irreconcilable (*adj.*)
,i-re-kən'sī-lə-bəl

not reconcilable; not able to be brought into friendly accord or compromise; incompatible

After Romeo and Juliet died, their families, who had been *irreconcilable* enemies, became friends.

irrelevant (*adj.*)
i're-lə-vənt

not relevant; inapplicable; off the topic; extraneous

Stick to the topic; don't make *irrelevant* remarks.

irrevocable (*adj.*)
,i're-və-kə-bəl

not revocable; incapable of being recalled or revoked; unalterable; irreversible

As an umpire's decision is *irrevocable*, it is useless to argue over a call.

EXERCISE 4.9: *IN-*, *IL-*, *IM-*, AND *IR-* WORDS

Fill each blank with the most appropriate word from group 13.

1. Half-frozen, the traveler knocked at a strange door, hoping the inhabitants would not be so __?__ as to turn him away from their fire.
2. Prior to their arrest, the gang had committed a number of thefts with __?__ .
3. The detective finally succeeded in clearing up the seemingly __?__ mystery by tracking down every clue.
4. On some of the very old tombstones in Boston's Granary Burying Ground, the inscriptions are almost __?__ .
5. Before the bridge was built, the island had been __?__ from the mainland, except by ferry.

14. BENE-: "good," "well"
15. MAL-, MALE-: "evil," "ill," "bad," "badly"

benediction (*n.*)
,be-nə'dik-shən

(literally, "good saying") blessing; good wishes; approbation
Robinson Crusoe ran off to sea against his parents' wishes and without their *benediction*.

malediction (*n.*)
,ma-lə'dik-shən

(literally, "evil saying") curse
With her dying breath, Queen Dido pronounced a *malediction* on Aeneas and all his descendants.

benefactor (*n.*)
'be-nə,fak-tə(r)

(literally, "one who does good") person who gives kindly aid, money, or a similar benefit
The museum could not have been built without the gift of ten million dollars by a wealthy *benefactor*.

malefactor (*n.*)
'ma-lə,fak-tə(r)

(literally, "one who does evil") offender; evildoer; criminal
Shortly after the crime, the *malefactor* was apprehended and brought to trial.

beneficial (*adj.*)
,be-nə'fi-shəl

productive of good; helpful; advantageous
Rest is usually *beneficial* to a person suffering from a bad cold.

beneficiary (*n.*)
,be-nə'fi-shē,e-rē

person receiving some good, advantage, or benefit
The sick and the needy will be the *beneficiaries* of your gift to the community fund.

benevolent (*adj.*)
bə'ne-və-lənt

(literally, "wishing well") disposed to promote the welfare of others; kind; charitable
Benevolent employers have a sincere concern for the welfare of their employees.

malevolent (*adj.*)
mə'le-və-lənt

(literally, "wishing ill") showing ill will; spiteful; malicious; vicious
In Robert Louis Stevenson's novel *Kidnapped*, David Balfour visits a *malevolent* uncle who tries to kill him.

maladjusted (*adj.*)
,ma-lə'jəs-təd

badly adjusted; out of harmony with one's environment
Beret was the most *maladjusted* person in the settlement; she was not suited for the hardships of pioneer life on the open prairie.

malice (*n.*)
'mal-əs

ill will; intention or desire to harm another; enmity; malevolence
My tire did not have a leak; someone had deflated it out of *malice*.

malnutrition (*n.*)
,mal-nyü'tri-shən

bad or faulty nutrition; poor nourishment
The lack of fresh fruit and vegetables in a person's diet may cause *malnutrition*.

maltreat (*v.*)
mal'trēt

treat badly or roughly; mistreat; abuse
Two news photographers were attacked by the mob, and their cameras were smashed. It is disgraceful that they were so *maltreated*.

EXERCISE 4.10: *BENE-*, *MAL-*, AND *MALE-* WORDS

Fill each blank with the most appropriate word from groups 14 and 15.

1. The Eskimo is at home in the Arctic, but I would probably be __?__ in that environment.
2. The hero of Charles Dickens' novel *Great Expectations* received considerable financial aid from an unknown __?__ .
3. Mrs. Adams will inherit a fortune, since she is named as the exclusive __?__ in her wealthy aunt's will.
4. Paula couldn't understand why anyone should bear her so much __?__ as to tear her notebook to bits.
5. Philip Nolan, in Edward Everett Hale's short story, "The Man Without a Country," is punished for uttering a __?__ on the United States.

16. DE-: "down," "down from," "opposite of"

decadent (*adj.*)
'de-kə-dənt

(literally, "falling down") deteriorating; growing worse; declining
The *decadent* rooming house was once a flourishing hotel.

deciduous (*adj.*)
də'si-jə-wəs

having leaves that fall down at the end of the growing season; shedding leaves
Maple, elm, birch, and other *deciduous* trees lose their leaves in the fall.

demented (*adj.*)
də'men-təd

out of one's mind; mad; insane; deranged
Whoever did this must have been *demented*; no sane person would have acted in such a way.

demolish (*v.*)
də'mä-lish

pull or tear down; destroy; raze; wreck
A wrecking crew is *demolishing* the old building.

demote (*v.*)
dē'mōt

move down in grade or rank; degrade; downgrade
For being absent without leave, the corporal was *demoted* to private.

dependent (*adj.*)
də'pen-dənt

(literally, "hanging down from") unable to exist without the support of another
Children are *dependent* on their parents until they are able to earn their own living.

depreciate (*v.*)
də'prē-shē,āt

1. go down in price or value
New automobiles *depreciate* rapidly, but antiques tend to go up in value.

2. speak slightingly of; belittle; disparage
The store manager would feel you are *depreciating* him if you refer to him as the "head clerk."

despise (*v.*)
də'spīz

look down on; scorn; feel contempt for; abhor; disdain
Benedict Arnold was *despised* by his fellow Americans for betraying his country.

deviate (*v.*)
'dē-vē,āt

turn aside, or down (from a route or rule); stray; wander; digress
Dr. Parker does not see a patient without an appointment, except in an emergency, and she does not *deviate* from this policy.

devour (*v.*)
də'vaů-ə(r)

(literally, "gulp down") eat greedily; eat like an animal
Wendy must have been starved; she *devoured* her food.

EXERCISE 4.11: *DE-* WORDS

Fill each blank with the most appropriate word from group 16.

1. The bus driver cannot take you to your door because he is not permitted to _?_ from his route.
2. Streets lined with _?_ trees are strewn with fallen leaves each autumn.
3. The patient's speech was not rational but like that of a _?_ person.
4. Retired people like to have an income of their own so as not to be _?_ on others.
5. By 400 A.D., the Romans were well past the peak of their glory and had become a _?_ people.

17. DIS-: "opposite of," "differently," "apart," "away"

discontent (*adj.*)
,dis-kən'tent

(usually followed by *with*) opposite of "content"; dissatisfied; discontented; disgruntled
Dan was *discontent* with the mark on his Spanish exam; he had expected at least 10 points more.

discredit (*v.*)
dəs'kre-dət

disbelieve; refuse to trust
The parents *discredited* the child's story, since he was in the habit of telling falsehoods.

discrepancy (*n.*)
də'skre-pən-sē

disagreement; difference; inconsistency; variation
Bea should have had $25 in her purse, instead of only $20. She could not account for the *discrepancy*.

disintegrate (*v.*)
də'sin-tə,grāt

do the opposite of "integrate" (make into a whole); break into bits; crumble; decay
The driveway needs to be resurfaced; it is beginning to *disintegrate*.

dispassionate (*adj.*)
,dəs'pa-shə-nət

opposite of "passionate" (showing strong feeling); calm; composed; impartial
For a *dispassionate* account of how the fight started, ask a neutral observer—not a participant.

disrepair (*n.*)
dis'rə-pe-ə(r)

opposite of good condition or repair; bad condition
The tape-player lent her was in good condition, but she returned it in *disrepair*.

dissent (*v.*)
də'sent

feel differently; differ in opinion; disagree
When the matter was put to a vote, 29 agreed and 4 *dissented*.

dissident (*adj.*)
'di-sə-dənt

(literally, "sitting apart") not agreeing; dissenting; nonconformist
The compromise was welcomed by all the strikers except a small *dissident* group who felt that the raises were too small.

distract (*v.*)
də'strakt

draw away, or divert the attention of; confuse; bewilder
When the bus is in motion, passengers should do nothing to *distract* the driver.

EXERCISE 4.12: *DIS-* WORDS

Fill each blank with the most appropriate word from group 17.

1. The leader conferred with several _?_ members of his party in an attempt to win them over to his views.
2. Add your marks for the different parts of the test to see if they equal your total mark. If there is a _?_, notify the teacher.
3. The negligent owner allowed her equipment to fall into _?_.
4. I had no reason to _?_ the information, since it came from a reliable source.
5. Turn off the television set while you are trying to concentrate, or it will _?_ your attention.

---

18. SE-: "apart"

---

secede (*v.*)
sə'sēd

(literally, "go apart") withdraw from an organization or federation
When Lincoln was elected President in 1860, South Carolina *seceded* from the Union.

secession (*n.*)
sə'se-shən

(literally, "a going apart") withdrawal from an organization or federation
South Carolina's *secession* was followed by that of ten other states and led to the formation of the Confederacy.

seclude (*v.*)
sə'klüd

keep apart from others; place in solitude; isolate; sequester
Monica was so upset over losing her job that she *secluded* herself and refused to see anyone.

secure (*adj.*)
sə'kyüə(r)

1. apart, or free, from care, fear, or worry; confident; assured
Are you worried about passing, or do you feel *secure*?

2. safe against loss, attack, or danger
Guests who want their valuables to be *secure* are urged to deposit them in the hotel vault.

sedition (*n.*)
sə'di-shən

going apart from, or against, an established government; action, speech, or writing to overthrow the government; insurrection; treason
The signers of the Declaration of Independence, if captured by the enemy, would probably have been tried for *sedition*.

segregate (*v.*)   (literally, "set apart from the herd") separate from the
'se-grə,gāt   main body; isolate
      During the swim period, the nonswimmers are *segre-gated* from the rest of our group to receive special instruction.

EXERCISE 4.13: *SE-* WORDS

Fill each blank with the most appropriate word from group 18.

1. The law forbids public institutions to __?__ people by race, sex, or religion.
2. In a dictatorship, anyone who criticizes the head of state may be charged with __?__ .
3. Three of the teams have threatened to __?__ from the league unless at least two umpires are assigned to each game.
4. As the storm approached, coastal residents were evacuated to more __?__ quarters in the interior.
5. Some prefer to study for a test with friends; others like to __?__ themselves with their books.

Review Exercises

REVIEW 17: LATIN PREFIXES 13–18

For each Latin prefix in column I, write the *letter* of its correct meaning from column II.

COLUMN I	COLUMN II
1. MAL, MALE	(A) opposite of, differently, apart, away
2. SE	(B) not, un-
3. BENE	(C) down, down from, opposite of
4. DIS	(D) apart
5. DE	(E) good, well
6. IN, IL, IM, IR	(F) evil, ill, bad, badly

REVIEW 18: WORDBUILDING

Fill in the prefix in column I and the complete word in column III.

	I		II		III
1.	_?_ *ill*	+	VOLENT *wishing*	=	_?_ *wishing ill; spiteful*
2.	_?_ *not*	+	LITERATE *able to read and write*	=	_?_ *unable to read and write*
3.	_?_ *down*	+	VOUR *gulp*	=	_?_ *eat greedily*
4.	_?_ *apart*	+	CURE *care*	=	_?_ *apart (free) from care*
5.	_?_ *not*	+	SOLUBLE *capable of being solved*	=	_?_ *incapable of being solved*
6.	_?_ *down*	+	SPISE *look*	=	_?_ *look down on; scorn*
7.	_?_ *good*	+	DICTION *saying*	=	_?_ *blessing*
8.	_?_ *not*	+	LEGIBLE *able to read*	=	_?_ *not able to be read*

9. ___?___   + INTEGRATE   = ___?___
   opposite of   *make into a whole*   *break into bits*

10. ___?___   + FACTOR   = ___?___
    evil   *one who does*   *evildoer*

11. ___?___   + MACULATE   = ___?___
    not   *spotted*   *unspotted; absolutely clean*

12. ___?___   + CREDIT   = ___?___
    opposite of   *believe*   *do opposite of believe;*
                                         refuse to trust

13. ___?___   + MOTE   = ___?___
    down   *move*   *move down in rank*

14. ___?___   + PUNITY   = ___?___
    not   *punishment*   *freedom from punishment*

15. ___?___   + SENT   = ___?___
    differently   *feel*   *feel differently; disagree*

16. ___?___   + NUTRITION   = ___?___
    bad   *nourishment*   *poor nourishment*

17. ___?___   + RELEVANT   = ___?___
    not   *applicable*   *not applicable; extraneous*

18. ___?___   + CEDE   = ___?___
    apart   *go*   *go apart; withdraw from*
                                         an organization

19. ___?___   + CADENT   = ___?___
    down   *falling*   *falling down; deteriorating*

20. ___?___   + MATURE   = ___?___
    not   *fully grown*   *not fully grown*

REVIEW 19: SENTENCE COMPLETION

Write the word from the list below that best fits the context.

benefactor   demented
demote   depreciate
discontent   discredit
disrepair   dissident
distract   illiterate
illogical   incessant
ingratitude   inhospitable
insoluble   malice
malnutrition   secede
seclude   secure

1. Worried that the daily events of the city would __?__ her from her work, the novelist __?__d herself in a mountain cabin.

2. The Southern states __?__d from the Union because they were __?__ with the policies of the Federal government.

3. The aunt never gets a visit from the nephews and nieces whom she put through college. Such __?__ to a(n) __?__ is indeed shocking.

4. When he said, "Madam, this is not a meal to ask a man to," Samuel Johnson __?__d the food his hostess had served. He considered her __?__ .

5. By her __?__ stress on the importance of reading, the superintendent hopes to ensure that no one in her district will remain __?__ .

6. The colonel has been a model officer. I can only guess that his superior was acting out of __?__ when he tried to __?__ him.

7. Those detectives who termed the case "__?__" did not adhere strictly to the principles of rational thinking. Their approach was __?__ .

8. The youngsters felt perfectly __?__ in a treehouse that was in such __?__ that its collapse was clearly imminent.

9. The survivor was not insane. He had not eaten for several days. His apparently __?__ state was solely the result of __?__ .

10. A group of __?__ stockholders tried to __?__ the company president by calling attention to his huge annual salary.

REVIEW 20: SYNONYMS

Avoid repetition by replacing the boldfaced word or expression with a synonym from the following words.

dependent	demolish(ing)
despise	deviate
discrepancy	dissent(ed)
immaculate	immature
inaccessible	inflexible

1. You deserve a medal for cleanliness; your room is **absolutely clean.**

2. They won't yield an inch. How can we reach a compromise if they are so **unyielding?**

3. We **feel contempt for** the vandals who did this contemptible thing.

4. Almost everyone agreed. I was one of the very few who **disagreed.**

5. You're acting like a child. Stop being **childish.**

6. The crash site is very **hard to get to,** but helicopters may be able to get there.

7. Now, they are **unable to exist without support from others,** but some-day they will be able to support themselves.

8. The account of the first eyewitness differs slightly from that of the second. Did you notice the **difference?**

9. One destructive child kept **destroying** what the others were trying to build.

10. Did the plane strictly adhere to its course, or did it **go off course** at any time?

REVIEW 21: ANTONYMS

Enter the word from the list below that is most nearly the opposite of the boldfaced word or words.

beneficial	decadent
deciduous	dispassionate
illegible	irrelevant
maladjusted	malediction
malevolent	maltreat

1. It is hard to believe that this __?__ place was once a **flourishing** mining town.

2. Most of the shrubs here are **evergreen;** only the azaleas are __?__ .

3. A **biased** observer may be unable to give a(n) __?__ account of what happened.

4. The medication is not entirely __?__ ; it has some **detrimental** side effects.

5. Some who are now **in harmony with their environment** might become __?__ if they were to find themselves in other surroundings.

6. Prisoners of war are to be **humanely treated;** they must not be __?__ed.

7. We tried to stay **on the topic;** little was said that was __?__ .

8. Did you get a **readable** copy? Mine is __?__ .

9. They came for a **blessing** but were sent off with a(n) __?__ .

10. Relatives could not understand how someone so **benevolent** to strangers could have been __?__ to his own kith and kin.

REVIEW 22: CONCISE WRITING

Express the thought of each sentence below in no more than four words.

1. The question that Terry is asking has nothing to do with the topic that we are discussing.

2. Maple trees lose their leaves at the end of the growing season.
3. The postcard that came in the mail from Bill is impossible to read.
4. Some did not tell the truth and were able to get away with it.
5. The destination that they are heading for seems hard to get to.

REVIEW 23: SYNONYM SUMMARY

Each line, when completed, should have three words similar in meaning. Write the *complete* words.

1. cr (1) m (1) nal   ev (1) ldoer   m (1) l (1) factor
2. diff (1) r (1) nce   inconsisten (1) y   (3) crepancy
3. charit (1) ble   k (1) nd   (4) volent
4. sc (1) rn   (2) hor   (2) spise
5. tr (2) son   ins (2) rection   (2) dition
6. (2) sane   (2) ranged   (2) mented
7. cr (1) mble   (2) cay   dis (2) tegrate
8. enm (1) ty   mal (1) volence   (3) ice
9. w (1) nder   d (1) gress   dev (2) te
10. (2) reversible   (2) alterable   irre (2) cable
11. advantag (2) us   help (3)   benefi (2) al
12. sep (1) rate   is (1) late   se (2) egate
13. inapplic (1) ble   extran (1) ous   irr (1) l (1) v (1) nt
14. (2) terminable   cease (4)   inces (2) nt
15. (2) rational   fallac (2) us   (2) logical
16. disp (1) r (1) ge   (2) little   (2) preciate
17. (3) fident   ass (1) red   sec (1) re
18. dis (2) tisfied   disgr (1) ntled   (3) content
19. r (1) ze   d (1) stroy   (2) molish
20. i (2) late   se (2) ester   (2) clude

REVIEW 24: ANALOGIES

Which lettered pair of words—*a, b, c, d,* or *e*—most nearly expresses the same relationship as the capitalized pair?

1. IRREVOCABLE : ALTER
   - (*a*) unique : match
   - (*b*) feasible : do
   - (*c*) disputable : question
   - (*d*) inconsequential : defer
   - (*e*) tractable : manage

2. BENEFACTOR : MALICE
   (a) perpetrator : offense
   (c) fledgling : experience
   (e) beneficiary : assistance
   (b) tutor : instruction
   (d) curator : museum

3. IMPUNITY : PUNISHMENT
   (a) merit : reward
   (c) insecurity : anxiety
   (e) susceptibility : disease
   (b) frailty : injury
   (d) infallibility : error

4. SWINDLER : MALEFACTOR
   (a) reader : subscriber
   (c) consumer : manufacturer
   (e) physician : pediatrician
   (b) infant : dependent
   (d) columnist : publisher

5. GLUTTONOUS : DEVOUR
   (a) lavish : conserve
   (c) dissident : agree
   (e) determined : waver
   (b) withdrawn : socialize
   (d) avaricious : hoard

6. DISPASSIONATE : PARTIALITY
   (a) merciless : cruelty
   (c) maltreated : resentment
   (e) malevolent : spite
   (b) indecisive : hesitation
   (d) indifferent : interest

7. MALNUTRITION : HEALTH
   (a) scandal : reputation
   (c) misinformation : inconvenience
   (e) enlightenment : knowledge
   (b) exercise : appetite
   (d) commendation :
       promotion

8. IRRATIONAL : LOGIC
   (a) loyal : allegiance
   (c) corrupt : ethics
   (e) contentious : controversy
   (b) facetious : laughter
   (d) sturdy : stamina

9. INCESSANT : INTERMITTENT
   (a) slovenly : untidy
   (c) robust : strong
   (e) permanent : transient
   (b) dormant : sluggish
   (d) meek : acquiescent

10. IMMACULATE : SPOT
   (a) airtight : weakness
   (c) noxious : harm
   (e) versatile : use
   (b) imperfect : flaw
   (d) priceless : worth

LATIN PREFIXES 19–24

Pretest 4

Write the *letter* of the best answer.

1. A *protracted* illness is not __?__ .
   (A) curable   (B) contagious   (C) brief

2. The term *"circumlocution"* in the margin of your composition paper indicates you have __?__ .
   (A) used too many words to express an idea   (B) wandered off the topic   (C) used a slang expression

3. Thoughts that *obsess* you __?__ your mind.
   (A) bypass   (B) trouble   (C) relax

4. Those who work in *collusion* are seeking to __?__ .
   (A) escape noise   (B) assist others   (C) commit fraud

5. A snowfall in Virginia in __?__ is *premature*.
   (A) December   (B) September   (C) March

6. If you make a *pertinent* comment, you are __?__ .
   (A) being rude   (B) delaying the discussion   (C) advancing the discussion

```
THE ANSWERS ARE

1. C  2. A  3. B  4. C  5. B  6. C
```

The following pages will introduce several additional words formed with the prefixes involved in the pretest: *circum-, con-, ob-, per-, pre-,* and *pro-*.

19. CIRCUM-: "around," "round"

WORD	MEANING AND TYPICAL USE
circumference (*n.*) sə(r)'kəm-fə-rəns	distance around a circle or rounded body; perimeter
	The *circumference* of the earth is greatest at the equator and diminishes as we go toward the North or South Pole.

circumlocution (*n.*)
,sər-kəm-lo'kyü-shən

roundabout way of speaking; use of excessive number of words to express an idea; verbiage; tautology

The *circumlocution* "the game ended with a score that was not in our favor" should be replaced by "we lost the game."

circumnavigate (*v.*)
,sər-kəm'na-və,gāt

sail around

Ferdinand Magellan's expedition was the first to *circumnavigate* the globe.

circumscribe (*v.*)
'sər-kəm,skrīb

1. draw a line around

On the composition I got back, the teacher had *circumscribed* a misspelled word to call it to my attention.

2. limit; restrict

The patient was placed on a very *circumscribed* diet; there are very few foods she is permitted to eat.

circumspect (*adj.*)
'sər-kəm,spekt

looking around and paying attention to all possible consequences before acting; cautious; prudent

Don't jump to a conclusion before considering all the facts. Be *circumspect*.

circumvent (*v.*)
'sər-kəm,vent

go around; get the better of; frustrate; skirt; bypass

To *circumvent* local sales taxes, shoppers buy in neighboring communities that do not have such taxes.

EXERCISE 4.14: *CIRCUM-* WORDS

Fill each blank with the most appropriate word from group 19.

1. A physician may decide to __?__ the physical activities and diet of a heart disease patient.
2. Obey the regulations; don't try to __?__ them.
3. If you had been __?__, you would have tested the used camera before buying it.
4. The __?__ of the earth at the equator is nearly 25,000 miles.
5. The rowers had expected to __?__ the island in a couple of hours, but by evening they were less than halfway around.

20. CON-, CO-, COL-, COR-: "together," "with"

coalesce (*v.*)
kō-ə'les

grow together; unite into one; join; combine
During the Revolutionary War, the thirteen colonies *coalesced* into one nation.

coherent (*adj.*)
kō'hi-rənt

sticking together; logically connected; consistent; logical
In *coherent* writing, every sentence is connected in thought to the previous sentence.

collaborate (*v.*)
kə'la-bə,rāt

work together with another or others, especially as a coauthor
George and Helen Papashvily *collaborated* on *Anything Can Happen* and several other books.

collusion (*n.*)
kə'lü-zhən

(literally, "playing together") secret agreement for a fraudulent purpose; conspiracy; plot
The federal agency claimed the price increases were due to *collusion* among the producers.

concord (*n.*)
'kän,ko(r)d

state of being together in heart or mind; agreement; harmony
Neighbors cannot live in *concord* if their children keep fighting with one another.

congenital (*adj.*)
kən'je-nə-təl

(literally, "born with") existing at birth; inborn; innate
Helen Keller's deafness and blindness were not *congenital* defects; she was normal at birth.

convene (*v.*)
kən'vēn

come together in a body; meet; assemble
The House and the Senate will *convene* at noon to hear an address by the President.

correspond (*v.*)
,kä-rə'spänd

1. (literally, "answer together") agree; be in harmony; match; tally
Helene's account of how the argument started does not *correspond* with Sam's version.

2. communicate by exchange of letters
Bill and I *correspond* regularly.

EXERCISE 4.15: *CON-*, *CO-*, *COL-*, AND *COR-* WORDS

Fill each blank with the most appropriate word from group 20.

1. Though elected in November of even-numbered years, the new Congress does not __?__ until the following January.
2. If your seat number does not __?__ to your ticket number, the usher may ask you to move.
3. When Billy Budd, the peacemaker, was aboard, there was perfect __?__ among the sailors.
4. Do you want to __?__ with me, or do you prefer to work alone?
5. Just above St. Louis, the Missouri and Mississippi rivers __?__ into a single waterway.

---

21. OB-: "against," "in the way," "over"

obliterate (*v.*) ə'bli-tə,rāt	(literally, "cover over letters") erase; blot out; destroy; remove all traces of Today's rain has completely *obliterated* yesterday's snow; not a trace remains.
obsess (*v.*) əb'ses	(literally, "sit over") trouble the mind of; haunt; preoccupy The notion that she had forgotten to lock the front door *obsessed* Mother all through the movie.
obstacle (*n.*) 'äb-sti-kəl	something standing in the way; hindrance; obstruction; impediment If Albert were to visit Rome, the language would be no *obstacle*; he knows Italian.
obstruct (*v.*) əb'strəkt	be in the way of; hinder; impede; block The disabled vehicles *obstructed* traffic until removed by a tow truck.
obtrude (*v.*) əb'trüd	(literally, "thrust against") thrust forward without being asked; intrude; impose It is unwise for outsiders to *obtrude* their opinions into a family quarrel.
obviate (*v.*) 'äb-vē,āt	(literally, "get in the way of") meet and dispose of; make unnecessary; forestall; avert By removing her hat, the woman in front *obviated* the need for me to change my seat.

EXERCISE 4.16: *OB-* WORDS

Fill each blank with the most appropriate word from group 21.

1. A dropout will discover that the lack of a high school diploma is a serious __?__ to employment.
2. The pickets sat on the front steps in an attempt to __?__ the entrance.
3. To __?__ waiting on line at the box office, order your tickets by mail.
4. Though Harry is a very careful driver, the possibility of his having a serious accident continues to __?__ his parents.
5. Claire tried to forget the incident, but she couldn't __?__ it from her mind.

---

22. PER-: "through," "to the end," "thoroughly"

---

perennial (*adj.*)
pə're-nē-əl
continuing through the years; enduring; unceasing
Authors have come and gone, but Shakespeare has remained a *perennial* favorite.

perennial (*n.*)
plant that lives through the years
Perennials like the azalea and forsythia bloom year after year.

perforate (*v.*)
'pər-fə,rāt
(literally, "bore through") make a hole or holes through; pierce; puncture
The tack I stepped on went through the sole of my shoe, but luckily did not *perforate* my skin.

permeate (*v.*)
'pər-mē,āt
pass through; penetrate; spread through; pervade
The aroma of freshly brewed coffee *permeated* the cafeteria.

perplex (*v.*)
pə(r)'pleks
confuse thoroughly; puzzle; bewilder
I need help with the fourth problem; it *perplexes* me.

persist (*v.*)
pə(r)'sist
(literally, "stand to the end")
1. continue in spite of opposition; refuse to stop; persevere
Dr. Brown warned Janet of the consequences if she *persisted* in smoking despite his warnings.

2. continue to exist; last; endure
The rain was supposed to end in the morning, but it *persisted* through the afternoon and evening.

pertinent (*adj.*)
'pər-tə-nənt

(literally, "reaching through to") connected with the matter under consideration; to the point; related; relevant

Stick to the point; don't give information that is not *pertinent*.

perturb (*v.*)
pə(r)'tərb

disturb thoroughly or considerably; make uneasy; agitate; upset

Sandra's folks were *perturbed* when they learned she had failed two subjects.

EXERCISE 4.17: *PER-* WORDS

Fill each blank with the most appropriate word from group 22.

1. The claim of wage earners that they are being overtaxed is by no means new; it has been their __?__ complaint.
2. Why do you __?__ in asking to see my notes when I have told you I don't have any?
3. Train conductors use hole punchers to __?__ passenger tickets.
4. We thought the news would upset Jane, but it didn't seem to __?__ her.
5. Road signs that __?__ residents of this community are even more confusing to out-of-town visitors.

23. PRE-: "before," "beforehand," "fore-"

precede (*v.*)
prē'sēd

go before; come before

Did your complaint follow or *precede* Jane's?

preclude (*v.*)
prē'klüd

put a barrier before; impede; prevent; make impossible

A prior engagement *precludes* my coming to your party.

precocious (*adj.*)
prə'kō-shəs

(literally, "cooked or ripened before its time") showing mature characteristics at an early age

If Nancy's three-year-old sister can read, she must be a *precocious* child.

preconceive (*v.*)
,prē-kən'sēv

form an opinion of beforehand, without adequate evidence

The dislike I had *preconceived* for the book disappeared when I read a few chapters.

prefabricated (*adj.*)   constructed beforehand
prē'fa-brə,kāt-əd   *Prefabricated* homes are quickly erected by putting together large sections previously constructed at a factory.

preface (*n.*)   foreword; preliminary remarks; author's introduc-
'pre-fəs   tion to a book
   The *preface* usually provides information that the reader should know before beginning the book.

premature (*adj.*)   before the proper or usual time; early; untimely
,prē-mə'tyu̇-ə(r)   Since less than half of the votes have been counted, my opponent's claims of victory are *premature*.

premeditate (*v.*)   consider beforehand
prē'me-də-tāt   The jury decided that the blow was struck in a moment of panic and had not been *premeditated*.

presume (*v.*)   (literally, "take beforehand") take for granted with-
prə'z(y)üm   out proof; assume; suppose
   Nineteen of the sailors have been rescued. One is missing and *presumed* dead.

preview (*n.*)   view of something before it is shown to the public
'prē,vyü   Last night Carole and Bob attended a *preview* of a play scheduled to open next Tuesday.

EXERCISE 4.18: *PRE-* WORDS

Fill each blank with the most appropriate word from group 23.

1. Mozart, who began composing at the age of five, was definitely __?__ .

2. The bills they have to pay do not __?__ their making further purchases; they can use their credit.

3. I __?__ the directions to Barbara's house are correct, since she gave them to me herself.

4. A group of distinguished specialists saw a __?__ of the exhibit before it was opened to the public.

5. The report that the President was in town was __?__ because his plane had not yet landed.

24. PRO-: "forward," "forth"

procrastinate (*v.*)
prō'kra-stə,nāt

(literally, "move forward to tomorrow") put things off from day to day; delay; dawdle

Start working on the assignment without delay. It doesn't pay to *procrastinate*.

proficient (*adj.*)
prə'fi-shənt

(literally, "going forward") well advanced in any subject or occupation; skilled; adept; expert

When I fell behind, the teacher asked one of the more *proficient* students to help me.

profuse (*adj.*)
prə'fyüs

pouring forth freely; exceedingly generous; extravagant; lavish

Despite a large income, the actor has saved very little because he is a *profuse* spender.

project (*v.*)
prə'jekt

throw or cast forward

The fireboat's powerful engines *projected* huge streams of water on the blazing pier.

prominent (*adj.*)
'prä-mə-nənt

(literally, "jutting forward") standing out; notable; important; conspicuous

The Mayor, the Governor, and several other *prominent* citizens attended the preview.

propel (*v.*)
prə'pel

impel forward; drive onward; force ahead; push; thrust

High winds *propelled* the flames, and they spread rapidly.

proponent (*n.*)
prə'pō-nənt

person who puts forth a proposal or argues in favor of something; advocate; supporter

At the budget hearing, both *proponents* and opponents of the tax increase will be able to present their views.

prospect (*n.*)
'prä,spekt

thing looked forward to; expectation; vision

To a first-year student, graduation is a distant but pleasant *prospect*.

prospects (*n. pl.*)
'prä,spekts

chances

The *prospects* of our winning are slim.

protract (*v.*)
prə'trakt

(literally, "drag forward") draw out; lengthen; extend; prolong

Our cousins stayed with us only for the day, though we urged them to *protract* their visit.

protrude (*v.*) thrust forth; stick out; bulge; jut
prō'trüd   Keep your feet under your desk; if they *protrude* into the aisle, someone may trip over them.

provoke (*v.*) 1. call forth; bring on; cause
prə'vōk   Jeff's account of his experiences as a dogcatcher *provoked* much laughter.

2. make angry; annoy; incense; irritate
There would have been no quarrel if Lisa hadn't *provoked* you by calling you a liar.

EXERCISE 4.19: *PRO-* WORDS

Fill each blank with the most appropriate word from group 24.

1. The __?__ of a sizable raise impelled the new employee to do her best.
2. Your enthusiastic supporters are __?__ in their praise of your merits.
3. George Stephenson was the first to use steam power to __?__ a locomotive.
4. You must not expect an apprentice to be as __?__ as an experienced worker.
5. The proposal to demolish the historic building is sure to __?__ a storm of protest.

Review Exercises

REVIEW 25: LATIN PREFIXES 19–24

For each Latin prefix in column I, write the *letter* of its correct meaning from column II.

COLUMN I

1. *per-*
2. *ob-*
3. *circum-*
4. *pro-*
5. *con-, co-, col-, cor-*
6. *pre-*

COLUMN II

(A) together, with
(B) through, to the end, thoroughly
(C) forward, forth
(D) before, beforehand, fore-
(E) around, round
(F) against, in the way, over

REVIEW 26: WORDBUILDING

Fill in the prefix in column I and the complete word in column III.

I	II	III
1. __?__ *together*	+ HERENT *sticking*	= __?__ *sticking together; logically connected*
2. __?__ *beforehand*	+ CONCEIVE *form an opinion*	= __?__ *form an opinion beforehand*
3. __?__ *around*	+ NAVIGATE *sail*	= __?__ *sail around*
4. __?__ *forward*	+ JECT *throw*	= __?__ *throw or cast forward*
5. __?__ *together*	+ LABORATE *work*	= __?__ *work together*
6. __?__ *through*	+ MEATE *pass*	= __?__ *pass through; penetrate*
7. __?__ *in the way*	+ STACLE *something standing*	= __?__ *something standing in the way; obstruction*
8. __?__ *beforehand*	+ FACE *something said*	= __?__ *something said beforehand; foreword*

9. ? *together*	+ VENE *come*	= ? *come together; assemble*
10. ? *through*	+ FORATE *bore*	= ? *bore through; pierce*
11. ? *against*	+ TRUDE *thrust*	= ? *thrust forward without being asked*
12. ? *forth*	+ VOKE *call*	= ? *call forth; cause*
13. ? *round*	+ LOCUTION *speaking*	= ? *roundabout way of speaking*
14. ? *before*	+ CLUDE *put a barrier*	= ? *put a barrier before; prevent*
15. ? *together*	+ RESPOND *answer*	= ? *match; agree*
16. ? *thoroughly*	+ TURB *disturb*	= ? *disturb thoroughly; upset*
17. ? *before*	+ CEDE *go*	= ? *go before; come before*
18. ? *forth*	+ PONENT *one who puts*	= ? *one who puts forth a proposal*
19. ? *beforehand*	+ FABRICATED *constructed*	= ? *constructed beforehand*
20. ? *over*	+ SESS *sit*	= ? *trouble the mind of; haunt*

REVIEW 27: SENTENCE COMPLETION

Fill each blank with the word from the list below that best fits the context.

circumlocution	circumspect
coalesce	collaborate
correspond	obliterate
obstruct	perplex
persist	preclude
preconceive	prefabricate
preface	premature
premeditate	presume
preview	prominent
prospect	provoke

1. The speaker's ineptitude, particularly his fondness for _?_, _?_d some in the audience to leave early.

2. The arrival of spring keeps _?_ing the experts. Sometimes it is late, and sometimes _?_.

3. Many of the people who plan to buy a home have the _?_d notion that _?_d houses are necessarily of low quality.

4. In the _?_ to their book, the authors describe how a chance meeting at a writers' conference led them to _?_.

5. The perpetrator was _?_ enough to _?_ all shreds of incriminating evidence.

6. When the noted reviewer began to get fewer invitations to _?_s, she _?_d it was because of her low ratings of many recent movies.

7. She is determined, nevertheless, to _?_ in writing honest reviews. After all, it was her candor that made her _?_.

8. A longer prison sentence was _?_d when the jury determined that the crime had not been _?_d.

9. So much political support has _?_d around the candidate that the _?_ of his being elected is much stronger.

10. The defense witness's testimony did not at all _?_ with that of the prosecution witness. Was it possibly an attempt to _?_ justice?

REVIEW 28: SYNONYMS

Avoid repetition by replacing the boldfaced word or expression with a synonym from the following words.

circumnavigate	circumvent
congenital	convene
perturb(ed)	precede
procrastinate	proficient
proponent(s)	protract

1. We have delayed too long; we must not **delay** any further.

2. Next month the board will **meet** in a new meeting place.

3. When you went sailing, did you **sail around** any of the islands in the sound?

4. I don't know who comes after me in the batting order, but I am sure that I **come before** you.

5. Drew did not support my proposal at first, but now he is one of its chief **supporters.**

6. Prejudice is not **inborn;** no one is born with it.

7. Someone must have said something to upset Amy; she is very **upset.**

8. A few wanted to **prolong** the discussion, but the majority refused to stay longer.

9. Those who try to **get around** the law may get into trouble.

10. Though Joyce had no computer skills when she was hired, she has become a highly **skilled** programmer.

REVIEW 29: ANTONYMS

Enter the word from the list below that is most nearly the opposite of the boldfaced word.

circumscribe	congenital
correspond	obstacle
persist	pertinent
proficient	prominent
proponent	protract

1. The poster, unfortunately, was **inconspicuous.** It should have been in a(n) more __?__ place.

2. I was criticized for omitting some __?__ details and including some that were quite **irrelevant.**

3. The scars on my arm were **acquired** through injuries. The birthmarks, of course, are __?__ .

4. The patient __?__ ed in smoking, though his physician had warned him to **desist.**

5. I am neither an **opponent** nor a(n) __?__ of the proposed changes.

6. The mediators seek to **curtail** the walkout, saying there is little to be gained by __?__ ing it.

7. Some graceful and __?__ dancers were once awkward and **inept.**

8. Sometimes, what we perceive as a(n) __?__ turns out to be an **advantage.**

9. The conclusions reached by two independent investigators should have __?__ ed, but they **disagreed.**

10. To allow him a greater variety of foods, the patient's strictly __?__ d diet has been somewhat **expanded.**

REVIEW 30: CONCISE WRITING

Express the thought of each sentence below in no more than four words.

1. Carefully consider all the possible consequences of what you intend to do before you do it.
2. It is obvious that a secret agreement was in existence for fraudulent purposes.
3. Those who are in favor of the proposal please say "aye."
4. The practice of using an excessive number of words to express an idea interferes with communication.
5. Does the question you are asking have anything to do with the matter that we are discussing?

REVIEW 31: SYNONYM SUMMARY

Each line, when completed, should have three words similar in meaning. Write the *complete* words.

1. p (1) sh	thr (1) st	pr (1) p (1) l
2. not (1) ble	(3) spicuous	(3) minent
3. agr (2) ment	h (1) rm (1) ny	c (1) nc (1) rd
4. p (2) rce	p (1) nct (1) re	p (1) rf (1) rate
5. comb (1) ne	j (2) n	(2) alesce
6. h (2) nt	(3) occupy	(2) sess
7. s (1) ppose	(2) sume	pr (1) s (1) me
8. l (1) st	(2) dure	pers (1) st
9. m (1) tch	(1) ally	(3) respond
10. ann (1) y	ir (2) tate	pr (1) v (1) ke
11. in (1) orn	(2) nate	(3) genital
12. ag (1) tate	(2) set	pert (1) rb
13. l (1) gical	cons (1) stent	co (2) rent
14. e (1) rly	(2) timely	pre (2) ture
15. sk (1) rt	b (1) pass	(6) vent
16. (1) vert	f (1) restall	(2) viate
17. pen (1) trate	perv (1) de	(3) meate
18. b (1) lge	j (1) t	(3) trude
19. end (1) ring	unc (2) sing	per (2) nial
20. verb (1) age	tautol (1) gy	(6) locution

REVIEW 32: ANALOGIES

Which lettered pair of words—*a, b, c, d,* or *e*—most nearly expresses the same relationship as the capitalized pair?

1. CORRESPOND : LETTERS
    - (*a*) obliterate : traces
    - (*b*) converse : words
    - (*c*) proofread : errors
    - (*d*) soundproof : noises
    - (*e*) economize : expenses

2. CURTAIL : PROTRACT
    - (*a*) attack : impugn
    - (*b*) inflate : expand
    - (*c*) separate : coalesce
    - (*d*) violate : contravene
    - (*e*) bicker : wrangle

3. COLLUSION : DEFRAUD
    - (*a*) prosecution : exonerate
    - (*b*) conservation : deplete
    - (*c*) condemnation : laud
    - (*d*) revolution : change
    - (*e*) recuperation : weaken

4. PREFACE : BOOK
    - (*a*) dawn : night
    - (*b*) footnote : page
    - (*c*) dessert : repast
    - (*d*) threshold : door
    - (*e*) overture : opera

5. CIRCUMSPECT : CAUTION
    - (*a*) objective : facts
    - (*b*) tolerant : bigotry
    - (*c*) gluttonous : restraint
    - (*d*) impulsive : patience
    - (*e*) hypocritical : sincerity

6. ADEPT : PROFICIENT
    - (*a*) manifest : evident
    - (*b*) clandestine : overt
    - (*c*) thrifty : wasteful
    - (*d*) compatible : uncongenial
    - (*e*) domesticated : wild

7. FATIGUE : PROFICIENCY
    - (*a*) intimidation : tension
    - (*b*) poverty : crime
    - (*c*) automation : drudgery
    - (*d*) exercise : longevity
    - (*e*) repetition : boredom

8. PROVOKE : ANGRY
    - (*a*) impoverish : indigent
    - (*b*) convince : suspicious
    - (*c*) placate : hostile
    - (*d*) absolve : blameworthy
    - (*e*) educate : ignorant

9. ENIGMA : PERPLEX
   - *(a)* license : prohibit
   - *(b)* forecast : guarantee
   - *(c)* rumor : reassure
   - *(d)* relapse : accelerate
   - *(e)* impediment : obstruct

10. PROFUSE : EXTRAVAGANCE
   - *(a)* frank : evasion
   - *(b)* nonconformist : compliance
   - *(c)* outgoing : seclusion
   - *(d)* indolent : procrastination
   - *(e)* uncharitable : benevolence

CHAPTER 5

Enlarging Vocabulary Through Latin Roots

What is a root?

A *root* is a word or basic element from which other words are derived. For example, *kind* is the root of *unkind, kindest, kindly,* and *unkindness.* As you can see, the *root* is the part of a word that is left after an addition, such as a prefix or a suffix, has been removed.

Sometimes a root has more than one form, as in the words *enjoy, rejoice, joyous,* and *enjoyable.* Here, the root is *joy* or *joi.*

Why study roots?

O nce you know what a particular root means, you have a clue to the meaning of words derived from that root. For example, when you have learned that the root *MAN* means "hand," you are better able to understand—and remember—that *manacles* are "handcuffs"; that to *manipulate* is to "handle" or "manage skillfully"; and that a *manual* operation is "something done by *hand.*"

Purpose of this unit

T his unit aims to enlarge your vocabulary by acquainting you with twenty Latin roots and some English words derived from them. Be sure to memorize the roots; they will help you unlock the meaning of numerous words beyond those discussed in this unit.

LATIN ROOTS 1–10

Pretest 1

Write the *letter* of the best answer.

1. Some people are *gregarious;* others __?__.
   (A) arrive late   (B) keep to themselves   (C) are ready to help
2. An *enamored* individual is __?__.
   (A) well rounded   (B) armed   (C) captivated
3. The *literal* meaning of a word is its __?__.
   (A) original meaning   (B) hidden meaning   (C) meaning in literature
4. A person with an *affinity* for sports is not __?__ them.
   (A) repelled by   (B) absorbed in   (C) talented in
5. Prices in *flux* __?__.
   (A) keep changing   (B) rise sharply   (C) drop rapidly
6. Don't be __?__. Give them a *lucid* answer.
   (A) frank   (B) misled   (C) vague
7. There can be no *animus* in a person of __?__ will.
   (A) good   (B) ill   (C) strong
8. There was __?__, instead of *cohesion.*
   (A) ignorance   (B) disunity   (C) uncertainty
9. Any *unilateral* action is a __?__ undertaking.
   (A) worldwide   (B) cooperative   (C) one-sided
10. A *regenerated* community __?__.
    (A) shows new life   (B) resists changes   (C) grows steadily worse

> THE ANSWERS ARE
>
> 6. C 7. A 8. B 9. C 10. A
> 1. B 2. C 3. A 4. A 5. A

In doing the pretest, you would have found it helpful to know the meaning of the roots *greg, amor, litera, fin, flux, luc, anim, hes, lateral* and *gen.* You will learn how to use these roots in the pages that follow.

1. AM, AMOR: "love," "liking," "friendliness"

WORD	MEANING AND TYPICAL USE

amateur (*n.*)
'a-mə-tə(r)

(literally, "lover")
1. person who follows a particular pursuit as a pastime, rather than as a profession
The performance was staged by a group of *amateurs* who have been studying dramatics as a hobby.

2. one who performs rather poorly; inexperienced person
When it comes to baking a cake, you are the expert; I'm only an *amateur*.

amiable (*adj.*)
'ā-mē-ə-bəl

likable; good-natured; pleasant and agreeable; obliging
Charlotte is an *amiable* person; everybody likes her.

amicable (*adj.*)
'a-mə-kə-bəl

characterized by friendliness rather than antagonism; friendly; neighborly; not quarrelsome
Let us try to settle our differences in an *amicable* manner.

amity (*n.*)
'a-mə-tē

friendship; goodwill; friendly relations
We must look ahead to the time when the dispute is over and *amity* is restored.

amorous (*adj.*)
'a-mə-rəs

strongly moved by love; loving; inclined to love; enamored
In the famous balcony scene, *amorous* Romeo expresses undying love for Juliet.

enamored (*adj.*)
ə'na-mə(r)d

(usually followed by "of") inflamed with love; charmed; captivated
John Rolfe, an English settler, became *enamored* of the Indian princess Pocahontas and married her.

2. ANIM: "mind," "will," "spirit"

animosity (*n.*)
,a-nə'mä-sə-tē

ill will (usually leading to active opposition); violent hatred; enmity; antagonism
Someday the *animosity* that led to the war will be replaced by amity.

animus (*n.*)
'a-nə-məs

ill will (usually controlled)
   Though Howard defeated me in the election, I bear no *animus* toward him; we are good friends.

equanimity (*n.*)
,ēk-wə'ni-mə-tē

evenness of mind or temper under stress; emotional balance; composure; calmness; equilibrium
   If you become extremely upset when you lose a game, it is a sign that you lack *equanimity*.

magnanimous (*adj.*)
mag'na-nə-məs

showing greatness or nobility of mind; chivalrous; forgiving; generous in overlooking injury or insult
   The first time I was late for practice, Ms. O'Neill excused me with the warning that she would not be so *magnanimous* the next time.

unanimity (*n.*)
,yü-nə'ni-mə-tē

oneness of mind; complete agreement
   In almost every discussion there is bound to be some disagreement. Don't expect *unanimity*.

unanimous (*adj.*)
yü'na-nə-məs

of one mind; in complete accord
   Except for one student, who voted "no," the class was *unanimous* in wanting the party.

EXERCISE 5.1: *AM, AMOR,* AND *ANIM* WORDS

Fill each blank with the most appropriate word from groups 1 and 2.

1. After his first success as a screen lover, the actor was cast only in __?__ roles.
2. The prospect of financial reward has induced many an __?__ to turn professional.
3. Don't brood over your defeat. Accept it with __?__ .
4. Narcissus was too conceited to like anyone else; he was __?__ of himself.
5. The 9–0 verdict shows that the judges were __?__ .

3. FIN: "end," "boundary," "limit"

affinity (*n.*)
ə'fi-nə-tē

(literally, condition of being "near the boundary" or "a neighbor") kinship; sympathy; liking; attraction
   Because they share the same language and ideals, the Americans and the English have an *affinity* for one another.

confine (*v.*)   keep within limits; restrict; limit
kən'fīn   I will *confine* my remarks to the causes of inflation; the
                       next speaker will discuss its effects.

definitive (*adj.*)   serving to end an unsettled matter; conclusive; final
də'fi-nə-tiv   The officials accused of bribery confessed when the
                            district attorney presented *definitive* evidence of their
                            guilt.

finale (*n.*)   end or final part of a musical composition, opera, play,
fə'na-lē   etc.; conclusion
                      The acting was superb from the opening scene to the
                      finale.

finis (*n.*)   end; conclusion
'fi-nəs   The word *finis* on the screen indicated that the film
                     had ended.

---

4. FLU, FLUC, FLUX: "flow"

---

fluctuate (*v.*)   flow like a wave; move up and down; change often and
'flək-chə-wāt   irregularly; be unsteady
                        Last week the stock *fluctuated* from a high of 19⅛ to a
                        low of 17½.

fluent (*adj.*)   ready with a flow of words; speaking or writing easily; ar-
'flü-ənt   ticulate; eloquent
                        Do you have to grope for words, or are you a *fluent*
                        speaker?

fluid (*n.*)   substance that flows
'flü-əd   Air, water, molasses, and milk are all *fluids*.

fluid (*adj.*)   not rigid; changeable; unstable
                       During November, the military situation remained *fluid*,
                       with advances and retreats by both sides.

flux (*n.*)   continuous flow or changing; unceasing change
'fləks   When prices are in a state of *flux*, many buyers delay
                    purchases until conditions are more settled.

influx (*n.*)   inflow; inpouring; inrush
'in,fləks   The discovery of gold in California in 1848 caused a large
                     influx of settlers from the East.

EXERCISE 5.2: *FIN*, *FLU*, *FLUC*, AND *FLUX* WORDS

Fill each blank with the most appropriate word from groups 3 and 4.

1. A diplomat who represents us in Russia should be __?__ in Russian.
2. During the late spring, beach resorts ready themselves for the expected __?__ of summer visitors.
3. The entire cast appeared on stage after the __?__, to acknowledge the applause.
4. Unlike a lower court ruling, which may be reversed on appeal, a Supreme Court decision is __?__ .
5. There is a(n) __?__ among classmates that is often as strong as loyalty to one's family.

---

5. GEN, GENER, GENIT: "birth," "kind," "class"

---

degenerate (*v.*)   sink to a lower class or standard; worsen; deteriorate
də'je-nə,rāt   But for the skill of the presiding officer, the debate would have *degenerated* into an exchange of insults.

engender (*v.*)   give birth to; create; generate; produce; cause
en'jen-də(r)   Name-calling *engenders* hatred.

genre (*n.*)   kind; sort; category
'zhän-rə   The writer achieved distinction in two literary *genres*— the short story and the novel.

progenitor (*n.*)   ancestor to whom a group traces its birth; forefather;
prō'je-nə-tə(r)   forebear
          The Bible states that Adam and Eve were the *progenitors* of the human race.

regenerate (*v.*)   cause to be born again; put new life into; reform com-
rē'je-nə,rāt   pletely; revive; reinvigorate
          The new manager *regenerated* the losing team and made it a strong contender.

---

6. GREG: "gather," "flock"

---

aggregate (*adj.*)   gathered together in one mass; total; collective
'a-grə-gət   The *aggregate* strength of the allies was impressive, though individually some were quite weak.

aggregation (*n.*) ,a-grə'gā-shən	gathering of individuals into a body or group; assemblage
	At the airport, the homecoming champions were welcomed by a huge *aggregation* of admirers.
congregation (*n.*) ,kän-grə'gā-shən	"flock" or gathering of people for religious worship
	The minister addressed the *congregation* on the meaning of brotherhood.
gregarious (*adj.*) grə'ga-rē-əs	inclined to associate with the "flock" or group; fond of being with others; sociable
	Human beings, as a rule, are *gregarious*; they enjoy being with other people.
segregation (*n.*) ,se-grə'gā-shən	separation from the "flock" or main body; setting apart; isolation; separation
	The warden believes in *segregation* of first offenders from hardened criminals.

EXERCISE 5.3: *GEN, GENER, GENIT,* AND *GREG* WORDS

Fill each blank with the most appropriate word from groups 5 and 6.

1. New housing developments, shopping centers, and schools can __?__ decadent neighborhoods.
2. Everyone in the __?__ rose to sing a hymn.
3. Unless healed soon, these animosities are sure to __?__ armed conflict.
4. The box score shows the points scored by each player, as well as the team's __?__ score.
5. When I first came here, I had no friends and kept to myself. I was not too __?__ .

---

7. HERE, HES: "stick"

---

adhere (*v.*) ad'hi-ə(r)	stick; hold fast; cling; be attached
	Apply the sticker according to the directions, or it will not *adhere*.
cohere (*v.*) kō'hi-ə(r)	stick together; hold together firmly
	I glued together the fragments of the vase, but they did not *cohere*.

coherence (*n.*)
kō'hi-rəns
state of sticking together; consistency; logical connection

If the relationship between the first sentence and what follows is not clear, the paragraph lacks *coherence*.

cohesion (*n.*)
kō'hē-zhən
act or state of sticking together; union; unity; bond

There can be no real *cohesion* in an alliance if the parties have little in common.

incoherent (*adj.*)
,in-kō-'hir-ənt
not logically connected; disconnected; unintelligible

The speech of a person in a rage may be *incoherent*.

inherent (*adj.*)
ən'hi-rənt
(literally, "sticking in") deeply infixed; intrinsic; essential

Because of her *inherent* carefulness, I am sure my sister will be a good driver.

---

8. LATERAL: "side"

---

bilateral (*adj.*)
bī'la-tə-rəl
involving two sides

A *bilateral* team of federal and local experts conducted the survey.

collateral (*adj.*)
kə'la-tə-rəl
situated at the side; accompanying; parallel; additional; supplementary

After voting for the road building program, the legislature took up the *collateral* issue of how to raise the necessary funds.

equilateral (*adj.*)
,ēk-wə'la-tə-rəl
having all sides equal

If one side of an *equilateral* triangle measures three feet, the other two must also be three feet each.

lateral (*adj.*)
'la-tə-rəl
of or pertaining to the side

The building plan shows both a front and a *lateral* view of the proposed structure.

multilateral (*adj.*)
,məl-tə'la-tə-rəl
having many sides

A parent plays a *multilateral* role as a nurse, housekeeper, shopper, cook, teacher, etc.

quadrilateral (*n.*)
,kwä-drə'la-tə-rəl
plane figure having four sides and four angles

A square is a *quadrilateral*.

unilateral (*adj.*)
,yü-nə'la-tə-rəl
one-sided; undertaken by one side only

Don't judge the matter by my opponent's *unilateral* statement, but wait till you have heard the other side.

EXERCISE 5.4: *HERE*, *HES*, AND *LATERAL* WORDS

Fill each blank with the most appropriate word from groups 7 and 8.

1. Most city blocks are shaped like a(n) __?__ .
2. Are you speaking for all the members of your club or giving only your __?__ views?
3. Some believe that might is right, but I do not __?__ to that doctrine.
4. When we were studying *Johnny Tremain*, our teacher assigned __?__ reading on the Revolutionary War.
5. The politician's __?__ role as champion of justice, defender of the poor, supporter of education, and friend of business attracted many adherents.

---

9. LITERA: ''letter''

---

alliteration (*n.*)
ə,li-tə'rā-shən

repetition of the same letter or consonant at the beginning of neighboring words
> Note the *alliteration* in the line ''Sing a song of sixpence.''

literacy (*n.*)
'li-tə-rə-sē

state of being lettered or educated; ability to read and write
> Research required a high degree of *literacy*.

literal (*adj.*)
'li-tə-rəl

following the letters or exact words of the original; verbatim; word-for-word
> We translate ''laissez-faire'' as ''absence of government interference,'' but its *literal* meaning is ''let do.''

literary (*adj.*)
'li-tə-re-rē

having to do with letters or literature
> Willa Cather is one of the great writers of novels in our *literary* history.

literate (*adj.*)
'li-tə-rət

lettered; able to read and write; educated
> The teacher's main goal in working with adults who can neither read nor write is to make them *literate*.

10. LUC, LUM: "light"

elucidate (*v.*) ə'lü-sə,dāt	throw light upon; make clear; explain; clarify I asked the teacher to *elucidate* a point that was not clear to me.
lucid (*adj.*) 'lü-səd	(literally, "containing light") clear; easy to understand; comprehensible To obviate misunderstanding, state the directions in the most *lucid* way possible.
luminary (*n.*) 'lü-mə,ne-rē	one who is a source of light or inspiration to others; famous person; notable; celebrity A number of *luminaries*, including a Nobel prize-winner, will be present.
luminous (*adj.*) 'lü-mə-nəs	emitting light; bright; shining; brilliant With this watch you can tell time in the dark because its hands and dial are *luminous*.
translucent (*adj.*) trans'lü-sənt	letting light through Lamp shades are *translucent* but not transparent.

EXERCISE 5.5: *LITERA*, *LUC*, AND *LUM* WORDS

Fill each blank with the most appropriate word from groups 9 and 10.

1. You need not prove that you can read and write. No one doubts your __?__ .

2. __?__ paint is used for road signs so that they may be visible to night drivers.

3. Gary tried to __?__ the matter, but he only made us more confused.

4. A host of admirers surrounded the sports __?__ to ask for her autograph.

5. Did you know that the __?__ meaning of Philip is "lover of horses"?

Review Exercises

REVIEW 1: LATIN ROOTS 1–10

For each Latin root in column I, write the *letter* of its definition from column II.

COLUMN I	COLUMN II
1. LATERAL	(A) light
2. FLU, FLUC, FLUX	(B) letter
3. AM, AMOR	(C) birth, kind, class
4. GREG	(D) side
5. HERE, HES	(E) flow
6. ANIM	(F) love, liking, friendliness
7. FIN	(G) gather, flock
8. LUC, LUM	(H) end, boundary, limit
9. GEN, GENER, GENIT	(I) stick
10. LITERA	(J) mind, will, spirit

REVIEW 2: WORDBUILDING

Fill in the *prefix* in column I, the *root* in column II, and the *missing letters* of the word in column III. Each blank stands for *one* missing letter.

	I PREFIX	II ROOT	III WORD
1.	(5) *through*	+ (3) *light*	= (8) ENT *letting light through*
2.	(2) *down from*	+ (5) *class*	= (7) ATE *sink to a lower class; deteriorate*
3.	(2) *again*	+ (5) *birth*	= (7) ATE *cause to be born again; reform completely*
4.	(2) *together*	+ (4) *stick*	= (6) *hold together firmly*
5.	(2) *in*	+ (4) *flow*	= (6) *inflow; inpouring*
6.	(3) *one*	+ (7) *side*	= (10) *one-sided*

7. (2)   + (4)   = (6) NT
    in   *stick*   *"sticking in"; deeply infixed; intrinsic*

8. (2)   + (4)   = (6) ATION
    apart   *flock*   *separation from the flock; isolation*

9. (2)   + (3)   = (5) ION
    together   *stick*   *act of sticking together; union*

10. (2)   + (6)   = (8) TE
    not   *letter*   *unlettered; unable to read or write*

REVIEW 3: SENTENCE COMPLETION

Fill each blank with the word from the list below that best fits the context.

adhere	affinity
alliteration	amateur
amicable	amorous
animosity	cohere
confine	congregation
definitive	degenerate
elucidate	engender
finale	fluent
gregarious	inherent
literary	luminary

1. A boundary dispute had __?__ed considerable __?__ between the two neighbors who formerly were friends.

2. Dad was once __?__ in French, but his proficiency in that language has __?__d because he has not used it for twenty years.

3. Being a(n) __?__ person, Roy lingered in the auditorium after the __?__ of the opera to chat with friends.

4. When he addresses the __?__, the spiritual leader is usually—but not always—brief; he does not have to __?__ to a time schedule.

5. The __?__ who had been invited to the convention announced that she would __?__ her oral reading to passages from her prize-winning book.

6. Sheldon is a lawyer by profession, but in painting he is just a(n) __?__, though he has a great __?__ for that calling.

7. In considering the suitor's proposal, Portia had to decide whether her feelings for him were truly __?__, or merely __?__.

8. The witness was asked to _?_ a statement she made that did not seem to _?_ with her earlier testimony.

9. In the line, "The furrow followed free," Samuel T. Coleridge uses the _?_ device known as _?_ .

10. The advice "Never make a generalization" cannot be regarded as _?_ because it contains a(n) _?_ contradiction: "Never make a generalization" is itself a generalization.

REVIEW 4: SYNONYMS

Avoid repetition by replacing the boldfaced word or expression with a synonym from the following words.

amiable	amity
animus	cohesion
fluctuate	literate
luminous	magnanimous
unanimity	unilateral

1. Many have forgiven and forgotten the suffering that former enemies caused, but others have not been so **forgiving.**

2. I don't like that scoundrel; he is not a(n) **likable** person.

3. The moon, which has no brightness of its own, is **bright** at night with light that shines on it from the sun.

4. If many members are resisting goals that a majority in their union supports, there is obviously a lack of **unity.**

5. This is just my **one-sided** opinion; it does not reflect the views of all sides to the dispute.

6. A nation that sets a low priority on education is not likely to have the world's most **educated** population.

7. The 11-to-1 vote shows how strongly the club agrees with your motion. If not for that one negative ballot, we would have had **complete agreement.**

8. There was no **friendship** between us when we were rivals. Lately, however, we have become friends.

9. Last month, there was little movement in stock prices. Usually, they **move up and down** quite a bit.

10. Linda is a person of good will; she has no **ill will** toward anyone.

REVIEW 5: ANTONYMS

Enter the word from the list below that is most nearly the opposite of the boldfaced word.

amateur	amicable
amity	definitive
degenerate	fluid
flux	literate
lucid	translucent

1. After a long interval of **stability,** we are now in a period of __?__ .
2. The early results are encouraging but **inconclusive;** more __?__ proof is needed before the researchers can claim a medical breakthrough.
3. Ours is a cast of talented __?__s, but we are not **professionals.**
4. Immediately after the operation, the patient was on a rigid diet of __?__s, with no **solids** whatsoever.
5. At last, the feud is over; __?__ has replaced **enmity.**
6. No light penetrates the walls because they are made of **opaque** materials; the windowpanes, of course, are __?__ .
7. This firm's prospects for recovery have __?__d rather than **improved.**
8. Explain what happened in __?__ English; don't be **vague.**
9. Earlier in the negotiations, the mood of both parties was __?__; now, it has turned **antagonistic.**
10. A bilingual person is __?__ in two languages but **illiterate** in all others.

REVIEW 6: SYNONYM SUMMARY

Each line, when completed, should have three words similar in meaning. Write the *complete* words.

1. chang (2) ble	unst (1) ble	flu (1) d
2. fr (2) ndly	n (2) ghborly	(1) mic (1) ble
3. fin (1) l	concl (1) sive	def (1) n (1) tive
4. w (1) rd-for-w (1) rd	verb (1) t (1) m	l (1) teral
5. cre (1) te	(1) ause	(2) gender
6. sep (1) ration	is (1) lation	(2) gregation
7. disc (2) nected	unintellig (1) ble	in (2) herent
8. (2) traction	l (1) king	(2) finity
9. (1) nion	b (1) nd	co (2) sion
10. accompan (1) ing	para (2) el	c (2) lateral

11. comp (1) sure	equ (1) librium	e (2) animity
12. k (1) nd	cat (1) gory	(2) nre
13. ant (1) g (1) nism	(2) mity	an (1) m (1) sity
14. c (1) l (1) brity	not (1) ble	l (1) min (1) ry
15. g (1) n (1) rous	chiv (1) lrous	mag (2) nimous
16. tot (1) l	c (2) lective	(2) gregate
17. (2) flow	inp (2) ring	infl (1) x
18. (2) sential	intr (1) nsic	(2) herent
19. (1) loquent	artic (1) late	fl (1) ent
20. wors (1) n	deter (2) rate	(2) generate

REVIEW 7: CONCISE WRITING

In no more than fifty words, rewrite the following passage, keeping all its ideas. Hint: Reduce each boldfaced expression to a single word.

The first sentence has been done to get you started. Go on from there.

A Rare Person

Bruce can be **pleasant and agreeable** when others are cranky. When they are unforgiving, he is usually **generous in overlooking injury or insult.** And when they get upset, he maintains his **evenness of mind and temper.** He is a rare person whose moods do not **change continually or vary in an irregular way.** Besides, he is **fond of being with others.** In conversation, he is not only **ready with a flow of words,** but logical, and **easy to understand.**

A Rare Person (concise version)

Bruce can be amiable when others are cranky.

REVIEW 8: ANALOGIES

Which lettered pair of words—*a, b, c, d,* or *e*—most nearly expresses the same relationship as the capitalized pair?

1. MALEVOLENT : ANIMUS
   - (*a*) blameless : guilt
   - (*b*) circumspect : foresight
   - (*c*) indigent : resources
   - (*d*) audacious : manners
   - (*e*) trustworthy : deception

2. SQUARE : QUADRILATERAL
- (a) hand : digit
- (b) weapon : missile
- (c) bulb : socket
- (d) access : passageway
- (e) eighth : fraction

3. FLUCTUATION : UNCERTAINTY
- (a) defect : malfunction
- (b) pain : inflammation
- (c) delay : fog
- (d) boredom : repetition
- (e) malnutrition : health

4. GREGARIOUS : COMPANY
- (a) reserved : communication
- (b) slovenly : neatness
- (c) frugal : waste
- (d) withdrawn : solitude
- (e) parsimonious : expenditure

5. INDIVIDUAL : AGGREGATION
- (a) particle : dust
- (b) chord : note
- (c) head : hair
- (d) oyster : pearl
- (e) message : word

6. LUCID : COMPREHEND
- (a) complex : grasp
- (b) indelible : erase
- (c) versatile : adapt
- (d) inequitable : justify
- (e) decadent : regenerate

7. MAGNANIMOUS : PARDON
- (a) headstrong : acquiesce
- (b) reasonable : compromise
- (c) meek : protest
- (d) insubordinate : obey
- (e) persistent : quit

8. TRANSLUCENT : LIGHT
- (a) opinionated : ideas
- (b) exclusive : people
- (c) airtight : leak
- (d) porous : liquid
- (e) conspicuous : attention

LATIN ROOTS 11–20

Pretest 2

Write the *letter* of the best answer.

1. *Video* signals have to do with __?__ .
   (A) sounds   (B) pictures   (C) music

2. In a *soliloquy*, you would be __?__ .
   (A) doing most of the talking   (B) questioning a group
   (C) talking to yourself

3. A *redundant* expression should be __?__ .
   (A) removed   (B) explained   (C) replaced

4. __?__ involves no *manual* operations.
   (A) Dining   (B) Typing   (C) Smiling

5. A *pendant* cannot __?__ .
   (A) translate   (B) adorn   (C) dangle

6. Now that my *veracity* has been questioned, I feel deeply __?__ .
   (A) honored   (B) insulted   (C) relieved

7. A *scribe* belongs to the __?__ profession.
   (A) teaching   (B) acting   (C) writing

8. We cannot tell whether their interest is *simulated* or __?__ .
   (A) real   (B) selfish   (C) pretended

9. The new regulation *imposes* additional __?__ on all.
   (A) responsibilities   (B) privileges   (C) benefits

10. If you are *insolvent*, you cannot __?__ .
    (A) vote   (B) pay your debts   (C) think logically

THE ANSWERS ARE

6. B 7. C 8. A 9. A 10. B
1. B 2. C 3. A 4. C 5. A

Had you known the meaning of the roots *vid, sol, unda, manu, pend, vera, scrib, simul, pos,* and *solv,* you would have had an advantage in the pretest. You will learn about these roots in the following pages.

---

11. MAN, MANU: "hand"

---

emancipate (*v.*)
ə'man-sə,pāt
(literally, "take from the hand" or power of another) release from bondage; free; liberate
The washing machine has *emancipated* millions of people from a great deal of drudgery.

manacle (*n.*)
'ma-nə-kəl
handcuff
The *manacles* were removed from the prisoner's wrists.

mandate (*n.*)
'man,dāt
(literally, something "given into one's hand")
1. authorization to act
The overwhelming vote for the reform slate is regarded as a *mandate* from the people to root out corruption.

2. command; order; injunction
By a close margin, the workers voted to comply with the court's *mandate* against a strike.

manipulate (*v.*)
mə'nip-yə,lāt
1. operate with the hands; handle or manage skillfully; maneuver
In today's lesson I learned how to *manipulate* the steering wheel.

2. manage unethically to serve a fraudulent purpose; falsify; rig
The defeated candidate charged that the election results had been *manipulated*.

manual (*n.*)
'man-yə-wəl
small, helpful book capable of being carried in the hand; handbook
Each student has a learner's permit and a copy of the "Driver's *Manual*."

manual (*adj.*)
relating to, or done with, the hands
Milking, formerly a *manual* operation, is now done by machine.

manuscript (*n.*)
'man-yə,skript
document written by hand, or typewritten
The author's *manuscript* is now at the printer.

12. PEND, PENS: "hang"

append (*v.*)
ə'pend

(literally, "hang on") attach; add as a supplement
If you hand in your report late, *append* a note explaining the reason for the delay.

appendix (*n.*)
ə'pen-diks

(literally, something "hung on") matter added to the end of a book or document
A school edition of a novel usually has an *appendix* containing explanatory notes.

impending (*adj.*)
əm'pen-diŋ

(literally, "overhanging") threatening to occur soon; imminent
At the first flash of lightning, we scurried for shelter from the *impending* storm.

pendant (*n.*)
'pen-dənt

hanging ornament
The *pendant* dangling from the chain around her neck looked like a medal, but it was really a timepiece.

pending (*adj.*)
'pen-diŋ

(literally, "hanging") waiting to be settled; not yet decided
Has a date been set for the game, or is the matter still *pending?*

pending (*prep.*)

until
Barbara agreed to conduct the meeting, *pending* the election of a presiding officer.

suspend (*v.*)
sə'spend

1. hang by attaching to something
Would you prefer to attach a lamp to the wall or *suspend* one from the ceiling?

2. stop temporarily; hold up; make inoperative for a while
Service will be *suspended* from midnight to 4 a.m. to permit repairs.

suspense (*n.*)
sə'spens

condition of being left "hanging" or in doubt; mental uncertainty; anxiety; apprehension
If you have seen the marks posted, please tell me whether I passed or failed; don't keep me in *suspense!*

EXERCISE 5.6: *MAN, MANU, PEND,* AND *PENS* WORDS

Write the most appropriate word from groups 11 and 12.

1. Can you operate this gadget? I don't know how to __?__ it.
2. As the enemy approached, the defenders got ready for the __?__ attack.
3. Because of a lengthy labor dispute, the city's daily newspapers had to __?__ publication.
4. Is it possible to __?__ addicts from their bondage to drugs?
5. The retiring manager has agreed to stay on, __?__ the choice of a successor.

---

13. PON, POS: "put"

depose (*v.*)
də'pōz

1. (literally, "put down") put out of office; dethrone
   Did the king abdicate or was he *deposed?*

2. state under oath; testify; swear
   He *deposed* on the witness stand that he had never taken a bribe.

impose (*v.*)
im'pōz

put on as a burden, duty, tax, etc.; inflict
Cleaning up after the job is the repair crew's responsibility. Don't let them *impose* it on you.

postpone (*v.*)
pōst'pōn

(literally, "put after") put off; defer; delay
Our instructor has *postponed* the test until tomorrow to give us an extra day to study.

superimpose (*v.*)
,sü-pə(r)-im'pōz

put on top of or over; attach as an addition
Today's snowfall *superimposed* a fresh two inches on yesterday's accumulation.

transpose (*v.*)
tranz'pōz

(literally, "put across") change the relative order of; interchange
There is a misspelled word on your paper, "strenght." Correct it by *transposing* the last two letters.

---

14. SCRIB, SCRIPT: "write"

conscript (*v.*)
kən'skript

enroll (write down) into military service by compulsion; draft

When there were not enough volunteers for the armed forces, the government had to *conscript* additional men and women.

inscription (*n.*)
in'skrip-shən

something inscribed (written) on a monument, coin, etc.
    The *inscription* on Paul's medal reads ''For excellence in English.''

prescribe (*v.*)
prə'skrīb

(literally, ''write before'')
1. order; dictate; direct
    The law *prescribes* that aliens may not vote.

2. order as a remedy
    Her physician *prescribed* some pills, a light diet, and plenty of rest.

proscribe (*v.*)
prō-'skrīb

condemn as harmful or illegal; prohibit; forbid
    The dumping of wastes into the waterways is *proscribed*.

scribe (*n.*)
'skrīb

person who writes; author; journalist
    Both candidates used professional *scribes* to prepare their campaign speeches.

script (*n.*)
'skript

1. written text of a play, speech, etc.
    How much time did the actors have to memorize the *script*?

2. handwriting; penmanship
    I knew the note was from Mabel because I recognized her *script*.

subscriber (*n.*)
səb'skrī-bə(r)

one who writes his or her name at the end of a document, thereby indicating approval; one who regularly receives a magazine, newspaper, etc.
    The petition to nominate Sue for president of the junior class already has forty-three *subscribers*.

EXERCISE 5.7: *PON, POS, SCRIB,* AND *SCRIPT* WORDS

Fill each blank with the most appropriate word from groups 13 and 14.

1. In his address, the President inserted some remarks that were not in the __?__ previously released to the press.
2. The insurgents aim to __?__ the dictator and establish a republic.
3. According to the __?__ on its cornerstone, this school was erected in 1969.
4. With war impending, the nation hastened to __?__ all able-bodied citizens.

5. You cannot __?__ your decision much longer; the deadline for submitting applications is Monday.

---

15. SIMIL, SIMUL: "similar," "like," "same"

assimilate (*v.*)
ə'si-mə,lāt

1. make similar or like
   The letter *n* in the prefix *in* is often *assimilated* with the following letter. For example, "in" plus "legible" becomes "illegible."

2. take in and incorporate as one's own; absorb
   A bright student *assimilates* knowledge rapidly.

dissimilar (*adj.*)
di'si-mə-lə(r)

opposite of *similar*; unlike; different
These gloves are not a pair; they are quite *dissimilar*.

similarity (*n.*)
si-mə'la-rə-tē

likeness; resemblance
The two pills are alike in color and shape, but there the *similarity* ends.

simile (*n.*)
'si-mə-lē

comparison of two different things introduced by "like" or "as"
"What happens to a dream deferred?" asks Langston Hughes in one of his poems. "Does it dry up/Like a raisin in the sun?" Note that the last six words are a *simile*.

simulate (*v.*)
'sim-yə,lāt

give the appearance of; feign; imitate
Nancy was the star of the show; she *simulated* the bewildered mother very effectively.

simultaneous (*adj.*)
,sī-məl'tā-nē-əs

existing or happening at the same time; contemporary; concurrent
The flash of an explosion comes to us before the sound, though the two are really *simultaneous*.

---

16. SOL, SOLI: "alone," "lonely," "single"

desolate (*v.*)
'de-sə,lāt

(literally, "make lonely or deprive of inhabitants"); lay waste; ravage; devastate
A large section of the neighborhood was *desolated* by the disastrous fire.

desolate (*adj.*)   left alone; deserted; forlorn; abandoned; forsaken
'de-sə-lət   At 5:30 a.m. the normally crowded intersection looks *desolate*.

sole (*adj.*)   one and only; single; lone
'sōl   Franklin D. Roosevelt was the *sole* candidate to be elected President for a fourth term.

soliloquy (*n.*)   speech made to oneself when alone
sə'li-lə-kwē   What an actor says in a *soliloquy* is heard by no one except the audience.

solitary (*adj.*)   opposite of *accompanied;* being or living alone; without
'sä-lə,te-rē   companions
     A hermit leads a *solitary* existence.

solitude (*n.*)   condition of being alone; loneliness; seclusion
'sä-lə,tüd   Though I like company, there are times when I prefer *solitude*.

solo (*n.*)   musical composition (or anything) performed by a sin-
'sō-lō   gle person
     Instead of singing a *solo*, Brenda would prefer to join with me in a duet.

EXERCISE 5.8: *SIMIL, SIMUL, SOL,* AND *SOLI* WORDS

Fill each blank with the most appropriate word from groups 15 and 16.

1. Did you know you were using a(n) __?__ when you said I was as sly as a fox?
2. After the chorus sang the first number, Stanley played a violin __?__ .
3. The closing of the huge factory did not __?__ the area, as few of the workers moved away.
4. Don't compare Jane with Peggy; the two are entirely __?__ .
5. If you speak too rapidly, your audience may be unable to __?__ what you are saying.

17. SOLV, SOLU, SOLUT: "loosen"

absolute (*adj.*)   1. completely free ("loosened") of constitutional or
'ab-sə,lüt   other restraint; autocratic; despotic
     A democratic ruler is restricted by a constitution, a legislature, and courts, but a dictator has *absolute* power.

2. utter; outright; unquestionable
I did everything wrong. I was an *absolute* failure.

dissolution
(*n.*)
,di-sə'lü-shən

act of "loosening" or breaking up into component parts; disintegration; ruin; destruction
When President Lincoln took office, the Union faced imminent *dissolution*.

dissolve (*v.*)
də'zälv

(literally, "loosen apart")
1. break up; disintegrate; disband
Since the members lack mutual interests, the group will probably *dissolve*.
2. cause to disappear; end
After our quarrel, Grace and I *dissolved* our friendship.

resolution (*n.*)
,re-sə'lü-shən

(literally, "act of unloosening") solving; solution; answer
The *resolution* of our air and water pollution problems will be difficult and costly.

resolve (*v.*)
rə'zälv

(literally, "unloosen") break up; solve; explain; unravel
A witness provided the clue that *resolved* the mystery.

soluble (*adj.*)
'säl-yə-bəl

(literally, "able to be loosened")
1. capable of being dissolved or made into a liquid
Sugar is *soluble* in water.
2. solvable
Someone would have found the answer by now if the problem were *soluble*.

solvent (*n.*)
'säl-vənt

substance, usually liquid, able to dissolve ("loosen") another substance, known as the solute
In a salt water solution, the water is the *solvent* and the salt is the solute.

solvent (*adj.*)

able to pay all one's debts
The examiners found the bank *solvent*, much to the relief of its depositors.

---

18. UND, UNDA: "wave," "flow"

---

abound (*v.*)
ə'baünd

(literally, "rise in waves" or "overflow")
1. (used with *in* or *with*) be well supplied; teem
Our nation *abounds* in (or with) opportunities for well-educated young men and women.

2. be plentiful; be present in great quantity

Fish *abound* in the waters off Newfoundland.

abundant (*adj.*)
ə'bən-dənt

(literally, "rising in waves") more than sufficient; plentiful

Before Christmas, the stores have *abundant* supplies of merchandise.

inundate (*v.*)
'i-nən,dāt

flood; overflow; deluge; overwhelm

On Election Night, the victor's offices were *inundated* by congratulatory messages.

redound (*v.*)
rə'daünd

flow back as a result; contribute

The success of so many of its graduates *redounds* to the credit of the school.

redundant (*adj.*)
rə'dən-dənt

(literally, "flowing back") exceeding what is necessary; superfluous; surplus; opposite of *concise*

Remove the last word of the following sentence because it is *redundant*: "My report is longer than Bob's report."

EXERCISE 5.9: *SOLV, SOLU, SOLUT, UND,* AND *UNDA* WORDS

Fill each blank with the most appropriate word from groups 17 and 18.

1. Mutual suspicion and jealousy led to the eventual __?__ of the alliance.
2. The blue whale, once __?__ in Antarctic waters, is becoming more and more scarce.
3. The firm is in no danger of bankruptcy; it is completely __?__ .
4. Several offshore areas __?__ in oil.
5. Either of the signers can __?__ the agreement by giving thirty days' written notice to the other.

19. VER, VERA, VERI: "true," "truth"

aver (*v.*)
əˈvə(r)
state to be true; affirm confidently; assert; depose; opposite of *deny*
Two eyewitnesses *averred* they had seen the defendant at the scene.

veracity (*n.*)
vəˈra-sə-tē
truthfulness
Since he has lied to us in the past, he should not wonder that we doubt his *veracity*.

verdict (*n.*)
ˈvər,dikt
(literally, something "truly said") decision of a jury; opinion; judgment
A hung jury is one that has been unable to reach a *verdict*.

verify (*v.*)
ˈve-rə,fī
prove to be true; confirm; substantiate; corroborate
So far, the charges have been neither disproved nor *verified*.

veritable (*adj.*)
ˈve-rə-tə-bəl
true; actual; genuine; real; authentic
As the pretended heirs of Peter Wilks were disposing of his fortune, the *veritable* heirs arrived.

verity (*n.*)
ˈve-rə-tē
truth (of things); something true; true statement
That smoking is injurious to health is a scientifically established *verity*.

20. VID, VIS: "see," "look," "sight"

envision (*v.*)
ənˈvi-zhən
foresee; envisage; have a mental picture of (something not yet a reality)
Mr. Brown *envisions* for Marcia a bright career as a fashion designer.

improvise (*v.*)
ˈim-prə,vīz
(literally, "do something without having prepared or seen it beforehand") compose, recite, or sing on the spur of the moment; invent offhand; extemporize
Did you prepare your jokes before the program or *improvise* them as you went along?

invisible (*adj.*)
inˈvi-zə-bəl
not able to be seen; imperceptible; indiscernible
The microscope enables us to see organisms *invisible* to the naked eye.

revise (*v.*)
rə'vīz
look at again to correct errors and make improvements; examine and improve
Before handing in your composition, be sure to *revise* it carefully.

video (*adj.*)
'vi-dē,ō
having to do with the transmission or reception of what is seen
The audio (sound) and *video* signals of a television program can be recorded on magnetic tape.

videotape (*v.*)
'vid-ē-ō-,tāp
make a video tape recording of an event or TV program
If we *videotape* the party, we can show it later to those who could not attend.

visibility (*n.*)
,vi-zə'bi-lə-tē
degree of clearness of the atmosphere, with reference to the distance at which objects can be clearly seen
With the fog rolling in and *visibility* approaching zero, it was virtually impossible for planes to land.

visual (*adj.*)
'vi-zhə-wəl
having to do with sight
Radar tells us of an approaching object long before *visual* contact is possible.

EXERCISE 5.10: *VER*, *VERA*, *VERI*, *VID*, AND *VIS* WORDS

Fill each blank with the most appropriate word from groups 19 and 20.

1. I am not much of a student, but Norma is a(an) __?__ scholar.
2. Since words alone may fail to convey an idea, teachers often use __?__ aids, such as pictures, charts, and films.
3. La Guardia Airport reports low clouds and reduced __?__ .
4. Since the speaker was not prepared, he had to __?__ his talk.
5. You may believe this statement; it comes from a person of unquestionable __?__ .

Review Exercises

REVIEW 9: WORDBUILDING

Fill in the *prefix* in column I, the *root* in column II, and the *missing letters* of the word in column III.

I		II		III
PREFIX		ROOT		WORD
1. (3)	+	(4)	=	(7) ED
apart		loosen		*separated into parts*
2. (2)	+	(3)	=	(5) IBLE
not		seen		*not able to be seen*
3. (2)	+	(3)	=	(5) ED
on		put		*put on as a burden; inflicted*
4. (3)	+	(4)	=	(8) ION
apart		loosen		*act of breaking up; disintegration*
5. (2)	+	(3)	=	(2) D (4) NT
back		flow		*exceeding what is necessary; superfluous*
6. (3)	+	(5)	=	(8) ED
before		write		*ordered as a remedy*
7. (2)	+	(3)	=	(5) ING
again		look		*looking at again to correct*
8. (2)	+	(4)	=	(6) TE
over		flow		*overflow; overwhelm*
9. (3)	+	(5)	=	(8) ER
under		write		*one who writes his or her name at the end of a document*
10. (2)	+	(3)	=	(5) ED
down		put		*put out of office; dethroned*

REVIEW 10: SENTENCE COMPLETION

Fill each blank with the word from the list on the next page that best fits the context.

1. Since the __?__ on my TV has gone out for the third time this week, I am afraid there may be no early __?__ of the problem. The only thing I see is "snow."

2. By closing her door, Jane was able to get the __?__ she needed to complete the __?__ of her term paper.

3. The owner's __?__ explains how to __?__ the controls on the air conditioner.

4. Gulliver, the _?_ survivor of a shipwreck, landed on an apparently _?_ coast, since there were no signs of other humans or dwellings.

5. One thing I had to do when I _?_d my paper was to eliminate all _?_ words and phrases.

abound	appendix
desolate	dissimilar
manipulate	manual
manuscript	pending
redundant	resolution
resolve	revise
simulate	simile
sole	soliloquy
solitude	veracity
verdict	video

6. Homer's *Iliad* _?_s in vivid _?_s. Here is a sample: "Achilles ran toward Hector as a hawk swoops for a trembling dove."

7. The _?_ to the annual report informs stockholders about _?_ lawsuits against the company.

8. The suspect's handwriting and the writing on the ransom note proved to be _?_. That was a blow to the detectives trying to _?_ the case.

9. Othello thinks Iago is his true friend. However, in a(n) _?_ later in the play, Iago reveals that his friendship for Othello is _?_d.

10. The jury's "not guilty" _?_ shows that they must have had confidence in the _?_ of the defense witness's testimony.

REVIEW 11: LATIN ROOTS 11–20

For each Latin root in column I, write the *letter* of its definition from column II.

COLUMN I	COLUMN II
1. SOL, SOLI	(A) hang
2. MAN, MANU	(B) see, look, sight
3. PEND, PENS	(C) put
4. SOLV, SOLU, SOLUT	(D) write
5. UND, UNDA	(E) alone, lonely, single
6. VER, VERA, VERI	(F) similar, like, same
7. SCRIB, SCRIPT	(G) wave, flow
8. VID, VIS	(H) hand
9. SIMIL, SIMUL	(I) true, truth
10. PON, POS	(J) loosen

REVIEW 12: SYNONYMS

Avoid repetition by replacing the boldfaced word or expression with a synonym from the following words.

absolute   abundant
emancipate   impending
postpone(d)   similarity
simultaneous   solvent
suspend(ed)   verify

1. In many respects, the partners do not resemble each other, but there is a striking **resemblance** in their voices.
2. Play will be **temporarily stopped** until it stops raining.
3. Her guilt is beyond question; there is **unquestionable** proof that she evaded the law.
4. Shouldn't we leave sooner? A storm is **threatening to occur soon.**
5. Since the two programs were **on at the same time,** I turned on one and videotaped the other.
6. Though the company is indebted to many suppliers, it is still **able to pay its debts.**
7. In late summer, there is plenty of fresh corn; the markets get **plentiful** supplies of it daily.
8. Several independent researchers are trying to **confirm** the scientist's claims. As yet, there is no confirmation.
9. The trial has already been **deferred** twice; now, the defendant is again requesting a deferment.
10. The revolution gave the people freedom from tyranny, but it did not **free** them from poverty.

REVIEW 13: ANTONYMS

Enter the word from the list below that is most nearly the opposite of the boldfaced word or words.

append   aver
depose   impose
inundate   manual
pending   proscribe
simultaneous   soluble

1. Before the clearance sale, the old price tickets were **detached** from the garments, and new ones were __?__ed.
2. Now that there is a promising clue, the case thought to be **beyond resolution** may indeed be __?__ .
3. The legislature voted to **remove** nuisance taxes that it had previously __?__d on business.
4. Two witnesses __?__ that the suspect tried to intimidate them, but he continues to **deny** that charge.
5. Engineers are working to **drain** the tunnel __?__d by last night's heavy rainstorm.
6. Most drivers prefer an **automatic** transmission rather than a(n) __?__ one because it allows them to shift gears without using their hands.
7. I can usually answer the telephone and the doorbell if they ring **at different times,** but not if they are __?__ .
8. Few who had seen the monarch **enthroned** were present when he was __?__d.
9. Is the matter already **decided,** or is it still __?__ ?
10. Most of the dumping that used to be **permitted** is now __?__d.

REVIEW 14: CONCISE WRITING

Using no more than sixty words, rewrite the following passage, keeping all its ideas.

The first sentence has been rewritten to get you started. Go on from there.

Broker vs. Clients

In one of the cases waiting to be settled, two clients are accusing a broker of managing their investments in a manner that is not ethical. They say that he has made huge profits, while they are now not able to pay their debts. The broker insists that he has never acted in a way that is fraudulent. When he was asked if he wanted to look back over his testimony to correct misstatements or make additions, he said "no." The decision of the jury is expected to be out in a short time.

Broker vs. Clients (Concise Version)

In a pending case, two clients are accusing a broker of manipulating their funds.

REVIEW 15: SYNONYM SUMMARY

Each line, when completed, should have three words similar in meaning. Supply the missing letters.

1. att (1) ch	(1) dd	app (1) nd
2. disint (1) grate	d (1) sband	d (2) solve
3. auth (1) r	journ (1) list	scr (1) be
4. lib (1) rate	(1) ree	eman (1) ipate
5. dev (1) state	r (1) vage	(2) solate
6. gen (1) ine	(2) thentic	v (1) r (1) table
7. fl (2) d	over (1) helm	in (2) date
8. c (1) mm (1) nd	(2) thorization	m (1) nd (1) te
9. d (1) rect	d (1) ctate	p (2) scr (1) be
10. utt (1) r	(3) right	abs (1) l (1) te
11. h (1) nd (1) riting	pen (3) ship	(2) ript
12. test (1) fy	(1) wear	(2) pose
13. s (1) l (1) tion	ans (1) er	res (1) l (1) tion
14. proh (1) b (1) t	(3) bid	pr (1) scribe
15. im (1) tate	f (2) gn	s (1) m (1) late
16. lon (1) l (1) ness	s (1) cl (1) sion	sol (1) t (1) de
17. anx (2) ty	appre (3) sion	(3) pense
18. abs (1) rb	inc (1) rp (1) rate	as (2) milate
19. conf (1) rm	substant (2) te	v (1) r (1) fy
20. c (1) nc (1) rr (1) nt	(3) temporary	s (1) multan (2) us

REVIEW 16: ANALOGIES

Which lettered pair of words—*a, b, c, d,* or *e*—most nearly expresses the same relationship as the capitalized pair?

1. ACTOR : SCRIPT
    - (a) physician : prescription
    - (b) composer : score
    - (c) navigator : course
    - (d) author : manuscript
    - (e) dramatist : play

2. GREGARIOUS : SOLITUDE
    - (a) economical : conservation
    - (b) contentious : argument
    - (c) autocratic : power
    - (d) conservative : change
    - (e) independent : freedom

3. EMANCIPATE : BONDAGE
  (a) indict : accusation
  (c) enlighten : ignorance
  (e) laud : commendation
  (b) promote : rank
  (d) commission : task

4. APPEND : DETACH
  (a) prohibit : ban
  (c) debilitate : weaken
  (e) curtail : protract
  (b) frustrate : circumvent
  (d) heed : mind

5. ENIGMA : RESOLVE
  (a) ball : roll
  (c) perfection : achieve
  (e) fish : swim
  (b) smoke : rise
  (d) rumor : spread

6. INSOLVENT : CURRENCY
  (a) magnanimous : generosity
  (c) undaunted : courage
  (e) solitary : company
  (b) amiable : cordiality
  (d) arrogant : pride

7. POSTPONEMENT : DEFERRAL
  (a) scarcity : abundance
  (c) redundancy : conciseness
  (e) impasse : resolution
  (b) exploit : feat
  (d) calamity : boon

8. PERJURER : VERACITY
  (a) bulldog : tenacity
  (c) jack-of-all-trades : versatility
  (e) monopolist : competition
  (b) celebrity : renown
  (d) upstart : resources

9. EARRING : PENDANT
  (a) water : solvent
  (c) moisture : sponge
  (e) animal : deer
  (b) ornament : ring
  (d) vegetable : asparagus

10. IMPROVISE : EXTEMPORANEOUS
  (a) obey : insubordinate
  (c) conspire : clandestine
  (e) sneeze : voluntary
  (b) lurk : conspicuous
  (d) rage : rational

CHAPTER 6

Enlarging Vocabulary Through Greek Word Elements

Why study Greek word elements?

English contains a substantial and growing number of words derived from Greek. Some of these words are general words in everyday use, e.g., *authentic, chronological, economical, homogeneous,* etc. Others are used in specialized fields. Certainly you have heard terms like *antibiotic, orthopedic,* and *pediatrician* in the field of medicine; *astronaut, protoplasm,* and *thermonuclear* in science; and *autonomous, demagogue,* and *protocol* in government.

These important words, and others like them in this unit, are constructed from Greek word elements. Once you know what a particular word element means, you have a clue to the meaning of words derived from it. When, for example, you have learned that *PAN* or *PANTO* means "complete" or "all," you are better able to understand—and remember— that a *panacea* is a "remedy for *all* ills," a *panorama* is a "*complete* and unobstructed view in *all* directions," and a *pantomime* is "*all* gestures and signs, i.e., a performance without words."

Purpose of this unit

This unit aims to enlarge your vocabulary by acquainting you with twenty Greek word elements and some English words derived from them. As you study each word group, make it a special point to memorize the meaning of the word element so that you will be able to recognize it in derivatives.

240

GREEK WORD ELEMENTS 1–10

Pretest 1

Write the *letter* of the best answer.

1. In a *plutocracy*, __?__ govern.
   (A) technical experts   (B) the wealthy   (C) the nobles

2. A *pedagogue* is mainly concerned with __?__ .
   (A) politics   (B) medicine   (C) teaching

3. *Pandemonium* is a condition of __?__ .
   (A) wild disorder   (B) poor nourishment   (C) absolute peace

4. People who lack *autonomy* are __?__ .
   (A) unreliable   (B) selfish   (C) not self-ruled

5. You study *orthography* mainly in your __?__ classes.
   (A) English   (B) mathematics   (C) social studies

6. A mistake in __?__ order is a mistake in *chronology*.
   (A) word   (B) alphabetical   (C) time

7. In a *homogeneous* group, the members are of __?__ ability.
   (A) similar   (B) varied   (C) high

8. A *kleptomaniac* is a menace mainly to __?__ .
   (A) liberty   (B) property   (C) life

9. The *odometer* on your automobile dashboard measures __?__ .
   (A) distance   (B) speed   (C) motor temperature

10. A *demagogue* stirs up the people __?__ .
    (A) when they forget their responsibilities   (B) to protect
    democratic principles   (C) for personal advantage

THE ANSWERS ARE

2. C   4. C   6. C   8. B   10. C
1. B   3. A   5. A   7. A   9. A

Each italicized word in the pretest came from a different word element: *plutocracy* from CRACY, meaning "government"; *pedagogue* from PED, meaning "child," etc. We shall now study ten such word elements and some words derived from them.

1. AUT, AUTO: "self"

WORD	MEANING AND TYPICAL USE
authentic (*adj.*) ȯ'then-tik	(literally, "from the master himself") genuine; real; reliable; trustworthy When you withdraw money, the bank may compare your signature with the one in its files to see if it is *authentic*.
autobiography (*n.*) ,ȯ-tə-bī'ä-grə-fē	story of a person's life written by the person himself or herself In her *autobiography* THE STORY OF MY LIFE, Helen Keller tells how unruly she was as a young child.
autocrat (*n.*) 'ȯ-tə,krat	ruler exercising self-derived, absolute power; despot; dictator The *autocrat* was replaced by a ruler responsible to the people.
autograph (*n.*) 'ȯ-tə-graf	person's signature written by himself or herself The baseball star wrote his *autograph* for an admirer who came up to him with a pencil and scorecard.
automatic (*adj.*) ȯ-tə'ma-tik	acting by itself; self-regulating You do not have to defrost a refrigerator equipped with an *automatic* defroster.
automation (*n.*) ,ȯ-tə'mā-shən	technique of making a process self-operating by means of built-in electronic controls Many workers have lost their jobs as a result of *automation*.
automaton (*n.*) ȯ'tä-mə-tən	(literally, "self-acting thing") purely mechanical person following a routine; robot An autocrat prefers subjects who are *automatons*, rather than intelligent human beings.
autonomous (*adj.*) ȯ'tä-nə-məs	self-governing; independent; sovereign The Alumni Association is not under the control of the school. It is a completely *autonomous* group.

autonomy (*n.*) ȯ'tä-nə-mē	right of self-government; independence; sovereignty After World War II, many former colonies were granted *autonomy* and became independent nations.
autopsy (*n.*) 'ȯ,täp-sē	(literally, ''a seeing for one's self'') medical examination of a dead body to determine the cause of death; postmortem examination The cause of the celebrity's sudden death will not be known until the *autopsy* has been performed.

EXERCISE 6.1: *AUT, AUTO* WORDS

Fill each blank with the most appropriate word from group 1.

1. Some members want to censure the president for ignoring the club's constitution and behaving like an __?__ .
2. You are no better than an __?__ if you act mechanically without using your intelligence.
3. The Prime Minister left her life story to others, for she had neither the time nor the desire to write an __?__ .
4. Elevator operators are not employed in buildings equipped with __?__ elevators.
5. For generations, colonial peoples who asked for __?__ were usually told that they were not ready to govern themselves.

2. CRACY: ''government''

aristocracy (*n.*) ,a-rəs'tä-krə-sē	1. (literally, ''government by the best'') government or country governed by a small privileged upper class Before 1789, France was an *aristocracy*. 2. ruling class of nobles; nobility; privileged class; gentry When the Revolution of 1789 began, many members of the French *aristocracy* fled to other lands.
autocracy (*n.*) ȯ'tä-krə-sē	government or country governed by one individual with self-derived, unlimited power Germany under Adolf Hitler was an *autocracy*.
bureaucracy (*n.*) byü'räk-rə-sē	government by bureaus or groups of officials; administration characterized by excessive red tape and routine

The Mayor was criticized for setting up an inefficient *bureaucracy* unresponsive to the needs of the people.

democracy (*n.*)   government or country governed by the people; rule
də'mäk-rə-sē   by the majority
   The Thirteen Colonies developed into the first *democracy* in the Western Hemisphere.

plutocracy (*n.*)   government or country governed by the rich
plü'täk-rə-sē   If only millionaires can afford to run for office, we may soon become a *plutocracy*.

technocracy (*n.*)   government or country governed by technical experts
tek'näk-rə-sē   In a *technocracy*, the governing class would consist largely of engineers.

The form *crat* at the end of a word means "advocate of a type of government," "member of a class," or, if the word is capitalized, "member of a political party." Examples:

aristocrat (*n.*)   1. advocate of aristocracy
ə'ris-tə,krat   An *aristocrat* would like to see members of the upper class in control of the government.

   2. member of the aristocracy; noble; patrician
   Winston Churchill was born an *aristocrat*; he was the son of Sir Randolph Churchill.

Democrat (*n.*)   member of the Democratic Party
'de-mə,krat   The Senator used to be a Republican but he is now a *Democrat*.

Also: **bureaucrat, plutocrat, technocrat**

EXERCISE 6.2: *CRACY* WORDS

Fill each blank with the most appropriate word from group 2.

1. It was most unusual for a member of the __?__ to marry someone not belonging to the nobility.
2. If you believe that only the affluent are fit to govern, you must be a(n) __?__.
3. In a(n) __?__, the ruler has absolute and unlimited power.
4. How can you call yourself a(n) __?__ if you do not believe in majority rule?
5. Many are opposed to a(n) __?__ because they do not wish to be ruled by technical experts.

3. DEM, DEMO: "people"

demagogue (*n.*)
'de-mə-gäg

political leader who stirs up the people for personal advantage; rabble-rouser

No responsible leader, only a *demagogue*, would make campaign speeches promising to solve all the people's problems.

democratic (*adj.*)
de-mə'kra-tik

based on the principles of democracy, or government by the people

A nation cannot be considered *democratic* unless its leaders are chosen by the people in free elections.

democratize (*v.*)
də'mä-krə,tīz

make democratic

The adoption of the 19th Amendment, giving women the franchise, greatly *democratized* our nation.

epidemic (*adj.*)
,e-pə'de-mik

(literally, "among the people") affecting many people in an area at the same time; widespread

Greater federal and state aid is needed in areas where unemployment is *epidemic*.

epidemic (*n.*)

outbreak of a rapidly spreading, contagious disease affecting many people at the same time; plague; rash

The high rate of absenteeism was caused by the flu *epidemic*.

EXERCISE 6.3: *DEM, DEMO* WORDS

Fill each blank with the most appropriate word from group 3.

1. Millions of people died in the 14th century as the result of a(n) __?__ known as the Black Death.
2. The election was not __?__ because some people voted more than once and others were prevented from voting.
3. An intelligent voter can distinguish the unselfish political leader from the __?__ .
4. To __?__ the country, a new constitution was drawn up, giving equal rights to all segments of the population.
5. It is more __?__ for a governor to be chosen by the people than to be appointed by the king.

4. PAN, PANTO: "all," "complete"

panacea (*n.*)
ˌpa-nə'sē-ə

remedy for all ills; cure-all; universal remedy; elixir
A two-week vacation is wonderful but will not cure baldness or improve vision. It is no *panacea*.

Pan-American (*adj.*)
ˌpa-nə'me-rə-kən

of or pertaining to all the countries of North, South, and Central America
The *Pan-American* Highway links all the countries of the Western Hemisphere from Alaska to Chile.

pandemonium (*n.*)
ˌpan-də'mō-nē-əm

(literally, "abode of all the demons," i.e., hell) wild uproar; very noisy din; wild disorder; tumult; racket
The huge crowds in Times Square grew noisier as the old year ticked away, and when midnight struck there was *pandemonium*.

panoply (*n.*)
'pa-nə-plē

complete suit of armor; complete covering or equipment; magnificent array
The opposing knights, mounted and in full *panoply*, awaited the signal for the tournament to begin.

panorama (*n.*)
ˌpa-nə'ra-mə

complete, unobstructed view
From the Verrazano-Narrows Bridge, you can get an excellent *panorama* of New York's harbor.

pantomime (*n.*)
'pan-tə,mīm

dramatic performance that is all signs and gestures without words
Not until *The Great Dictator* did Charlie Chaplin play a speaking part. All his previous roles were in *pantomime*.

EXERCISE 6.4: *PAN, PANTO* WORDS

Fill each blank with the most appropriate word from group 4.

1. When Karen scored the tie-breaking goal with five seconds left to play, __?__ broke out.
2. Many regard education as the __?__ that will cure all of society's ills.
3. The top of 3605-foot Mt. Snow in Vermont offers a fine __?__ of the Green Mountains.
4. In a __?__, the actors express themselves only by facial expressions, bodily movements, and gestures.
5. The woods in their full __?__ of autumn color are a breathtaking sight.

5. CHRON, CHRONO: "time"

anachronism (*n.*) error in chronology or time order
ə'na-krə,ni-zəm It would be an *anachronism* to say that Joan of Arc rode to battle in a jeep.

chronicle (*n.*) historical account of events in the order of time; his-
'krä-nə-kəl tory; annals
One of the earliest accounts of King Arthur occurs in a 12th-century *chronicle* of the kings of Britain by Geoffrey of Monmouth.

chronological (*adj.*) arranged in order of time
,krä-nə'lä-jə-kəl The magazines in this file are not in *chronological* order. I found the February issue after the October one.

chronology (*n.*) arrangement of data or events in order of time of
krə'nä-lə-jē occurrence
In the *chronology* of American Presidents, Ulysses S. Grant comes after Andrew Johnson.

synchronize (*v.*) cause to agree in time; make simultaneous
'siŋ-krə,nīz The clocks in the library need to be *synchronized;* one is a minute and a half behind the other.

EXERCISE 6.5: *CHRON, CHRONO* WORDS

Fill each blank with the most appropriate word from group 5.

1. Can you recall the World Series champions of the last five years in the correct __?__ ?

2. To say that the ancient Greeks watched the siege of Troy on television would be an amusing __?__ .

3. The film begins near the climax and then goes back to the hero's childhood, violating the usual __?__ order.

4. The townspeople used to __?__ their timepieces with the clock outside the village bank.

5. The current *World Almanac* gives a(n) __?__ of last year's events.

6. MANIA: "madness," "insane impulse," "craze"

kleptomania (*n.*)   insane impulse to steal
,klep-tə'mā-nē-ə   The millionaire arrested for shoplifting was found to
                          be suffering from *kleptomania*.

mania (*n.*)   1. madness; insanity
'mā-nē-ə   For a student with an A average to quit school two
                          months before graduation is sheer *mania*.

                          2. excessive fondness; craze
                             Though I still read science fiction, I no longer have
                          the *mania* for it that I originally had.

maniac (*n.*)   raving lunatic; mad or insane person; crackpot
'mā-nē,ak   The deranged behavior of the narrator in "The Tell-
                          Tale Heart" leaves little doubt that he is a *maniac*.

maniacal (*adj.*)   characterized by madness; insane; raving
mə'nī-ə-kəl   You protested in such a loud, violent, and *maniacal*
                          manner that onlookers must have thought you had lost
                          your sanity.

pyromania (*n.*)   insane impulse to set fires
,pī-rō'mā-nē-ə   The person charged with setting the fire had been
                          suspected of *pyromania* on two previous occasions.

The form *maniac* at the end of a word means "person affected by an insane impulse or craze." Examples: **kleptomaniac, pyromaniac.**

EXERCISE 6.6: *MANIA* WORDS

Fill each blank with the most appropriate word from group 6.

1. The weird, __?__ shrieks and groans coming from the house might have made one believe that it was inhabited by a raving lunatic.
2. Sharon has a __?__ for chocolates; she will finish a whole box in no time at all if not restrained.
3. Herb can't help taking things belonging to others; he is a __?__.
4. Officials believe the recent series of small fires to be the work of a __?__.
5. The spoiled brat raved like a __?__ when he didn't get his way.

7. PED: "child"

encyclopedia (*n.*)
ən,sī-klə'pē-dē-ə

(literally, "well-rounded rearing of a child") work offering alphabetically arranged information on various branches of knowledge

There are four different *encyclopedias* in the reference section of our school library.

orthopedic (*adj.*)
,ȯ(r)-thə'pē-dik

(literally, "of the straight child") having to do with *orthopedics*, the science dealing with the correction and prevention of deformities, especially in children

Patients recovering from broken limbs are treated in the hospital's *orthopedic* ward.

pedagogue (*n.*)
'pe-də,gäg

(literally, "leader of a child") teacher of children

The new teacher received a great deal of help from the more experienced *pedagogues*.

pedagogy (*n.*)
'pe-də,gō-jē

art of teaching

Dr. Dworkin's lessons are usually excellent. She is a master of *pedagogy*.

pediatrician (*n.*)
,pē-dē-ə'tri-shən

physician specializing in the treatment of babies and children

When the baby developed a fever, the parents telephoned the *pediatrician*.

pediatrics (*n.*)
,pē-dē'a-triks

branch of medicine dealing with the care, development, and diseases of babies and children

From the number of baby carriages outside the office, you can tell that Dr. Enders specializes in *pediatrics*.

EXERCISE 6.7: *PED* WORDS

Fill each blank with the most appropriate word from group 7.

1. __?__ deals with diseases that afflict the young.
2. Charlotte doesn't have to go to the library as often as I because she has a twenty-two volume __?__ at home.
3. A teacher's professional training includes courses in __?__ .
4. Until the age of six months, the baby was taken to the __?__ every month.
5. A(n) __?__ specialist performed the operation to correct the deformity of the child's spinal column.

8. ORTHO: "straight," "correct"

orthodontist (*n.*)
,ȯ(r)-thə'dän-təst

dentist specializing in *orthodontics,* a branch of dentistry dealing with straightening and adjusting of teeth

A teenager wearing braces is obviously under the care of an *orthodontist.*

orthodox (*adj.*)
'ȯ(r)-thə,däks

(literally, "correct opinion") generally accepted, especially in religion; conventional; approved; conservative

There was no religious liberty in the Massachusetts Bay Colony. Roger Williams, for example, was banished because he did not accept *orthodox* Puritan beliefs.

orthography (*n.*)
ȯ(r)'thä-grə-fē

(literally, "correct writing") correct spelling

American and English *orthography* are very much alike. One difference, however, is in words like "honor" and "labor," which the English spell "honour" and "labour."

orthopedist (*n.*)
,ȯ(r)-thə'pē-dəst

physician specializing in the correction and prevention of deformities, especially in children

A deformity of the spine is a condition that requires the attention of an *orthopedist.*

unorthodox (*adj.*)
ən'ȯ(r)-thə,däks

not orthodox; not in accord with accepted, standard, or approved belief or practice; unconventional; heretical

Vaccination was rejected as *unorthodox* when Dr. Jenner first suggested it.

EXERCISE 6.8: *ORTHO* WORDS

Fill each blank with the most appropriate word from group 8.

1. It is __?__ to begin a meal with the dessert.
2. Phyllis has won the spelling bee again. She excels in __?__.
3. The young patient is under the care of a well-known __?__ for a leg deformity.
4. The infant gets up at 4 a.m. We should prefer him to wake at a more __?__ hour, such as 7 a.m.
5. Laura's parents have been assured by an __?__ that her teeth can be straightened.

9. GEN, GENO, GENEA: "race," "kind," "birth"

genealogy (*n.*)
ˌjē-nē′ä-lə-jē

(literally, "account of a race or family") history of the descent of a person or family from an ancestor; lineage; pedigree

Diane can trace her descent from an ancestor who fought in the Mexican War. I know much less about my own *genealogy*.

genesis (*n.*)
′je-nə-səs

birth or coming into being of something; origin

According to legend, the Trojan War had its *genesis* in a dispute among three Greek goddesses.

heterogeneous (*adj.*)
ˌhe-tə-rə′jē-nē-əs

differing in kind; dissimilar; not uniform; varied

Many different racial and cultural groups are to be found in the *heterogeneous* population of a large American city.

homogeneous (*adj.*)
ˌhō-mə′jē-nē-əs

of the same kind; similar; uniform

All the dancers in the ballet corps wore the same costume to present a *homogeneous* appearance.

homogenize (*v.*)
hō′mä-jə,nīz

make homogeneous

If dairies did not *homogenize* milk, the cream would be concentrated at the top instead of being evenly distributed.

EXERCISE 6.9: *GEN, GENO, GENEA* WORDS

Fill the blank with the appropriate word from group 9.

1. The class consists of intermediate and advanced dancers, as well as a few beginners. It is a __?__ group.
2. A family Bible in which births, marriages, and deaths have been recorded for generations is a source of information about a person's __?__ .
3. There are always lumps in the cereal when you cook it. You don't know how to __?__ it.
4. When every house on the block has the same exterior, the result is a __?__ dullness.
5. Democracy is not an American creation; it had its __?__ in ancient Greece.

10. METER, METR: "measure"

barometer (*n.*)
bə′rä-mə-tə(r)

instrument for measuring atmospheric pressure as an aid in determining probable weather changes

When the *barometer* indicates a rapid drop in air pressure, it means a storm is coming.

chronometer (*n.*)
krə′nä-mə-tə(r)

instrument for measuring time very accurately

Unlike ordinary clocks and watches, *chronometers* are little affected by temperature changes or vibration.

diameter (*n.*)
dī-′a-mə-tə(r)

(literally, "measure across") straight line passing through the center of a body or figure from one side to the other; length of such a line; thickness; width

Some giant redwood trees measure up to 30 feet (9.14 meters) in *diameter*.

meter (*n.*)
′mē-tə(r)

1. device for measuring

When water *meters* are installed, it will be easy to tell how much water each home is using.

2. unit of measure in the metric system; 39.37 inches

A *meter* is 3.37 inches longer than a yard.

odometer (*n.*)
ō′dä-mə-tə(r)

instrument attached to a vehicle for measuring the distance traversed

All eyes, except the driver's, were fastened on the *odometer* as it moved from 9,999.9 to 10,000 miles.

photometer (*n.*)
fō′tä-mə-tə(r)

instrument for measuring intensity of light

The intensity of a source of light, such as an electric light bulb, can be measured with a *photometer*.

speedometer (*n.*)
spē′dä-mə-tə(r)

instrument for measuring speed; tachometer

I advised Ann to slow down as we were in a 30-mile-an-hour zone and her *speedometer* registered more than 40.

symmetry (*n.*)
′si-mə-trē

correspondence in measurements, shape, etc., on opposite sides of a dividing line; well-balanced arrangement of parts; harmony; balance

As the planes passed overhead, we were impressed by the perfect *symmetry* of their V-formation.

EXERCISE 6.10: *METER, METR* WORDS

Fill each blank with the most appropriate word from group 10.

1. Every apple in this package has a(n) __?__ of no less than 2¼ inches.
2. We couldn't tell how fast we were going because the __?__ was out of order.
3. Notice the __?__ of the human body. The right side is the counterpart of the left.
4. You can tell how many miles a car has been driven since its manufacture if you look at its __?__ .
5. In the 100-__?__ dash, the course is more than 100 yards long.

Review Exercises

REVIEW 1: GREEK WORD ELEMENTS 1–10

For each Greek word element in column I, write the *letter* of its correct meaning from column II.

COLUMN I	COLUMN II
1. ORTHO	(A) child
2. MANIAC	(B) all; complete
3. GEN, GENO, GENEA	(C) madness; insane impulse; craze
4. CHRON, CHRONO	(D) straight; correct
5. CRAT	(E) government
6. AUT, AUTO	(F) race; kind; birth
7. METER, METR	(G) people
8. PAN, PANTO	(H) advocate of a type of government
9. MANIA	(I) measure
10. CRACY	(J) self
11. PED	(K) time
12. DEM, DEMO	(L) person affected by an insane impulse

REVIEW 2: WORDBUILDING

Write the word defined below.

DEFINITION	WORD
1. arranged in order of time	(6) LOGICAL
2. technique of making a process self-operating	(4) MATION
3. instrument for measuring atmospheric pressure	BARO (5)
4. remedy for all ills	(3) ACEA
5. differing in kind	HETERO (3) EOUS
6. person affected by an insane impulse to set fires	PYRO (6)
7. government by small privileged upper class	ARISTO (5)
8. dentist specializing in straightening teeth	(5) DONTIST
9. teacher of children	(3) AGOGUE
10. self-governing	(4) NOMOUS
11. correspondence in shape, size, etc.	SYM (4) Y

12. complete equipment   (3) OPLY
13. contrary to approved or conservative   UN (5) DOX
    practice
14. physician specializing in treatment of   (3) IATRICIAN
    children
15. member of wealthy class   PLUTO (4)
16. of the same kind   HOMO (3) EOUS
17. affecting many people in an area at the same   EPI (3) IC
    time
18. characterized by madness   (5) CAL
19. cause to agree in time   SYN (5) IZE
20. government by the people   (4) CRACY

REVIEW 3: SENTENCE COMPLETION

Fill each blank with the word from the list below that best fits the context.

anachronism	aristocracy
authentic	autobiography
autocrat	autograph
chronological	democracy
encyclopedia	genesis
heterogeneous	homogeneous
maniacal	panacea
pandemonium	pedagogue
pedagogy	pyromaniac
synchronize	unorthodox

1. In his __?__, the famous teacher describes some personal experiences that taught him the art of __?__.
2. When the home team won the championship, __?__ broke out, and thousands of __?__ fans charged the goal posts to knock them down.
3. A handwriting expert was called in to determine whether the __?__ of Babe Ruth on the old baseball was __?__.
4. Hoping to oust the __?__ ruling the country with an iron fist, the conspirators __?__d their watches and moved cautiously toward the palace.
5. The psychiatrist treating the __?__ is trying to discover the __?__ of his urge to set fires.
6. Only if I were a "walking __?__" could I have recited the names of all the kings and queens of England in perfect __?__ order.

7. The __?__ explained to her class that the striking of the clock in *Julius Caesar* is a(n) __?__, since the play is set in ancient Rome.
8. Though the young man had grown up among the __?__, his father had instilled in him the principles of __?__.
9. The __?__ candidate readily admitted to the voters that he had no __?__ for their problems.
10. The athletes participating in the international meet were __?__ in ethnic origin, but __?__ in their quest for glory.

REVIEW 4: SYNONYMS

Avoid repetition by replacing the boldfaced word or expression with a synonym from the following words.

automatic	automaton
autonomous	chronology
diameter	genealogy
kleptomania	orthography
pantomime	pediatrician(s)

1. The helper was a(n) **purely mechanical person** who mechanically repeated everything that the boss said.
2. Posts with a **thickness** of six inches are much sturdier than those that are only four inches thick.
3. **Physicians who specialize in the treatment of children** see more cases of measles than most other physicians.
4. Once we set the temperature, the heating system is **self-regulating;** we don't have to regulate it.
5. Most colonies governed by a mother country eventually became **self-governing.**
6. Jack would be a better speller if he learned some of the rules of **spelling.**
7. If you say that something happened at an earlier time than it really did, you are making an error in **time sequence.**
8. The defendant claims she took to stealing not because of greed, but because of **an insane impulse to steal.**
9. From history and from conversations with your grandparents and great-grandparents, you may learn a good deal about your **family history.**
10. Not a word was spoken; the performers used **signs and gestures, but no words.**

REVIEW 5: ANTONYMS

Write the word from the list below that is most nearly the opposite of the boldfaced word or words.

aristocrat	authentic
automatic	democratic
genesis	heterogeneous
homogeneous	maniac
symmetry	unorthodox

1. In the olden days, it was rare for a **commoner** to marry a(n) __?__ .
2. The insurgents hope to topple the **authoritarian** regime and replace it with a(n) __?__ government.
3. From its __?__ to its **cessation,** the epidemic took a heavy toll.
4. Is the car equipped with a(n) __?__ transmission, or a **manual** one?
5. I cannot believe that a **sane person** could suddenly turn into a(n) __?__ .
6. Is the class __?__ , or does it consist of students of **dissimilar** ability?
7. An occasional **lack of balance** in the marching formations somewhat marred the __?__ of the parade.
8. The documents would have seemed __?__ to most people, but experts knew they were **false.**
9. The establishment favors **conventional** ways of dealing with the crisis and frowns on __?__ approaches.
10. We looked through a(n) __?__ assortment of lamps reduced for final sale, in which no two were **of the same kind.**

REVIEW 6: CONCISE WRITING

In no more than eighty words, rewrite the following passage.

The Peloponnesian War: 431–404 B.C.

In 431 B.C., Athens, a small **country governed in accordance with the wishes of the majority of its citizens,** went to war with Sparta, a **nation governed by a small privileged upper class.** Athens would have won if not for two misfortunes. First, it was devastated in 430–428 B.C. by a **rapidly spreading contagious disease** that killed a quarter of its population. Then, because of **political leaders who stirred up the people for their own selfish advantage,** it undertook reckless offensives on which it squandered its finest troops. As a result, Athens lost not only the war, but its **right to govern itself.**

Most of the above facts were recorded by Thucydides in his **historical account of the events, in the order of time,** of the Peloponnesian War.

REVIEW 7: SYNONYM SUMMARY

Each line, when completed, should have three words similar in meaning. Write the *complete* words.

1. dictat (1) r	d (1) spot	(2) tocrat
2. ins (1) ne	r (1) ving	(2) niacal
3. b (1) rth	(1) rigin	genes (2)
4. w (1) dth	th (1) ckness	d (1) ameter
5. tr (1) stworthy	gen (1) ine	aut (2) ntic
6. l (1) natic	cr (1) ckp (1) t	man (2) c
7. ind (1) pend (1) nt	self-gov (2) ning	aut (1) n (1) mous
8. sim (1) l (1) r	un (1) form	homogen (2) us
9. n (1) b (1) lity	g (1) ntry	a (3) tocracy
10. (2) sanity	m (1) dness	(2) nia
11. b (1) lance	harm (1) ny	s (2) metry
12. convent (2) nal	(3) servative	(2) thodox
13. t (1) mult	r (1) cket	(3) demonium
14. (2) story	ann (1) ls	chr (1) n (1) cle
15. ped (1) gree	lin (2) ge	gene (1) logy
16. n (1) ble	patri (2) an	(1) r (1) st (1) crat
17. (2) dependence	sover (2) gnty	aut (1) n (1) my
18. (2) conventional	h (1) retical	(2) ortho (3)
19. plag (2)	r (1) sh	ep (1) d (1) mic
20. (3) similar	v (1) ried	h (1) t (1) r (1) geneous

REVIEW 8: ANALOGIES

Which lettered pair of words—*a, b, c, d,* or *e*—most nearly expresses the same relationship as the capitalized pair?

1. DUCHESS : ARISTOCRACY
   - (*a*) retiree : staff
   - (*c*) voter : electorate
   - (*e*) alien : citizenry
   - (*b*) student : faculty
   - (*d*) employment : management

2. PANDEMONIUM : HEARING
   - (*a*) glare : sight
   - (*c*) abundance : scarcity
   - (*e*) disharmony : agreement
   - (*b*) praise : learning
   - (*d*) fog : collision

   Hint: **pandemonium** makes **hearing** difficult.

3. DEMAGOGUE : POLITICS
  (a) civilian : warfare   (b) quack : medicine
  (c) amateur : sports   (d) clown : circus
  (e) apprentice : trade
   Hint: A **demagogue** is an unscrupulous person in **politics**.

4. AUTHENTIC : ACCEPTANCE
  (a) futile : effort   (b) corrupt : contempt
  (c) incredible : belief   (d) insignificant : concern
  (e) demagogic : trust

5. AUTOMATION : PRODUCTIVITY
  (a) air conditioning : temperature   (b) rest : fatigue
  (c) bickering : amity   (d) resentment : achievement
  (e) refrigeration : shelf life

6. SUBJUGATE : AUTONOMY
  (a) demote : authority   (b) initiate : membership
  (c) vindicate : innocence   (d) gag : censorship
  (e) elevate : prestige

7. BIOGRAPHY : CHRONOLOGICAL
  (a) height : vertical   (b) index : alphabetical
  (c) novel : fictional   (d) width : horizontal
  (e) news story : factual

8. ORTHODONTICS : DENTISTRY
  (a) astronomy : physics   (b) orthopedics : fractures
  (c) biology : zoology   (d) pyrotechnics : fireworks
  (e) pediatrics : childhood

9. GENESIS : BEGINNING
  (a) diagnosis : disease   (b) prognosis : recovery
  (c) crisis : downfall   (d) status : promotion
  (e) metamorphosis : change

GREEK WORD ELEMENTS 11–20

Pretest 2

Write the *letter* of the best answer.

1. If a product is *synthetic*, it was not made by __?__ .
   (A) hand   (B) nature   (C) humans

2. A *thermostat* __?__ .
   (A) regulates temperature   (B) keeps liquids warm   (C) provides heat

3. The reference mark __?__ is called an *asterisk*.
   (A) [;]   (B) [']   (C) [*]

4. An *anonymous* poem is __?__ .
   (A) by an unknown author   (B) humorous   (C) a nursery rhyme

5. The __?__ in a series of similar things is the *prototype*.
   (A) latest   (B) first   (C) best

6. Usually, a *nemesis* brings __?__ .
   (A) defeat   (B) luck   (C) victory

7. A *phenomenon* can be __?__ .
   (A) a ghost or a shadow only   (B) an extraordinary fact only
   (C) any observable fact or event

8. A *dermatologist* is a __?__ specialist.
   (A) skin   (B) foot   (C) heart

9. If you have an *antipathy* to a subject, you have a(n) __?__ for it.
   (A) enthusiasm   (B) dislike   (C) talent

10. __?__ is an *anagram* of "meat."
    (A) "Meet"   (B) "Flesh"   (C) "Team"

```
+-----------------------------------+
|         THE ANSWERS ARE           |
|                                   |
|   2. A   4. A   6. A   8. A   10. C |
|   1. B   3. C   5. B   7. C   9. B  |
+-----------------------------------+
```

Each italicized word in the pretest came from a different word element: *synthetic* from THET, meaning "put"; *thermostat* from THERMO, meaning "heat," etc. In the following pages you will learn about ten such word elements and some of their derivatives.

11. ANT, ANTI: "against," "opposite"

antagonist (*n.*)
an'ta-gə,nəst

one who is against, or contends with, another in a struggle, fight, or contest; opponent; adversary; foe
Great Britain was our *antagonist* in the War of 1812.

antibiotic (*n.*)
,an-tə,bī'ä-tik

substance obtained from tiny living organisms that works against harmful bacteria
The *antibiotic* penicillin stops the growth of bacteria that cause pneumonia, tonsillitis, and certain other diseases.

antibody (*n.*)
,an-ti'bä-dē

substance manufactured in the body that works against germs or poisons produced by germs
When the body is invaded by foreign agents, such as bacteria or viruses, the *antibodies* go to work against them.

antidote (*n.*)
'an-ti,dōt

1. remedy that acts against the effects of a poison
By telephone, the physician prescribed the exact *antidote* to be given immediately to the poison victim.

2. countermeasure
Heavy fines are an *antidote* to illegal parking.

antihistamine (*n.*)
,an-tə'hist-ə,mən

drug used against certain allergies and cold symptoms
The *antihistamine* prescribed for my cold was not too effective.

antipathy (*n.*)
an'ti-pə-thē

feeling against; distaste; repugnance; dislike; enmity
A few of the neighbors have an *antipathy* to dogs, but most are fond of them.

antiseptic (*n.*)
,an-tə'sep-tik

(literally, "against decaying") substance that prevents infection by checking the growth of microorganisms; germicide
The wound was carefully washed; then hydrogen peroxide was applied as an *antiseptic*.

antitoxin (*n.*)
,an-ti'täk-sən

substance formed in the body as the result of the introduction of a toxin (poison) and capable of acting against that toxin
We are injected with diphtheria *antitoxin* produced in horses because the *antitoxin* manufactured by our bodies may not be enough to prevent diphtheria.

antonym (*n.*)
'an-tə,nim

word meaning the opposite of another word
"Temporary" is the *antonym* of "permanent."

EXERCISE 6.11: *ANT, ANTI* WORDS

Fill each blank with the most appropriate word from group 11.

1. An __?__ prescribed by a physician may give temporary relief to some cold and allergy sufferers.
2. Our armed forces must be capable of defending us against any foreign __?__ .
3. Streptomycin, an __?__ developed from living microorganisms, is used in the treatment of tuberculosis.
4. The infection would not have developed if an __?__ had been used.
5. I have had an __?__ to ship travel ever since I became seasick on a lake cruise.

---

12. ONYM, ONOMATO: "name," "word"

---

acronym (*n.*)
'a-krə,nim

name formed from the first letter or letters of other words
> The word "radar" is an *acronym* for *RA*dio *D*etecting *A*nd *R*ange.

anonymous (*adj.*)
ə'nä-nə-məs

nameless; unnamed; unidentified
> An *anonymous* American killed in combat in World War I lies in the Tomb of the Unknown Soldier.

homonym (*n.*)
'hä-mə,nim

word that sounds like another but differs in meaning
> "Fair" and "fare" are *homonyms*.

onomatopoeia (*n.*)
,ä-nə,ma-tə'pē-ə

use of words whose sound suggests their meaning
> Notice the *onomatopoeia* in these lines by the poet John Dryden: "The double, double, double beat/Of the thundering drum."

pseudonym (*n.*)
'sü-də,nim

(literally, "false name") fictitious name used by an author; pen name; alias
> Because of antipathy to female authors in her time, Mary Ann Evans wrote under the *pseudonym* "George Eliot."

synonym (*n.*)
'si-nə,nim

word having the same meaning as another word
> "Building" is a *synonym* for "edifice."

EXERCISE 6.12: *ONYM, ONOMATO* WORDS

Fill each blank with the most appropriate word from group 12.

1. "Deer" and "dear" are __?__s.
2. There is no need to use a(n) __?__, unless you wish to conceal your identity.
3. Anzac is a(n) __?__ for Australian and New Zealand Army Corps.
4. I was embarrassed when the __?__ test paper my teacher spoke about turned out to be mine. I had forgotten to put my name on it.
5. "Hiss," "mumble," and "splash" are good one-word examples of __?__.

---

13. DERM, DERMATO: "skin"

---

dermatologist (*n.*) dər-məˈtä-lə-jəst	physician specializing in *dermatology*, the science dealing with the skin and its diseases
	The patient with the skin disorder is under the care of a *dermatologist*.
dermis (*n.*) ˈdər-məs	inner layer of the skin
	The tiny cells from which hairs grow are located in the *dermis*.
epidermis (*n.*) ˌe-piˈdər-məs	outer layer of the skin
	Although very thin, the *epidermis* protects the underlying dermis.
hypodermic (*adj.*) ˌhī-pəˈdər-mik	beneath the skin
	A *hypodermic* syringe is used for injecting medication beneath the skin.
taxidermist (*n.*) ˈtak-sə-ˌdər-məst	one who practices *taxidermy*, the art of preparing, stuffing, and mounting the skins of animals in lifelike form
	The lifelike models of animals that you see in museums are the work of skilled *taxidermists*.

EXERCISE 6.13: *DERM, DERMATO* WORDS

Fill each blank with the most appropriate word from group 13.

1. The __?__ stretched the skin over a plastic cast of the animal's body.
2. Was the antibiotic taken by mouth or administered by __?__ injection?

3. There are numerous tiny openings, or pores, in the __?__, or outer layer of the skin.

4. It took three visits for the __?__ to remove Rita's painful wart in the skin of her left sole.

5. The sweat glands are located in the __?__, or inner layer of the skin.

---

14. NOM, NEM: "management," "distribution," "law"

agronomy (*n.*)
ə'grä-nə-mē

(literally, "land management") branch of agriculture dealing with crop production and soil management; husbandry
   The science of *agronomy* helps farmers obtain larger and better crops.

astronomical (*adj.*)
,a-strə'nä-mi-kəl

1. having to do with *astronomy* (literally, "distribution of the stars") the science of the sun, moon, planets, stars, and other heavenly bodies
   The first *astronomical* observations with a telescope were made by the Italian scientist Galileo.

2. inconceivably large
   It is difficult to conceive of so *astronomical* a sum as a trillion dollars.

economic (*adj.*)
,e-kə'nä-mik

having to do with *economics* (literally, "household management") the social science dealing with production, distribution, and consumption
   The President's chief *economic* adviser expects that production will continue at the same rate for the rest of the year.

economical (*adj.*)
,e-kə'nä-mi-kəl

managed or managing without waste; thrifty; frugal; sparing
   Which is the most *economical* fuel for home heating—gas, electricity, or oil?

gastronome (*n.*)
'gas-trə,nōm

one who follows the principles of *gastronomy*, the art or science of good eating (literally, "management of the stomach") lover of good food; epicure; gourmet
   Being a *gastronome*, my uncle is well acquainted with the best restaurants in the city.

nemesis (*n.*)
'ne-mə-səs

(from *Nemesis*, the Greek goddess of vengeance who distributes or deals out what is due)
1. person that inflicts just punishment for evil deeds; avenger; scourge

The tyrant Macbeth was invincible in combat until he faced Macduff, who proved to be his *nemesis*.

2. formidable and usually victorious opponent
We would have ended the season without a defeat if not for our old *nemesis*, Greeley High.

EXERCISE 6.14: *NOM, NEM* WORDS

Fill each blank with the most appropriate word from group 14.

1. The villain had engineered several robberies before encountering his __?__ in the person of Sherlock Holmes.
2. Overproduction is a serious __?__ problem.
3. Some museums and art collectors have gone to __?__ expense to acquire famous paintings.
4. Underdeveloped nations are trying to improve the yield and quality of their crops by applying the principles of __?__ .
5. The acknowledged __?__ cheerfully aided her dining companions in making their selections from the menu.

15. PHAN, PHEN: "show," "appear"

cellophane (*n.*) 'se-lə,fān	cellulose substance that "shows" through or permits seeing through; transparent cellulose substance used as a wrapper When used as a wrapper, *cellophane* lets the purchaser see the contents of the package.
diaphanous (*adj.*) dī'af-ə-nəs	of such fine texture as to permit seeing through; sheer; transparent Pedestrians on the sidewalk could see some of the inside of the restaurant through its *diaphanous* curtains.
fancy (*n.*) 'fan-sē	imagination; illusion We must be able to distinguish between fact and *fancy*.
fantastic (*adj.*) fan'tas-tik	based on fantasy rather than reason; imaginary; unreal; odd; unbelievable Robert Fulton's proposal to build a steamboat was at first regarded as *fantastic*.

fantasy (*n.*)   illusory image; play of the mind; imagination; fancy
'fan-tə-sē   Selma is not sure whether she saw a face at the window. Perhaps it was only a *fantasy*.

phantom (*n.*)   something that has appearance but no reality; appar-
'fan-təm   ition; ghost; specter
    The *phantom* of the slain Caesar appeared to Brutus in a dream.

phenomenal (*adj.*)   extraordinary; remarkable; exceptional; unusual
fə'nä-mə-nəl   Bernadine has a *phenomenal* memory; she never forgets a face.

phenomenon (*n.*)   (literally, "an appearance")
fə'nä-mə,nän   1. any observable fact or event
    We do not see many adults traveling to work on bicycles, but in some foreign cities it is a common *phenomenon*.
    2. extraordinary person, event, or thing; wonder; prodigy
    Renowned as a composer and performer while yet in his teens, Mozart was a musical *phenomenon*.

EXERCISE 6.15: *PHAN, PHEN* WORDS

Fill each blank with the most appropriate word from group 15.

1. Sarah Bernhardt was no ordinary actress; she was a __?__.
2. Though these conclusions may seem __?__, I can show you they are based on reason.
3. If the apples are in a __?__ bag, you can tell how many there are without opening it.
4. Joan was sure someone was behind the door, but no one was there. It was just a __?__.
5. Mrs. Potter thought Christine's performance was __?__, but I found nothing extraordinary or remarkable in it.

---

16. THERM, THERMO: "heat"

---

diathermy (*n.*)   generation of heat in body tissues through high-
'dī-ə,thər-mē   frequency electric currents for medical purposes
    Diathermy may be used to treat arthritis, bursitis, and other conditions requiring heat treatment.

thermal (*adj.*)
'thər-məl

pertaining to heat; hot; warm
   At Lava Hot Springs in Idaho, visitors may bathe in the *thermal* mineral waters.

thermometer (*n.*)
thə(r)'mä-mə-tə(r)

instrument for measuring temperature
   At 6 a.m. the *thermometer* registered 32° Fahrenheit (0° Celsius).

thermonuclear (*adj.*)
,thər-mō'nü-klē-ə(r)

having to do with the fusion (joining together) at an extraordinarily high temperature, of the nuclei of atoms (as in the hydrogen bomb)
   It is believed that the sun gets its energy from *thermonuclear* reactions constantly taking place within it.

thermostat (*n.*)
'thər-mə,stat

automatic device for regulating temperature
   You can set the *thermostat* to shut off the heat when the room reaches a comfortable temperature.

EXERCISE 6.16: *THERM, THERMO* WORDS

Fill each blank with the most appropriate word from group 16.

1. The room was cold because the __?__ had been set for only 59° Fahrenheit (19° Celsius).
2. If you have a __?__ mounted outside your window, you don't need to go outside to learn what the temperature is.
3. The unbelievably intense heat required to start the __?__ reaction in a hydrogen bomb is obtained by exploding an atomic bomb.
4. Drugs, hot baths, and __?__ are some of the means used to relieve the pain of arthritis.
5. Hot Springs, Arkansas, derives its name from its numerous __?__ springs.

17. PROT, PROTO: "first"

protagonist (*n.*)
prō'ta-gə,nəst

the leading ("first") character in a play, novel, or story
   Brutus is the *protagonist* in William Shakespeare's *Julius Caesar*, and Anthony is the antagonist.

protocol (*n.*)
prō-tə,kȯl

1. first draft or record (of discussions, agreements, etc.) from which a treaty is drawn up; preliminary memorandum

The *protocol* initiated by the representatives of the three nations is expected to lead to a formal treaty.

2. rules of etiquette of the diplomatic corps, military services, etc.

It is a breach of *protocol* for a subordinate publicly to question the judgment of a superior officer.

protoplasm (*n.*)   (literally, "first molded material") fundamental sub-
'prō-tə,pla-zəm   stance of which all living things are composed
The presence of *protoplasm* distinguishes living from nonliving things.

prototype (*n.*)   first or original model of anything; model; pattern
'prō-tə,tīp   The crude craft in which the Wright brothers made the first successful flight in 1903 was the *prototype* of the modern airplane.

protozoan (*n.*)   (literally, "first animal") animal consisting only of a
,prō-tə'zō-ən   single cell
The tiny *protozoan* is believed to be the first animal to have appeared on earth.

EXERCISE 6.17: *PROT*, *PROTO* WORDS

Fill the blank with the appropriate word from group 17.

1. At the opening game of the baseball season in Washington, D.C., the President, according to __?__, is invited to throw out the first ball.
2. The ameba, a one-celled animal living in ponds and streams, is a typical __?__ .
3. Our Constitution has served as the __?__ of similar documents in democratic nations all over the world.
4. The movie star will not accept a minor part; she wants the role of the __?__ .
5. Living plants and animals consist of __?__ .

18. THESIS, THET: "set," "place," "put"

antithesis (*n.*)   (literally, "a setting against") direct opposite; contrary;
an'ti-thə-səs   reverse
I cannot vote for a candidate who stands for the *antithesis* of what I believe.

epithet (*n.*)
'e-pə,thet

(literally, something "placed on" or "added") characterizing word or phrase; descriptive name or title

Anna Mary Robertson Moses earned the *epithet* "Grandma" because she did not begin to paint until her late seventies.

hypothesis (*n.*)
hī'pä-thə-səs

(literally, "a placing under" or "supposing") supposition or assumption made as a basis for reasoning or research

When Columbus first presented his *hypothesis* that the earth is round, very few believed it.

synthesis (*n.*)
'sin-thə-səs

(literally, "putting together") combination of parts or elements into a whole

Much of the rubber we use is not a natural product but a *synthesis* of chemicals.

synthetic (*adj.*)
sin'the-tik

(literally, "put together") artificial; factitious; not of natural origin

Cotton is a natural fiber, but rayon and nylon are *synthetic*.

thesis (*n.*)
'thē-səs

1. claim put forward; proposition; statement; contention

Do you agree with Ellen's *thesis* that a student court would be good for our school?

2. essay written by a candidate for an advanced degree

Candidates for Ph.D. degrees usually must write a *thesis* based on original research.

Note: To form the plural of a word ending in *is*, change the *is* to *es*. Examples: *antitheses, hypotheses, theses*, etc.

EXERCISE 6.18: *THESIS, THET* WORDS

Fill each blank with the most appropriate word from group 18.

1. __?__ rubber is superior to natural rubber in some respects and inferior in others.
2. Jonathan's jalopy is a(n) __?__ of parts from several old cars.
3. In the *Odyssey*, you will often find the __?__ "wily" before Ulysses' name because he had a reputation for cunning.
4. Anyone who undertakes to write a(n) __?__ must know how to do research.
5. Their leader, timid, complaining, and weak, is the __?__ of what a leader should be.

19. ASTER, ASTR, ASTRO: "star"

aster (*n.*)
'as-tə(r)

plant having small, starlike flowers
Most *asters* bloom in the fall.

asterisk (*n.*)
'as-tə,risk

(literally, "little star") star-shaped mark (*) used to call attention to a footnote, omission, etc.
The *asterisk* after "Reduced to $9.95" refers the shopper to a footnote reading "Small and medium only."

asteroid (*n.*)
'as-tə,ròid

1. very small planet resembling a star in appearance
Compared to planet Earth, some *asteroids* are tiny, measuring less than a mile in diameter.

2. starfish
If an *asteroid* loses an arm to an attacker, it can grow back the missing arm.

astrologer (*n.*)
ə'strä-lə-jə(r)

person who practices *astrology*, a study professing to interpret the supposed influence of the moon, sun, and stars on human affairs
An *astrologer* would have people believe that their lives are regulated by the movements of the stars, planets, sun, and moon.

astronaut (*n.*)
'as-trə,nòt

(literally, "star sailor") traveler in outer space
Yuri Gagarin, the world's first *astronaut*, orbited the earth in an artificial satellite on April 12, 1961.

astronomer (*n.*)
ə'strä-nə-mə(r)

expert in *astronomy*, science of the stars, planets, sun, moon, and other heavenly bodies
Because the stars are so far away, *astronomers* measure their distance from Earth in "light-years" (one light-year equals about six trillion miles).

disaster (*n.*)
də'zas-tə(r)

(literally, "contrary star") sudden or extraordinary misfortune; calamity; catastrophe
The attack on Pearl Harbor was the worst *disaster* in the history of the U.S. Navy.

EXERCISE 6.19: *ASTER, ASTR, ASTRO* WORDS

Fill each blank with the most appropriate word from group 19.

1. Some __?__s are regarded as pests because they feed on oysters.
2. __?__s claim that your life is influenced by the position of the stars at the moment of your birth.

3. __?__s undergo a long and difficult period of training that equips them for the challenges of space travel.

4. Nations that continue to spend beyond their means are headed for economic __?__ .

5. A(n) __?__ alerts the reader to look for additional information at the foot of the page.

---

20. GRAM, GRAPH: "letter," "writing"

anagram (*n.*)
'a-nə,gram

word or phrase formed from another by transposing the letters
"Moat" is an *anagram* for "atom."

cartographer (*n.*)
kä(r)'tä-grə-fə(r)

(literally, "map writer") person skilled in *cartography*, the science or art of mapmaking
Ancient *cartographers* did not know of the existence of the Western Hemisphere.

cryptogram (*n.*)
'krip-tə,gram

something written in secret code
Military leaders, diplomats, and industrialists use *cryptograms* to relay secret information.

electrocardiogram (*n.*)
ə,lek-trō'kà(r)-dē-ō-,gram

"writing" or tracing made by an *electrocardiograph*, an instrument that records the amount of electricity the heart muscles produce during the heartbeat
After reading Henrietta's *electrocardiogram*, the physician assured her that her heart was working properly.

epigram (*n.*)
'e-pə,gram

(literally, something "written on" or "inscribed") bright or witty thought concisely and cleverly expressed
"The more things a man is ashamed of, the more respectable he is" is one of George Bernard Shaw's *epigrams*.

graphic (*adj.*)
'gra-fik

written or told in a clear, lively manner; vivid; picturesque
The reporter's *graphic* description made us feel that we were present at the scene.

graphite (*n.*)
'gra,fīt

soft black carbon used in lead pencils
"Lead" pencils do not contain lead, but rather a mixture of clay and *graphite*.

monogram (*n.*)
'mä-nə,gram

(literally, "one letter") person's initials interwoven or combined into one design
My *monogram* appears on the front of my warm-up jacket.

monograph (*n.*)
'mä-nə,graf

written account of a single thing or class of things
For her thesis, my sister wrote a *monograph* on the life of an obscure 19th-century composer.

stenographer (*n.*)
stə'nä-grə-fə(r)

person skilled in, or employed to do, *stenography* (literally, "narrow writing") the art of writing in shorthand
A court *stenographer* has to be able to take down more than 250 words a minute.

typographical (*adj.*)
,tī-pə'gra-fə-kəl

pertaining to or occurring in printing or *typography* (literally, "writing with type")
Proofs submitted by the printer should be carefully checked to eliminate *typographical* errors.

EXERCISE 6.20: *GRAM, GRAPH* WORDS

Fill each blank with the most appropriate word from group 20.

1. Modern __?__s use aerial photography to aid in mapmaking.
2. There is a(n) __?__ account of London in the 1580's in Marchette Chute's *Shakespeare of London.*
3. The patient's physicians cannot be certain that a heart attack has occurred until they have studied his __?__ .
4. "Reform" is a(n) __?__ for "former."
5. I knew it was Annabel's handkerchief because her __?__ was on it.

Review Exercises

REVIEW 9: GREEK WORD ELEMENTS 11–20

For each Greek word element in column I, write the *letter* of its correct meaning from column II.

COLUMN I	COLUMN II
1. NOM, NEM	(A) heat
2. ASTER, ASTR, ASTRO	(B) first
3. THERM, THERMO	(C) skin
4. ANT, ANTI	(D) management, distribution, law
5. DERM, DERMATO	(E) name, word
6. GRAM, GRAPH	(F) star
7. ONYM, ONOMATO	(G) show, appear
8. THESIS, THET	(H) against, opposite
9. PROT, PROTO	(I) letter, writing
10. PHAN, PHEN	(J) set, place, put

REVIEW 10: WORDBUILDING

Write the word defined below.

DEFINITION	WORD
1. putting together of parts into a whole	SYN (6)
2. remedy against the effects of a poison	(4) DOTE
3. punishment distributor	(3) ESIS
4. outer layer of the skin	EPI (4) IS
5. skilled writer of shorthand	STENO (5) ER
6. of unnamed origin	AN (4) OUS
7. first draft leading to a treaty	(5) COL
8. feeling against	(4) PATHY
9. expert in the science of the stars	(5) NOMER
10. any observable fact or event	(4) OMENON
11. automatic temperature-regulating device	(6) STAT
12. managing without waste	ECO (3) ICAL
13. first or original model	(5) TYPE
14. small star-resembling planet	(5) OID

15. use of words whose sound suggests their meaning   (7) POEIA
16. something having appearance but no reality   (4) TOM
17. word formed of transposed letters of another   ANA (4)
18. characterizing name added to ("put on") a person   EPI (4)
19. pertaining to heat   (5) AL
20. beneath the skin   HYPO (4) IC

REVIEW 11: SENTENCE COMPLETION

Fill each blank with the word from the list that best fits the context.

anonymous	antagonist
antidote	antipathy
antithesis	asterisk
asteroid	astrology
astronomy	epigram
gastronome	homonym
hypodermic	nemesis
phenomenal	protagonist
protocol	pseudonym
thesis	typographical

1. Henry's _?_ in the finals was the longtime _?_ who had defeated him in all six of their previous matches.
2. Nadine is the _?_ of a(n) _?_; she doesn't go to fancy restaurants, and she will eat any food that is wholesome and nourishing.
3. Pip, the _?_ of *Great Expectations*, has his education financed by a(n) _?_ benefactor who later identifies himself as Abel Magwitch.
4. The _?_ of this article is that dinosaurs became extinct after the earth collided with a(n) _?_ .
5. Unfortunately, many people know more about the false science of _?_ than about the true science of _?_ .
6. Because the author has a(n) _?_ to being in the public eye, she wrote her best-selling novels under a(n) _?_ .
7. The sentence ends with *mens sana in corpore sano**. The _?_ leads to a footnote explaining that the words are a Latin _?_ meaning "a healthy mind in a healthy body."
8. Because of a(n) _?_ error in the phonetic spelling of *wary* in my dictionary, I pronounced it as if it were a(n) _?_ of weary.
9. The patient who had accidentally swallowed the poisonous liquid was given a(n) _?_ injection of the appropriate _?_ .
10. Sending an undersecretary to greet the visiting foreign potentate was a breach of _?_ , as well as a(n) _?_ diplomatic blunder.

REVIEW 12: SYNONYMS

Avoid repetition by replacing the boldfaced word or expression with a synonym from the following words.

antiseptic	astronomical
cryptogram(s)	disaster
epithet	graphic
hypothesis	phenomenon
prototype	synthetic

1. The flowers were artificial. The fruit in the basket was artificial. The whole place had a(n) **artificial** appearance.
2. If no **substance to prevent infection** is applied, the wound may become infected.
3. Our enormous national debt keeps growing larger and larger; it has become **inconceivably large.**
4. Dealers had catastrophic losses in the fall. If sales had not picked up before Christmas, the year would have ended in financial **catastrophe.**
5. What **descriptive title** can better describe America than ''the Beautiful''?
6. Their **coded messages** were undecipherable only so long as no one else knew their code.
7. Her **lively** manner of expression makes everything she describes come to life.
8. The return of spring is truly a(n) **extraordinary event.** Unfortunately, some people are so used to it that they rarely think it is extraordinary.
9. Sometimes a movie is so successful that it becomes the **original model** on which a series of later films is modeled.
10. The alchemists assumed that a way could be found to turn base metals into gold, but they were never able to verify their **assumption.**

REVIEW 13: ANTONYMS

Enter the word from the list below that is most nearly the opposite of the boldfaced word or words.

anonymous	antagonist
antipathy	antonym
economical	fancy
homonym	phenomenal
protagonist	synthetic

1. When those that we have befriended become intolerable, our **affection** for them may turn to __?__ .
2. Since last summer's drought, we have reduced our **extravagant** uses of water and become more __?__ .
3. When we read fairy tales, we leave **reality** and enter the realm of __?__ .
4. "Authentic" is a **synonym** of "genuine," and "fraudulent" is one of its __?__s.
5. The soles are made of **natural** leather, but the heels are __?__ .
6. In last year's play, Sheila was a **minor** character, but in this one she is the __?__ .
7. Joan of Arc had an **ordinary** peasant background, but she provided France with __?__ leadership.
8. **Words that do not sound alike** cannot be called __?__s.
9. The donors have asked not to be **named**; they prefer to remain __?__ .
10. Many a nation that was once our __?__ in the United Nations is now our **supporter**.

REVIEW 14: CONCISE WRITING

Express the thought of each sentence below in no more than four words.

1. What assumption did you make as a basis for reasoning?
2. No one can predict when sudden or extraordinary misfortunes will strike.
3. Is he the one with whom you have been contending?
4. Letters that do not disclose the name of the writer are not worthy of trust.
5. No one who practices the art of good eating devours food.
6. Everyone enjoys witty thoughts that are concisely and cleverly expressed.
7. Gail is taking courses in crop production and soil management.
8. Amebas are animals that consist only of a single cell.
9. People who do not conform to generally accepted patterns of behavior pay no attention to the rules of etiquette.
10. Our bodies manufacture substances that counteract the effects of disease-causing germs and their poisons.

REVIEW 15: SYNONYM SUMMARY

Each line, when completed, should have three words similar in meaning. Enter the missing letters.

1. unbel (2) vable — (2) real — (3) tastic
2. fr (1) g (1) l — sp (1) ring — eco (3) ical
3. (2) ponent — advers (1) ry — (2) tagonist
4. w (1) rm — h (1) t — th (1) rm (1) l
5. rev (1) rse — opp (1) s (1) te — (4) thesis
6. v (1) v (1) d — pictur (2) que — gr (1) ph (1) c
7. artifi (2) al — facti (2) ous — syn (2) etic
8. (1) nmity — rep (1) gn (1) nce — (2) tipathy
9. s (1) pposition — as (3) ption — (2) pothesis
10. n (1) meless — (2) identified — an (2) ymous
11. w (1) nder — pr (1) d (1) gy — phe (3) enon
12. c (1) l (1) mity — (2) tastrophe — dis (2) ter
13. sh (2) r — transp (1) rent — (2) aphanous
14. m (1) del — patt (1) rn — (2) ototype
15. app (1) r (1) tion — (1) host — ph (1) nt (1) m
16. r (1) m (1) dy — c (2) ntermeasure — an (2) dote
17. ill (1) sion — (1) magination — f (2) cy
18. prop (1) s (1) tion — cont (1) ntion — th (1) s (1) s
19. g (2) rmet — ep (1) c (1) re — gastr (1) n (1) me
20. av (1) nger — sc (2) rge — n (1) m (1) sis

REVIEW 16: ANALOGIES

Which lettered pair of words—*a, b, c, d,* or *e*—most nearly expresses the same relationship as the capitalized pair?

1. ASTEROID : PLANET
   (a) skyscraper : edifice
   (b) deluge : shower
   (c) crowd : gathering
   (d) microbe : organism
   (e) age : interval

2. FANTASY : FACT
   (a) significance : meaning
   (b) warmth : cordiality
   (c) antipathy : affection
   (d) celerity : speed
   (e) equity : justice

3. DERMATOLOGY : SKIN
- (a) chronology : story
- (b) psychology : mind
- (c) anthology : volume
- (d) biology : science
- (e) apology : blame

4. ASTRONOMICAL : LARGE
- (a) immature : old
- (b) nominal : significant
- (c) extraordinary : common
- (d) priceless : cheap
- (e) infinitesimal : small

5. STEEL : STEAL
- (a) ribbon : bow
- (b) here : there
- (c) friend : foe
- (d) peace : piece
- (e) flaw : defect

6. SYNTHETIC : ARTIFICIAL
- (a) restive : restful
- (b) healthful : deleterious
- (c) partial : objective
- (d) toxic : antiseptic
- (e) sagacious : wise

7. PROTAGONIST : STORY
- (a) standard-bearer : cause
- (b) tenor : opera
- (c) finalist : tournament
- (d) professor : faculty
- (e) soprano : choir

8. PHANTOM : EXISTENCE
- (a) river : source
- (b) progenitor : descendant
- (c) statue : mobility
- (d) cryptogram : solution
- (e) chaos : disorder

9. THERMOSTAT : COMFORT
- (a) alarm : security
- (b) pandemonium : harmony
- (c) digression : direction
- (d) defection : unity
- (e) lamp : electricity

   Hint: A **thermostat** provides **comfort**.

10. HYPOTHESIS : REASONING
- (a) unpacking : moving
- (b) landing : flying
- (c) review : learning
- (d) rebuttal : debating
- (e) soil preparation : planting

CHAPTER 7

Expanding Vocabulary Through Derivatives

Suppose you have just learned a new word—*literate,* meaning "able to read and write; educated." If you know how to form derivatives, you have in reality learned not one new word but several: you have learned *literate, illiterate,* and *semiliterate; literately, illiterately,* and *semiliterately; literacy, illiteracy,* and *semiliteracy,* etc.

This unit will help you to expand your vocabulary by teaching you how to form and spell important derivatives.

What is a derivative?

A derivative is a word formed by adding a prefix, or a suffix, or both a prefix and a suffix, to a word or root.

PREFIX		WORD		DERIVATIVE
with	+	hold	=	withhold
(*back*)				(*hold back*)

PREFIX		ROOT		DERIVATIVE
in	+	flux	=	influx
(*in*)		(*flow*)		(*inflow; inpouring*)

WORD		SUFFIX		DERIVATIVE
literate	+	ly	=	literately
(*educated*)		(*manner*)		(*in an educated manner*)

	ROOT		SUFFIX		DERIVATIVE
	leg	+	ible	=	legible
	(read)		*(able to be)*		*(able to be read)*

PREFIX		WORD		SUFFIX		DERIVATIVE
semi	+	literate	+	ly	=	semiliterately
(half; partly)						*(in a partly educated manner)*

PREFIX		ROOT		SUFFIX		DERIVATIVE
il	+	leg	+	ible	=	illegible
(not)						*(not able to be read)*

Terms used in this unit

A derivative may be a noun, an adjective, a verb, or an adverb.

A **noun** is a word naming a person, place, thing, or quality. In the following sentences, all the italicized words are nouns:

1. The enthusiastic *student* very quickly read the partially finished *composition* to the amused *class*.
2. *Knowledge* is *power*.

An **adjective** is a word that modifies (describes) a noun. The following words in sentence 1 are adjectives: *enthusiastic, finished, amused*.

A **verb** is a word that expresses action or a state of being. The verbs in the sentences above are *read* (sentence 1) and *is* (sentence 2).

An **adverb** is a word that modifies a verb, an adjective, or another adverb. In sentence 1 above, *quickly* is an adverb because it modifies the verb "read"; *partially* is an adverb because it modifies the adjective "finished"; and *very* is an adverb because it modifies the adverb "quickly."

Vowels are the letters *a, e, i, o,* and *u.*

Consonants are all the other letters of the alphabet.

FORMING DERIVATIVES BY ATTACHING PREFIXES AND SUFFIXES

1. Attaching Prefixes

When you add the prefix *mis* to the word *spelled,* does the new word have one *s* or two? For help with problems of this sort, learn the following rule:

Rule: Do not add or omit a letter when attaching a prefix to a word. Keep *all* the letters of the prefix and *all* the letters of the word. Example:

PREFIX		WORD		DERIVATIVE
mis	+	spelled	=	misspelled
mis	+	informed	=	misinformed

EXERCISE 7.1

Write the derivative formed by attaching the prefix to the word.

	PREFIX		WORD			PREFIX		WORD
1.	over	+	ripe		14.	dis	+	interred
2.	dis	+	integrate		15.	semi	+	circle
3.	un	+	necessary		16.	un	+	nerve
4.	anti	+	aircraft		17.	pre	+	existence
5.	in	+	audible		18.	dis	+	solution
6.	under	+	rated		19.	extra	+	curricular
7.	fore	+	seen		20.	un	+	navigable
8.	extra	+	ordinary		21.	over	+	run
9.	un	+	noticed		22.	in	+	appropriate
10.	with	+	held		23.	semi	+	autonomous
11.	e	+	migrate		24.	dis	+	satisfied
12.	mis	+	spent		25.	un	+	abridged
13.	over	+	estimated					

2. Attaching the Prefix *IN*

Sometimes, the N in the prefix IN changes to another letter. To learn when this occurs, study the following rule:

Rule: Before *l*, IN becomes IL, as in *illegal, illiterate,* etc.
Before *m* or *p*, IN becomes IM, as in *immature, impure,* etc.
Before *r*, IN becomes IR, as in *irrational, irregular,* etc.

EXERCISE 7.2

Write the negative word by attaching the prefix *in, il, im,* or *ir* to the word in column II.

I. NEGATIVE PREFIX		II. WORD	I. NEGATIVE PREFIX		II. WORD
1. __?__	+	gratitude	9. _____	+	personal
2. _____	+	patiently	10. _____	+	legible
3. _____	+	responsible	11. _____	+	plausible
4. _____	+	equitable	12. _____	+	articulate
5. _____	+	moderate	13. _____	+	material
6. _____	+	literacy	14. _____	+	reversible
7. _____	+	replaceable	15. _____	+	security
8. _____	+	consistently			

3. Attaching Suffixes

What happens when you add the suffix *ness* to *stubborn?* Does the new word have one *n* or two? Questions of this sort will never bother you once you have learned this simple rule:

Rule: Do not omit, add, or change a letter when attaching a suffix to a word—unless the word ends in *y* or silent *e.* Keep *all* the letters of the word and *all* the letters of the suffix. Examples:

WORD		SUFFIX		DERIVATIVE
stubborn	+	ness	=	stubbornness
conscious	+	ness	=	consciousness
punctual	+	ly	=	punctually
anonymous	+	ly	=	anonymously
disagree	+	able	=	disagreeable

EXERCISE 7.3

Attach the suffix to the word.

WORD		SUFFIX		WORD		SUFFIX
1. govern	+	ment	**6.**	embarrass	+	ment
2. tail	+	less	**7.**	sudden	+	ness
3. synonym	+	ous	**8.**	room	+	mate
4. radio	+	ed	**9.**	ski	+	er
5. unilateral	+	ly	**10.**	foresee	+	able

---

4. Attaching Suffixes to Words Ending in Y

Final *y* can be troublesome. Sometimes it changes to *i*; sometimes it does not change at all. To learn how to deal with final *y*, follow these helpful rules:

Rule 1: If the letter before final *y* is a consonant, change the *y* to *i* before attaching a suffix.

WORD		SUFFIX		DERIVATIVE
comply	+	ed	=	complied
sturdy	+	est	=	sturdiest
costly	+	ness	=	costliness
ordinary	+	ly	=	ordinarily

Exception A: Except before *ing*.

comply	+	ing	=	complying

Exception B. Learn these special exceptions: dryly, dryness, shyly, shyness, babyish, jellylike.

Rule 2: If the letter before final *y* is a vowel, do *not* change the *y* before attaching a suffix.

destroy	+	ed	=	destroyed
play	+	ful	=	playful

Exceptions: laid, paid, said, and their compounds (mislaid, underpaid, unsaid, etc.); daily.

EXERCISE 7.4

Write the derivatives. Watch your spelling.

	WORD		SUFFIX		WORD		SUFFIX
1.	decay	+	ed	11.	ceremony	+	ous
2.	fancy	+	ful	12.	deny	+	al
3.	stealthy	+	ly	13.	momentary	+	ly
4.	foolhardy	+	ness	14.	crafty	+	er
5.	magnify	+	ing	15.	display	+	ed
6.	plucky	+	est	16.	bury	+	al
7.	defy	+	ance	17.	shy	+	ly
8.	overpay	+	ed	18.	oversupply	+	ing
9.	accompany	+	ment	19.	harmony	+	ous
10.	costly	+	ness	20.	disqualify	+	ed

EXERCISE 7.5

Two words have been omitted from each line except the first. Complete each of the other lines so that it will correspond to the first.

	I. ADJECTIVE	II. ADJECTIVE ENDING IN ER	III. ADJECTIVE ENDING IN EST
1.	clumsy	clumsier	clumsiest
2.	?	noisier	?
3.	?	?	sturdiest
4.	uneasy	?	?
5.	?	greedier	?
6.	flimsy	?	?
7.	?	wearier	?
8.	?	?	heartiest
9.	wary	?	?
10.	?	unhappier	?

5. Attaching Suffixes to Words Ending in Silent *E*

When you add a suffix to a word ending in silent *e*, what happens to the *e*? Is it kept or dropped? Here are the rules:

Rule 1: Drop silent *e* if the suffix begins with a vowel.

WORD		SUFFIX		DERIVATIVE
blame	+	able	=	blamable
secure	+	ity	=	security
innovate	+	or	=	innovator

Exception A: If the word ends in *ce* or *ge*, and the suffix begins with *a* or *o*, keep the *e*.

service	+	able	=	serviceable
courage	+	ous	=	courageous

Exception B: Learn these special exceptions: acreage, mileage, singe-ing, canoeing, hoeing, shoeing.

Rule 2: Keep silent *e* if the suffix begins with a consonant.

hope	+	ful	=	hopeful
profuse	+	ly	=	profusely
postpone	+	ment	=	postponement

Exceptions: argument, awful, duly, truly, wholly, ninth.

EXERCISE 7.6

Write the derivatives. Watch your spelling.

WORD		SUFFIX		WORD		SUFFIX
1. depreciate	+	ion	10. dawdle	+	er
2. survive	+	al	11. reverse	+	ible
3. suspense	+	ful	12. immaculate	+	ly
4. fatigue	+	ing	13. spine	+	less
5. censure	+	able	14. outrage	+	ous
6. acquiesce	+	ent	15. demote	+	ion
7. nine	+	th	16. homogenize	+	ed
8. hostile	+	ity	17. recharge	+	able
9. malice	+	ious	18. abate	+	ment

19. emancipate + or
20. dispute   + able
21. whole   + ly
22. provoke   + ing

23. argue   + ment
24. fragile   + ity
25. replace   + able

---

6. Attaching the Suffix *LY*

Rule: To change an adjective into an adverb, add *ly*.

ADJECTIVE	SUFFIX		ADVERB
close	+ ly	=	closely
firm	+ ly	=	firmly
usual	+ ly	=	usually

Exception A: If the adjective ends in *y*, remember to change *y* to *i* before adding *ly*.

easy	+ ly	=	easily

Exception B: If the adjective ends in *ic*, add *al* plus *ly*.

tragic	+ al	+ ly	=	tragically
heroic	+ al	+ ly	=	heroically

However, *public* has only *ly*:

public	+ ly	=	publicly

Exception C: If the adjective ends in *le* preceded by a consonant, simply change the *le* to *ly*.

ADJECTIVE	ADVERB
able	ably
simple	simply
idle	idly

EXERCISE 7.7

Change the following adjectives into adverbs.

ADJECTIVE

1. overwhelming	11. punctual
2. normal	12. exclusive
3. interscholastic	13. unwary
4. mutual	14. chronic
5. ample	15. synthetic
6. conspicuous	16. intermittent
7. economic	17. manual
8. outspoken	18. heavy
9. graphic	19. infallible
10. incontrovertible	20. frantic

EXERCISE 7.8

For each noun, write an adjective ending in *ic* and an adverb ending in *ally*; for example: **democracy, democratic, democratically.**

1. autocracy	6. astronomy
2. stenography	7. diplomacy
3. antagonist	8. bureaucracy
4. pedagogy	9. autobiography
5. economics	10. symmetry

7. Doubling Final Consonants Before Suffixes

Why is the *r* in *defer* doubled (defe*rr*ed) when *ed* is added, whereas the *r* in *differ* is not (differed)? Why is the *n* in *plan* doubled (pla*nn*ing) before *ing*, whereas the *n* in *burn* is not (bur*n*ing)?

To clear up these matters, review two rules for doubling final consonants.

Rule 1: In a one-syllable word, double the final consonant before a suffix beginning with a vowel.

WORD		SUFFIXES		DERIVATIVES
plan	+	ing, er	=	planning, planner
stop	+	ed, age	=	stopped, stoppage
big	+	er, est	=	bigger, biggest

Exception A: If the final consonant comes right after two vowels, do not double it.

fail	+	ed, ing	=	failed, failing
stoop	+	ed, ing	=	stooped, stooping

Exception B: If the final consonant comes right after another consonant, do not double it.

warm	+	er, est	=	warmer, warmest
last	+	ed, ing	=	lasted, lasting

Rule 2. In a word of two or more syllables, double the final consonant only if it is in an *accented* syllable before a suffix beginning with a vowel.

deFER'	+	ed, ing, al	=	deferred, deferring, deferral
resubMIT'	+	ed, ing	=	resubmitted, resubmitting

Note carefully that the rule does not apply if the final consonant is in an *unaccented* syllable.

DIF'fer	+	ed, ing, ent	=	differed, differing, different
BEN'efit	+	ed, ing	=	benefited, benefiting

Exception A: The rule does not apply if the final consonant comes right after two vowels.

obTAIN'	+	ed, ing	=	obtained, obtaining
conCEAL'	+	ed, ing	=	concealed, concealing

Exception B: The rule does not apply if the final consonant comes right after another consonant.

abDUCT'	+	ed, ing, or	=	abducted, abducting, abductor
comMEND'	+	ed, ing, able	=	commended, commending, commendable

Exception C: The rule does not apply if the accent shifts back to the first syllable.

$$conFER' + ence = CON'ference$$
$$preFER' + ence = PREF'erence$$
$$reFER' + ence = REF'erence$$

However: $exCEL' + ence = EX'cellence$

EXERCISE 7.9

Write the derivatives, paying careful attention to the spelling.

WORD		SUFFIX	WORD		SUFFIX
1. concur	+	ing	14. defer	+	ence
2. entail	+	ed	15. propel	+	ant
3. abhor	+	ent	16. inter	+	ing
4. flat	+	er	17. append	+	age
5. retract	+	able	18. covet	+	ous
6. refer	+	al	19. discredit	+	ed
7. dispel	+	ed	20. adapt	+	able
8. deter	+	ent	21. cower	+	ing
9. ungag	+	ed	22. disinter	+	ed
10. drum	+	er	23. pilfer	+	er
11. elicit	+	ing	24. slim	+	est
12. imperil	+	ed	25. excel	+	ent
13. absorb	+	ent			

8. Troublesome Suffixes

Why should *dispensable* end in *able* but *sensible* in *ible*? Why should *foreigner* end in *er* but *debtor* in *or*? Unhappily, there are no simple rules to guide you in these matters. You will have to learn individually each word with a troublesome suffix and consult the dictionary when in doubt. The following review should prove helpful:

1. Attaching *able* or *ible*. Study the following adjectives:

ABLE	IBLE
amiable	accessible
changeable	credible
equitable	fallible
formidable	flexible
hospitable	illegible
impregnable	incompatible
indomitable	incontrovertible
lovable	invincible
noticeable	reversible
unquenchable	visible

Note that adjectives ending in *able* become nouns ending in *ability*. On the other hand, adjectives ending in *ible* become nouns ending in *ibility*.

ADJECTIVE	NOUN	ADJECTIVE	NOUN
incapable	incapability	audible	audibility
pliable	pliability	resistible	resistibility

2. Attaching suffixes meaning "one who" or "that which": *er, or, ent,* or *ant*. Study these nouns:

ER	OR	ENT	ANT
abstainer	aggressor	adherent	assistant
abuser	benefactor	antecedent	consultant
commuter	bisector	belligerent	contestant
contender	collaborator	correspondent	defendant
dispenser	duplicator	current	deodorant
retainer	exhibitor	dependent	immigrant
typographer	interceptor	insurgent	inhabitant
underseller	precursor	opponent	participant
withholder	reflector	precedent	pendant
wrangler	transgressor	proponent	tenant

3. Attaching *ant* or *ent*. Study these adjectives:

ANT	ENT
defiant	adjacent
discordant	affluent
dormant	coherent
extravagant	decadent
hesitant	fluent
ignorant	imminent
incessant	latent
irrelevant	negligent
reliant	permanent
vigilant	vehement

Note that adjectives ending in *ant* become nouns ending in *ance* or *ancy*. On the other hand, adjectives ending in *ent* become nouns ending in *ence* or *ency*.

ADJECTIVE	NOUN
defiant	defiance
coherent	coherence
dormant	dormancy
fluent	fluency
hesitant	hesitance, hesitancy
permanent	permanence, permanency

EXERCISE 7.10

Supply the missing letter, and write the complete word.

1. inflex __?__ ble
2. ten __?__ ncy
3. vehem __?__ nce
4. benefact __?__ r
5. self-reli __?__ nce
6. vis __?__ bility
7. dispens __?__ r
8. relev __?__ nce
9. infall __?__ bility
10. unchange __?__ ble
11. collaborat __?__ r
12. impregn __?__ bility
13. reflect __?__ r
14. curr __?__ ncy
15. correspond __?__ nce
16. contend __?__ r
17. imperman __?__ nt
18. irrevers __?__ ble
19. inaccess __?__ bility
20. semidepend __?__ nt

EXERCISE 7.11

For each noun, write the corresponding adjective. (The first adjective is **capable.**)

NOUN

1. capability	11. inconstancy
2. urgency	12. malevolence
3. resistance	13. indefatigability
4. infallibility	14. observance
5. subservience	15. cogency
6. compatibility	16. adaptability
7. eminence	17. incandescence
8. truancy	18. unavailability
9. audibility	19. compliance
10. opulence	20. transiency

CHAPTER 8

Understanding Word Relationships and Word Analogies

Word Relationships

ROBIN : BIRD

What relationship is there between *robin* and *bird*? Obviously, a *robin* is a *bird*. So, too, is a sparrow, a woodpecker, a crow, a gull, a pigeon, a blue jay, etc. *Bird*, clearly, is the large category of which *robin* is one member.

If we call *robin* word A and *bird* word B, we may express the *robin* : *bird* relationship by saying "A is a member of the B category."

Here are some additional pairs of words with an explanation of the relationship in each pair. As in the above, let us call the first word A and the second B.

MINE : COAL

Mine is the source from which we obtain the substance *coal*. To express the *mine* : *coal* relationship, we may say "A is the source of B."

SPADE : DIGGING

A *spade* is a kind of shovel that is used for *digging*. The relationship here is "A is used for B."

TEMPERATURE : THERMOMETER

> *Temperature* is measured by a *thermometer*. The relationship in this pair is "A is measured by B."

MEEK : SUBMIT

> Anyone who is *meek* ("yielding without resentment when ordered about") will usually *submit* ("give in"). We may express this relationship as "An A person is likely to B."

To find the relationship between a pair of words, go through the kind of reasoning shown in the preceding paragraphs. When you have determined the relationship, sum it up in a very short sentence using A and B, as in the following examples:

WORD PAIR	RELATIONSHIP
PAUPER : MEANS	A lacks B.
FOUNDATION : EDIFICE	A supports B.
SECURITY GUARD : THEFT	A guards against B.
BLINDFOLD : VISION	A interferes with B.
LITERATE : READ	One who is A can B.
ILLNESS : ABSENCE	A may cause B.
SEIZING : TAKING	A is a sudden, forcible form of B.
GREGARIOUS : COMPANY	One who is A likes B.
PEBBLE : STONE	A is a small B.
PAINTER : EASEL	A uses B.

Word Analogy Questions

So far, we have been dealing only with one relationship at a time. A *word analogy question*, however, tests your ability to see that the relationship between one pair of words is the same as the relationship between another pair of words. Here is a typical word analogy question.

Directions: Write the *letter* of the pair of words related to each other in the same way that the capitalized words are related to each other.

PREFACE : INDEX :: ___?___

(A) tool : drill
(B) departure : trip
(C) famine : drought
(D) appetizer : dessert
(E) water : well

Solution: The first step is to find the relationship in the capitalized pair *preface : index*. Since a *preface* comes at the beginning of a book, and an *index* at the end, the relationship here is "A begins that which B ends."

The next step is to analyze the five suggested answers to see which has the same relationship as *preface : index*. Since an *appetizer* comes at the beginning of dinner and a *dessert* at the end, the correct answer is obviously D.

EXERCISE 8.1   Select the lettered pair that best expresses a relationship similar to that expressed in the capitalized pair. Write the *letter* A, B, C, D, or E.

1. NEEDLE : STITCH :: _?_

(A) shears : prune   (D) stake : bush
(B) rake : mow   (E) wrench : soak
(C) spade : level

2. FATHOM : DEPTH :: _?_

(A) calorie : temperature   (D) dive : surface
(B) search : treasure   (E) base : height
(C) minute : time

3. DAM : FLOW :: _?_

(A) research : information   (D) autocracy : liberty
(B) laws : justice   (E) education : opportunity
(C) reporters : news

4. FOREST : TIMBER :: _?_

(A) magnet : filings   (D) clay : earth
(B) art : museum   (E) zoo : spectators
(C) quarry : stone

5. NECK : BOTTLE :: _?_

(A) bonnet : head   (D) metal : leather
(B) rim : wheel   (E) chain : link
(C) roof : cellar

6. TYRO : EXPERIENCE :: _?_

(A) despot : power   (D) coward : courage
(B) razor : sharpness   (E) farewell : welcome
(C) artisan : skill

7. GRAVEL : PIT :: __?__

(A) oil : well
(B) cement : sand
(C) tunnel : cave
(D) asphalt : road
(E) crest : mountain

8. FACULTY : TEACHER :: __?__

(A) congregation : clergy
(B) crew : captain
(C) act : play
(D) choir : singer
(E) election : candidate

9. KITTEN : CAT :: __?__

(A) ewe : lamb
(B) tiger : cub
(C) seedling : flower
(D) fawn : deer
(E) napkin : towel

10. MICROSCOPE : BIOLOGIST :: __?__

(A) horoscope : scientist
(B) medicine : druggist
(C) lens : photography
(D) telescope : astronomer
(E) spectacles : optometry

11. LIEUTENANT : OFFICER :: __?__

(A) actor : understudy
(B) moon : planet
(C) veteran : newcomer
(D) sophomore : undergraduate
(E) passenger : conductor

12. BIRTH : DECEASE :: __?__

(A) takeoff : flight
(B) negligence : dismissal
(C) opera : finale
(D) dawn : sunset
(E) competition : defeat

13. FOG : VISION :: __?__

(A) superstition : ignorance
(B) evidence : testimony
(C) malnutrition : growth
(D) rain : overflow
(E) vigilance : safety

14. PLANT : HARVEST :: __?__

(A) factory : equipment
(B) launch : decommission
(C) sow : irrigate
(D) clump : shrub
(E) mishap : carelessness

15. COD : FISH :: __?__

(A) immunity : disease
(B) band : trumpet
(C) mutiny : authority

(D) penalty : offense
(E) pneumonia : illness

Working Backwards in Completing Analogies

Sometimes you may find it difficult to determine the exact relationship between word A and word B in a given pair. In such cases it is advisable to work backwards from the five choices suggested for the answer. The chances are that one of these choices will lead you to the A : B relationship. Consider the following question:

BANKRUPTCY : PROFIT ::

(A) population : housing
(B) fatigue : effort
(C) congestion : space

(D) memory : knowledge
(E) flood : thaw

Suppose you are having trouble finding the relationship between *bankruptcy* and *profit*. Try the back door: find the relationship of each suggested pair and discover which relationship applies also to the capitalized pair. This method is illustrated below.

BANKRUPTCY : PROFIT ::

(A) population : housing. The relationship is ''A needs B'' (*population needs housing*). But bankruptcy does not need profit; once bankruptcy has occurred, it is too late for profit to be of help. Therefore, choice A is incorrect.

BANKRUPTCY : PROFIT ::

(B) fatigue : effort. The relationship is ''A results from too much B'' (*fatigue results from too much effort*). Since bankruptcy does not result from too much profit, choice B is incorrect.

BANKRUPTCY : PROFIT ::

(C) congestion : space. The relationship is ''A results from a lack of B'' (*congestion results from a lack of space*). Bankruptcy results from a lack of profit. Choice C looks correct, but let's test the remaining choices.

BANKRUPTCY : PROFIT ::

(D) memory : knowledge. The relationship is "A stores B" (*memory stores knowledge*). Since bankruptcy does not store profit, choice D is incorrect.

BANKRUPTCY : PROFIT ::

(E) flood : thaw. The relationship is "A may result from B" (*a flood may result from a thaw*). But bankruptcy does not result from profit. Therefore, choice E is incorrect.

Answer: C

EXERCISE 8.2 The following questions are more difficult than those in the previous exercise. If you cannot readily find the relationship between word A and word B in the given pair, try the "working backwards" method described above.

1. SOLVENT : PAY ::

(A) indigent : thrive
(B) innocent : acquit
(C) loyal : adhere
(D) punctual : tardy
(E) lavish : economize

2. ANTISEPTIC : BACTERIA ::

(A) soldier : nation
(B) hair : scalp
(C) pseudonym : author
(D) prescription : cure
(E) education : ignorance

3. INTERMEDIARY : SETTLEMENT ::

(A) belligerent : peace
(B) prosecutor : conviction
(C) adherent : pact
(D) strife : recess
(E) rumor : discovery

4. GENEROUS : FORGIVE ::

(A) pliable : yield
(B) spineless : resist
(C) opinionated : change
(D) conspicuous : hide
(E) impatient : delay

5. DISTANCE : ODOMETER ::

(A) weight : scale
(B) heat : barometer
(C) quiz : knowledge
(D) map : compass
(E) clock : time

6. GUILTLESS : BLAME ::

(A) unbiased : prejudice
(B) bankrupt : debt
(C) sincere : honesty

(D) apprehensive : worry
(E) verdict : acquittal

7. AUTOMATON : ORIGINALITY ::

(A) ambassador : goodwill
(B) pioneer : foresight
(C) hothead : equanimity

(D) guest : hospitality
(E) benefactor : generosity

8. CONJUNCTION : CLAUSES ::

(A) barrier : neighbors
(B) paragraph : phrases
(C) door : hinges

(D) bridge : shores
(E) preposition : nouns

9. IRREVOCABLE : ALTER ::

(A) irreproachable : trust
(B) available : obtain
(C) audible : hear

(D) intelligible : comprehend
(E) pressing : defer

10. SMOG : POLLUTANTS ::

(A) fog : travel
(B) wars : destruction
(C) ambition : diligence

(D) contagion : disinfectants
(E) exhaustion : overwork

11. MANACLE : MOVEMENT ::

(A) sailor : crew
(B) pendant : chain
(C) gag : speech

(D) manual : information
(E) invalid : vigor

12. EROSION : WATER ::

(A) earthquake : destruction
(B) ocean : wind
(C) inauguration : presidency

(D) aging : time
(E) solid : liquid

13. ARISTOCRAT : COUNT ::

(A) flower : leaf
(B) senator : voter
(C) professional : amateur

(D) civilian : soldier
(E) insect : ant

14. DESPOTIC : DOMINEER ::

(A) disgruntled : rejoice
(B) cordial : rebuff
(C) timorous : withdraw

(D) aggressive : tremble
(E) malcontent : cooperate

15. HOLD : VESSEL ::

(A) tail : airplane
(B) vault : security
(C) site : edifice

(D) garage : vehicle
(E) basement : house

Alternate-Type Analogy Questions

In the following alternate type of analogy question, you are given the first pair and the first word of the second pair. You are asked to complete the second pair by selecting one of five suggested words.

EXERCISE 8.3   Write the *letter* of the word that best completes the analogy.

1. *Justice* is to *judge* as *health* is to

    (A) lawyer   (C) physician   (E) jury
    (B) nutrition   (D) disease

2. *Dentist* is to *teeth* as *dermatologist* is to

    (A) heart   (C) eyes   (E) lungs
    (B) feet   (D) skin

3. *Quart* is to *gallon* as *week* is to

    (A) pint   (C) liquid   (E) measure
    (B) year   (D) month

4. *Horse* is to *stable* as *dog* is to

    (A) leash   (C) bone   (E) kennel
    (B) curb   (D) muzzle

5. *Pear* is to *potato* as *peach* is to

    (A) carrot   (C) nectarine   (E) tomato
    (B) cucumber   (D) melon

6. *Composer* is to *symphony* as *playwright* is to

   (A) essay   (C) novel   (E) copyright
   (B) cast   (D) drama

7. *Friction* is to *rubber* as *repetition* is to

   (A) skill   (C) literacy   (E) knowledge
   (B) novelty   (D) memory

8. *Pond* is to *lake* as *asteroid* is to

   (A) moon   (C) planet   (E) meteor
   (B) comet   (D) orbit

9. *Bear* is to *fur* as *fish* is to

   (A) seaweed   (C) scales   (E) gills
   (B) fins   (D) water

10. *Condemn* is to *criticize* as *scald* is to

    (A) praise   (C) freeze   (E) burn
    (B) heat   (D) thaw

11. *Pearl* is to *oyster* as *ivory* is to

    (A) piano   (C) tusks   (E) tortoise
    (B) crocodile   (D) elephant

12. *Sheep* is to *fold* as *bluefish* is to

    (A) boat   (C) bait   (E) shore
    (B) line   (D) school

13. *Drama* is to *intermission* as *conflict* is to

    (A) feud   (C) reconciliation (E) stage
    (B) truce   (D) intervention

14. *War* is to *hawk* as *peace* is to

    (A) eagle   (C) dove   (E) owl
    (B) gull   (D) falcon

15. *Ballistics* is to *projectiles* as *genealogy* is to

    (A) exploration (C) minerals   (E) missiles
    (B) lineage   (D) causes

16. *Pistol* is to *holster* as *airliner* is to

    (A) fuselage   (C) runway   (E) landing
    (B) hangar   (D) fuel

17. *Frugal* is to *waste* as *infallible* is to

   (A) dread   (C) criticize   (E) err
   (B) save   (D) prosper

18. *Toothpaste* is to *tube* as *graphite* is to

   (A) pencil   (C) coal   (E) tar
   (B) lead   (D) cable

19. *State* is to *traitor* as *plant* is to

   (A) soil   (C) leaf   (E) moisture
   (B) absorption (D) pest

20. *Spot* is to *immaculate* as *name* is to

   (A) autonomous (C) anonymous   (E) illegible
   (B) illiterate   (D) dependent

CHAPTER *9*

Dictionary
of Words
Taught in This Text

The following pages contain a partial listing of the words presented in this book. The words included are those likely to offer some degree of difficulty. The definitions given have in many cases been condensed.

The numeral following a definition indicates the page on which the word appears. Roman type (e.g., abate, 57) is used when the word appears in the first column on that page. Italic type (e.g., abandon, *34*) is used when the word appears in the second column.

Use this dictionary as a tool of reference and review. It is a convenient means of restudying the meanings of words that you may have missed in the exercises. It is also a useful device for a general review before an important vocabulary test. Bear in mind, however, that you will get a fuller understanding of these words from the explanations and exercises of the foregoing chapters.

abandon: give up completely *34*
abate: become less; make less 57
abatement: slackening; letup 57
abdicate: give up 149
abduct: carry off by force 149
abhor: hate 149, *181*
abnormal: unusual 150
abode: home *111*
abound: be well supplied; be plentiful 230
abrasion: scraping or wearing away of the skin by friction 150
abroad: in or to a foreign land or lands 110
abrupt: broken off 150
abscond: steal off and hide 150

absolute: free from control or restriction; utter; outright 229
absolve: set free from some duty or responsibility; declare free from guilt or blame *15*, *150*
absorbing: extremely interesting 150
abstain: withhold oneself from doing something 150
abundant: plentiful *5*, *231*
abut: be in contact with *152*
accede: agree 87
accessible: easy to approach *177*
accommodate: hold without crowding or inconvenience; do a favor for 49

accord: agreement; agree   57, 88
accumulate: pile up   77
acquiesce: accept, agree, or give implied consent by keeping silent or by not making objections   87, 113
acquiescent: disposed to acquiesce   114
acquit: exonerate; absolve   15
acronym: name formed from the first letter or letters of other words   262
adapt: adjust; make suitable for a different use   151
adaptable: capable of changing so as to fit a new or specific use or situation   114
addicted: given over (to a habit)   151
adept: highly skilled or trained   198
adequate: enough; sufficient   7, 151
adhere: stick   49, 213
adherent: faithful supporter   151
adjacent: lying near   152
adjoin: be next to   152
adjourn: close a meeting; put off to another day   14, 152
adroit: expert in using the hands   74
adroitness: skill in the use of the hands   75
advantageous: helpful   179
advent: approach   152
adversary: opponent   152, 261
adverse: unfavorable   152
advocate: supporter   198
affinity: sympathy   210
affirm: declare to be true   232
affluence: abundance of wealth or property   77
affluent: very wealthy   76
aggravate: make worse   57
aggregate: gathered together in one mass   212
aggregation: gathering of individuals into a body or group   213
aggression: unprovoked attack   32
aggressor: person or nation that begins a quarrel   32
agitate: disturb   196
agronomy: branch of agriculture dealing with crop production and soil management   264
alertness: watchfulness   103
alias: assumed name; otherwise called   85, 262
alienate: turn (someone) from affection to dislike or enmity; make hostile or unfriendly   89
allegiance: loyalty   113
alleviate: lessen; relieve   6
alliteration: repetition of the same letter or consonant at the beginning of consecutive words   215
altercation: noisy, angry dispute   89
alternative: choice   65
altitude: height; elevation   32

amass: pile up   77
amateur: person who follows a particular pursuit because he likes it, rather than as a profession; person who performs rather poorly   209
ambidextrous: able to use both hands equally well   74
ambush: trap in which concealed persons lie in wait to attack by surprise   86
amiable: lovable   209
amicable: characterized by friendliness rather than antagonism   209
amity: friendship   209
amorous: having to do with love   209
amplify: enlarge   42
anachronism: error in chronology or time order   247
anagram: word or phrase formed from another by transposing the letters   271
ancestry: line of descent   66
animosity: violent hatred   209
animus: ill will   210
annals: record of events arranged in yearly sequence   247
annul: cancel   50
anonymous: of unnamed or unknown origin   262
antagonist: one who is against, or contends with, another in a struggle, fight, or contest; main opponent of the principal character in a play, novel, or story   152, 261
antagonize: make an enemy of   89
antecedents: ancestors   152
antechamber: an outer room leading to another usually more important room   153
antedate: assign a date before the true date; precede   152
ante meridiem: before noon   153
anteroom: room placed before and forming an entrance to another   153
antibiotic: substance obtained from tiny living organisms that works against harmful bacteria   261
antibody: substance in the blood or tissues that works against germs or poisons produced by germs   261
anticipate: foresee   49
antidote: remedy that acts against the effects of a poison; countermeasure   261
antihistamine: drug used against certain allergies and cold symptoms   261
antipathy: dislike   261
antiseptic: substance that prevents infection   261
antithesis: direct opposite   268
antitoxin: substance formed in the body as the result of the introduction of a toxin and capable of acting against that toxin   261

antonym: word meaning the opposite of another word 261

anxiety: painful uneasiness of mind usually over an anticipated ill *103, 225*

apathy: lack of interest or concern *136*

apparition: ghost *266*

append: attach 225

appendix: matter added to the end of a book or document 225

apprehend: anticipate with fear; arrest 49

apprehension: alarm; uneasiness *49, 225*

apprehensive: expecting something unfavorable *49, 78*

apprentice: person learning an art or trade under a skilled worker *6, 75*

apprise: inform 86

appropriate: fitting; proper 15

aptitude: talent; bent 75

archetype: prototype; original *6*

aristocracy: government, or country governed, by a small privileged upper class; ruling class of nobles 243

aristocrat: advocate of aristocracy; member of the aristocracy 244

articulate: able to speak effectively *211*

artisan: skilled workman *75*

aspersion: discredit *34*

assailant: one who attacks violently with blows or words *32*

assemblage: gathering *213*

assent: agree *87*

assert: maintain as true *41, 232*

assimilate: make similar; take in and incorporate as one's own 228

aster: plant having small starlike flowers 270

asterisk: star-shaped mark (*) used to call attention to a footnote, omission, etc. 270

asteroid: very small planet resembling a star in appearance; starfish 270

astrologer: person who practices astrology 270

astrology: study dealing with the supposed influence of the stars and planets on human affairs 270

astronaut: outer-space traveler 270

astronomer: expert in astronomy 270

astronomical: having to do with the science of the sun, moon, planets, stars, and other heavenly bodies; inconceivably large 264

astronomy: science of the sun, moon, planets, stars, and other heavenly bodies *264, 270*

astute: shrewd; wise 14

audacious: bold; too bold 79

audacity: nerve; rashness 79

authentic: genuine *5, 232, 242*

autobiography: story of a person's life written by the person 242

autocracy: government, or country governed, by one individual with self-derived, unlimited power 243

autocrat: ruler exercising self-derived, absolute power 242

autocratic: ruling with absolute power and authority *23, 229*

autograph: person's signature 242

automation: technique of making a process self-operating by means of built-in electronic controls 242

automaton: robot 242

autonomous: self-governing 242

autonomy: right of self-government 243

autopsy: medical examination of a dead body to determine the cause of death *153, 243*

avarice: excessive desire for wealth 76

avaricious: greedy 76

aver: state to be true 232

averse: opposed 150

avert: turn away *150, 194*

avocation: hobby 150

avowal: open acknowledgment 86

ban: forbid *16*

banish: compel to leave *164*

barometer: instrument for measuring atmospheric pressure as an aid in determining probable weather changes 252

beguile: deceive by means of flattery or by a trick or lie *127*

belittle: speak of in a slighting way *181*

belligerent: fond of fighting *41, 57*

benediction: blessing 179

benefactor: person who gives kindly aid, money, or a similar benefit 179

beneficial: productive of good 179

beneficiary: person receiving some good, advantage, or benefit 179

benevolent: disposed to promote the welfare of others 179

beverage: drink 65

bewilder: confuse *182, 195*

bicameral: consisting of two chambers or legislative houses 154

bicentennial: two-hundredth anniversary 154

bicker: quarrel in a petty way *90*

biennial: occurring every two years 154

bilateral: having two sides 154, 214

bilingual: speaking two languages equally well; written in two languages 154

bimonthly: occurring every two months 154

bipartisan: representing two political parties 155

bisect: divide into two equal parts 155

blunder: mistake caused by stupidity or carelessness *65, 127*

brawl: quarrel noisily *90*

breach: violation of a law or duty   *112*
bulwark: wall-like defensive structure   *100*
bureaucracy: government by bureaus or groups of officials   *243*
bureaucrat: member of a bureaucracy   *244*

cache: hiding place to store something   *23*
calamitous: disastrous   *32*
calamity: great misfortune   *32, 270*
capsize: overturn   *41*
captivated: charmed   *209*
cartographer: person skilled in the science or art of mapmaking   *271*
catastrophe: great misfortune   *270*
category: kind; sort   *212*
cautious: wary; circumspect   *103, 192*
cede: relinquish   *34*
celerity: speed   *43*
cellophane: transparent cellulose substance   *265*
censure: act of blaming; find fault with   *14, 16*
chasm: split; division   *89*
check: hold back   *24*
chivalrous: generous and high-minded   *210*
chronic: marked by long duration and frequent recurrence; having a characteristic, habit, disease, etc., for a long time   *114*
chronicle: historical account of events in the order of time   *247*
chronological: arranged in order of time   *247*
chronology: arrangement of data or events in order of time of occurrence   *247*
chronometer: instrument for measuring time very accurately   *252*
chum: crony; associate   *32*
circumference: distance around a circle or rounded body   *191*
circumlocution: roundabout way of speaking   *192*
circumnavigate: sail around   *192*
circumscribe: draw a line around; limit   *192*
circumspect: careful to consider all circumstances and possible consequences   *192*
circumvent: go around   *192*
citadel: fortress   *100*
civilian: person not a member of the armed forces, or police, or fire-fighting forces   *5*
clandestine: carried on in secrecy and concealment   *86*
cleavage: split   *89*
cleave: stick   *49*
cling: stick   *49, 213*
coalesce: grow together   *193*
coerce: force; compel   *33*
cogent: convincing   *100*

cogitation: thought   *34*
cohere: stick together   *213*
coherence: state of sticking together   *214*
coherent: sticking together   *193*
cohesion: act or state of sticking together   *214*
coincide: agree   *5*
collaborate: work together   *193*
collateral: situated at the side   *214*
collective: of a group of individuals as a whole   *212*
collusion: secret agreement for a deceitful purpose   *193*
colossal: huge   *97*
combative: eager to fight   *57*
comestible: eatable   *90*
commencing: beginning   *115*
commend: praise   *23*
commendable: praiseworthy   *23*
commodious: spacious and comfortable   *97*
commute: travel back and forth daily, as from a home in the suburbs to a job in the city   *110*
commuter: person who travels back and forth daily   *111*
compact: agreement   *88*
compatible: able to exist together harmoniously   *88*
compelling: forceful   *100*
compete: take part in a contest   *41*
complex: hard to analyze or solve   *5*
complicated: hard to understand   *5*
comply: act in accordance with another's wishes or in obedience to a rule   *88, 113*
comprehensible: understandable   *216*
compromise: settlement reached by a partial yielding on both sides   *88*
compulsory: required by authority   *116*
con: against; opposing argument   *167*
conclusive: final   *211*
concord: state of being together in heart or mind   *193*
concur: agree   *5*
concurrent: occurring at the same time   *115, 228*
concurrently: at the same time   *42*
condiment: something added to or served with food to enhance its flavor   *90*
confine: keep within limits   *211*
confirm: state or prove the truth of   *5*
confirmation: proof   *5*
confirmed: habitual   *114*
conform: be in agreement or harmony with   *88*
congenial: agreeable; pleasant   *88*
congenital: existing at birth   *193*
congregate: come together into a crowd   *32*
congregation: gathering of people for religious worship   *213*

conscientious: having painstaking regard for what is right   *103*

conscript: enroll into military service by compulsion   *226*

conservative: tending or disposed to maintain existing views, conditions, or institutions   *250*

consistency: harmony   *214*

consistent: keeping to the same principles throughout   *88, 193*

consonant: in agreement   *88*

conspicuous: noticeable   *58, 163, 198*

conspiracy: plot   *193*

constant: steady; unchanging   *115*

contemplate: consider carefully and for a long time   *50*

contend: take part in a contest; argue   *41*

content: satisfied   *49*

contentious: inclined to argue   *23, 41*

contraband: merchandise imported or exported contrary to law   *167*

contrary: opposite   *268*

contravene: go or act contrary to   *167*

controversial: open to argument; debatable   *65*

controversy: dispute   *65, 167*

convene: meet in a group for a specific purpose   *32, 193*

convention: treaty; agreement   *32*

conventional: customary   *250*

cordial: warm and friendly   *32*

cordiality: friendliness   *32*

correspond: be in harmony; communicate by exchange of letters   *88, 193*

corroborate: confirm   *232*

counter: contrary   *167*

countermand: cancel (an order) by issuing a contrary order   *167*

covenant: agreement   *88*

covert: secret   *86*

covet: crave, especially something belonging to another   *76*

cow: make afraid   *33, 78*

cower: draw back tremblingly   *78*

craft: skill; cunning   *58*

craftsperson: skilled workman   *75*

crafty: clever   *14, 58*

craven: cowardly; coward   *58, 78*

craze: fad   *248*

cringe: shrink in fear   *78*

crony: close companion   *32*

crouch: cower   *78*

cryptogram: something written in secret code   *271*

culprit: one guilty of a fault or crime   *50*

cunning: clever   *14, 58*

cupidity: greediness   *76*

cur: worthless dog   *23*

curb: hold back   *24, 140*

cure-all: remedy for all ills   *246*

currency: something in circulation as a medium of exchange   *58*

custody: care   *65*

dastardly: cowardly and mean   *58, 78*

dauntless: fearless   *79*

dawdle: waste time   *67, 115, 198*

debate: discussion or argument carried on between two sides   *65, 167*

debilitate: impair the strength of   *99*

decadent: marked by decay or decline   *99, 180*

decease: death   *41*

deciduous: having leaves that fall down at the end of the growing season   *180*

declining: growing worse   *99, 180*

decrepit: broken down or weakened by old age or use   *99*

default: failure to do something required; fail to pay or appear when due   *102*

defer: yield to another out of respect, authority, or courtesy   *113, 152, 226*

defiance: refusal to obey authority   *112*

definitive: serving to end an unsettled matter   *211*

deft: skillful   *74*

deftness: skill   *75*

degenerate: sink to a lower class or standard   *212*

degrade: downgrade   *181*

delectable: delicious   *91*

deliberately: in a carefully thought out manner; slowly   *32*

delude: lead from truth or into error   *127*

deluge: flood   *42, 231*

demagogue: political leader who stirs up the people for personal advantage   *245*

demented: out of one's mind   *180*

demise: death   *41*

democracy: government, or country governed, by the people   *244*

Democrat: member of the Democratic Party   *244*

democratic: based on the principles of government by the people   *245*

democratize: make democratic   *245*

demolish: tear down; destroy   *14, 181*

demolition: destruction   *14*

demote: move down in grade or rank   *181*

denizen: inhabitant   *111*

dependent: unable to exist without the support of another   *181*

depletion: using up   *163*

depose: bear witness; put out of office   *226, 232*

depreciate: go down in price or value; speak slightingly of   *181*

deranged: insane *180*
dermatologist: physician specializing in the diseases of the skin 263
dermatology: science dealing with the skin and its diseases 263
dermis: inner layer of the skin 263
desist: cease to proceed or act *150*
desolate: make lonely; left alone 228
despise: look down on 181
despite: in spite of *141*
despot: ruler with absolute power and authority *242*
despotic: domineering 23, *229*
despotism: tyranny 23
destitute: not possessing the necessaries of life 76
deter: turn aside through fear 58
deteriorate: make or become worse *212*
deteriorating: becoming worse or of less value 99, *180*
deterioration: worsening; wearing away *163*
detest: loathe; hate *149*
devastate: ravage; lay waste *228*
deviate: turn aside or down (from a route or rule) *5*, 181
devotion: loyalty *113*
devour: eat up greedily 90, 181
dexterity: skill in using the hands or mind 75
dexterous: skillful with the hands 74
diameter: straight line passing through the center of a body or figure from one side to the other 252
diaphanous: of such fine texture as to permit seeing through; transparent 265
diathermy: method of treating disease by generating heat in body tissues by high-frequency electric currents 266
dictatorial: domineering 23
differentiate: tell apart *41*
digress: turn aside; get off the main subject in speaking or writing *5, 181*
dilapidated: falling to pieces 99
diminish: become less 57
diminutive: below average size 66
din: loud noise 41
disable: make unable or incapable *100*
disaster: sudden or extraordinary misfortune 270
disband: break up the organization of *14, 203*
disbelieve: refuse to believe *182*
discharge: unload; dismiss 14
discipline: train in obedience *113*
disclose: make known 87
discontent: dissatisfied 182
discord: lack of agreement or harmony 89
discredit: refuse to trust *182*
discreet: wisely cautious 103

discrepancy: difference 89, 182
disdain: scorn; despise *181*
disencumber: free from encumbrances *15*
disentangle: straighten out *15*
disgruntled: discontented; dissatisfied *182*
disinclined: unwilling *150*
disintegrate: break into bits 182, *230*
disparage: speak slightingly of *181*
dispassionate: calm 182
dispel: drive away by scattering 66
dispense: deal out; distribute 33
dispense with: do without 33
disperse: scatter 66
disputatious: contentious; controversial 23, *65*
dispute: argue about 23
disregard: pay no attention to *102*
disrepair: bad condition 182
dissension: discord; conflict; strife 14, *89*
dissent: differ in opinion 14, 89, 182
dissident: not agreeing 182
dissimilar: unlike 228, *251*
dissolution: act of breaking up into component parts 230
dissolve: break up; cause to disappear 230
distinguish: tell apart 41, *163*
distract: draw away (the mind or attention) 182
divert: turn the attention away *182*
divulge: make known 41, 87
docile: easily taught *113*
domain: region; sphere of influence *50*
domicile: home 111
domineering: ruling in an overbearing way 23, *128*
dormant: inactive, as if asleep 66, *86*
dovetail: to fit together with, so as to form a harmonious whole 88
dowry: money, property, etc., that a bride brings to her husband 77
draft: enroll into military service *226*
drought: long period of dry weather 41
dubious: doubtful 33
duplicate: copy 58
dynamic: forceful 100

economic: having to do with the social science dealing with production, distribution, and consumption 264
economical: thrifty; frugal 76, 264
economics: the social science dealing with production, distribution, and consumption 264
economize: reduce expenses 76
edible: fit for human consumption 90
edifice: building, especially a large or impressive building 23
eject: force out; expel 164
elaborate: complex; intricate *5*

electrocardiogram: tracing showing the amount of electricity the heart muscles produce during the heartbeat 271

electrocardiograph: instrument that records the amount of electricity the heart muscles produce during the heartbeat *271*

elevation: height 32

elicit: draw forth 87, *163*

eliminate: get rid of 50

elucidate: make clear 216

emancipate: set free 224

embroil: involve in conflict 89

emigrate: move out of a country or region to settle in another 163

eminence: a natural elevation *32*

eminent: standing out 163

enamored: inflamed with love 209

encyclopedia: work offering alphabetically arranged information on various branches of knowledge 249

endurance: ability to withstand strain, suffering, or hardship *59, 79*

endure: hold out; last *141, 195*

enduring: lasting *115, 195*

enervate: lessen the vigor or strength of 99, *136, 163*

enfeeble: weaken *99, 163*

engender: give birth to 212

engrave: cut or carve on a hard surface *163*

engrossing: taking up the whole interest of *150*

enigma: puzzle 86

enigmatic: puzzling 86

enlighten: shed the light of truth and knowledge upon 87

enmity: hatred *180, 209, 261*

enrage: fill with anger 42

entail: involve as a necessary consequence 116

entomb: bury *6*

envisage: have a mental picture of especially in advance of realization *232*

envision: foresee 232

ephemeral: not lasting; passing soon *16*

epicure: person with sensitive or discriminating tastes in food or wine *264*

epidemic: affecting many people in an area at the same time; outbreak of a disease affecting many people at the same time 245

epidermis: outer layer of the skin 263

epigram: bright or witty thought concisely and cleverly expressed 271

epithet: characterizing word or phrase 269

epoch: age; period *23*

equanimity: evenness of mind or temper 210

equilateral: having all sides equal 214

equilibrium: emotional balance *210*

equitable: fair to all concerned 14

era: historical period 23

eradicate: remove by or as if by uprooting *139*

erosion: gradual wearing away 163

essence: most necessary or significant part, aspect, or feature 116

essential: necessary 117, *214*

estrange: turn from affection to dislike or enmity 89

evidence: show *87*

evident: clear; obvious 87

evoke: bring out *87*, 163

excise: cut out 163

exclude: shut out *50*

exclusive: shutting out, or tending to shut out, others; not shared with others 66, 164

exclusively: without sharing with others 66

exculpate: free from blame *150*

exempt: released from an obligation to which others are subject 66, *150*

exemption: freedom from something which others are subject to 66

exhibit: show 164

exonerate: free from blame 15, *150*

expectation: something expected *198*

expel: drive out; eject 164

exploit: heroic act 79

extemporaneous: composed or spoken without preparation 15

extract: draw forth 87

extraction: descent 66

extracurricular: outside the regular curriculum, or course of study 165

extraneous: coming from or existing outside 165, *178*

extravagant: outside the bounds of reason; spending lavishly 166, *198*

extremity: very end 33

extricate: free from difficulties 15

facetious: given to joking 50

fallacious: illogical *177*

famish: starve 41

fancy: imagination 265

fantastic: based on imagination rather than reason 127, 265

fantasy: illusory image 266

fatigue: tire; exhaust; weariness 50

feat: deed notable especially for courage 79

feebleness: weakness; frailty *100*

feign: give an imitation *228*

fictitious: imaginary; false 58

fidelity: loyalty *113*

finale: end or final part of a musical composition, opera, play, etc. 211

financial: having to do with money matters 77

finis: end 211

fiscal: having to do with financial matters 77

fleece: deprive or strip of money or belongings by fraud 77

fleeting: passing rapidly 16

flimsy: lacking strength or solidity 100

flinch: draw back involuntarily 34

fluctuate: flow like a wave 211

fluent: ready with a flow of words 211

fluid: substance that flows; not rigid 211

flux: continuous flow or changing 211

foe: enemy 152, 261

forcible: showing force 100

forearm: part of the arm from the wrist to the elbow 125

forebear: ancestor 125, 152, 212

foreboding: feeling beforehand of coming trouble 125, 126

forecast: predict 33, 125

forefather: ancestor 125, 212

forefront: foremost place or part 125

foregoing: preceding 125

foremost: standing at the front 125

foreshadow: indicate beforehand 125

foresight: power of seeing beforehand what is likely to happen 125

forestall: prevent; avert 150, 194

foreword: introduction at the beginning of a book 33, 125, 197

forfeit: lose or have to give up as a penalty for some error, neglect, or fault 15

forlorn: deserted 229

formidable: exciting fear by reason of strength, size, difficulty, etc. 100

forsaken: abandoned; desolate 229

forte: strong point 100

forthcoming: about to appear 139

fortitude: courage in facing danger, hardship, or pain 79

fragile: easily broken; breakable 5, 100

frail: not very strong 100

frailty: weakness 100

frank: free and forthright in expressing one's feelings and opinions 128

friction: conflict of ideas between persons or parties of opposing views 89

frugal: barely enough; avoiding waste 76, 264

frustrate: bring to nothing 192

furious: intense; vehement 101

furtive: stealthy; catlike 86

fusion: joining together 267

galore: plentiful 5

gamut: entire range of anything from one extreme to another 98

gastronome: a lover and expert judge of excellence in food and drink 264

gastronomy: art or science of good eating 264

genealogy: history of the descent of a person or family from an ancestor 251

generate: bring into existence 212

genesis: birth or coming into being 251

genre: category 212

gentry: upper class 243

genuine: real; authentic 5, 232, 242

glutton: greedy eater; person with a great capacity for enduring or doing something 91

gluttonous: greedy in eating 91

gourmet: expert judge of good food and drink 264

graphic: written or told in a clear, lifelike manner 271

graphite: soft black carbon used in lead pencils 271

gratuitous: uncalled for 116

gregarious: fond of being with others 213

guile: deceitful slyness 58

gutless: cowardly 58

habitual: according to habit 114

habituated: accustomed 151

harmony: agreement 88, 193, 252

haunt: come to mind frequently 194

heed: pay attention 103

heedless: careless 102, 136

heterogeneous: differing in kind 251

hibernate: spend the winter 33

hinder: hold back; obstruct 58, 194

hindrance: something that obstructs or impedes 194

hoard: save and conceal 77

homogeneous: of the same kind 251

homogenize: make uniform 251

homonym: word that sounds like another but differs in meaning 262

horde: great crowd 24

hospitable: kind to guests and strangers 178

host: person who receives or entertains a guest or guests; large number 33

hostile: of or relating to an enemy or enemies; unfriendly 6, 152

husbandry: agriculture 264

hypodermic: beneath the skin 263

hypothesis: supposition or assumption made as a basis for reasoning or research 269

ignore: disregard; overlook 102

illegible: not able to be read; very hard to read 15, 177

illiterate: unable to read and write 177

illogical: not observing the rules of correct reasoning 177

illuminate: light up 41

immaculate: spotless 58, 177

immature: not fully grown or developed 177

immigrate: move into a foreign country or region as a permanent resident 163

imminent: about to happen 115, 163, 225

immoderate: too great 98

immunity: condition of being not susceptible 66, 177

impartial: fair 14, 182

impatient: not willing to bear delay 6

impede: block 196

impediment: obstruction 194

impel: drive on 164

impending: threatening to occur soon 163, 225

imperative: not to be avoided 116

imperil: endanger 42, 66

impetuous: impulsive 79

implicate: show to be part of or connected with 164

impose: put on as a burden, duty, tax, etc. 194, 226

impoverish: make very poor 76

impregnable: incapable of being taken by assault 101

impromptu: without previous thought or preparation 15

improvise: compose, recite, or sing on the spur of the moment 232

improvised: composed, recited, or sung on the spur of the moment 15

impudent: marked by a bold disregard of others 79

impugn: call in question 164

impunity: freedom from punishment, harm, loss, etc. 66, 177

inaccessible: not able to be reached 177

inadvertent: careless 102

inadvertently: not done on purpose 15

inappropriate: not fitting 15

inaudible: incapable of being heard 42

inborn: born in or with one 193

incapacitate: render incapable or unfit 100

incarcerate: put into prison 164

incense: make extremely angry 42, 199

incessant: not ceasing 115, 177

incipient: beginning to show itself 115

incise: cut into 163

inclusive: including the limits mentioned; broad in scope 164

incoherent: unintelligible 214

incompatible: not capable of being brought together in harmonious or agreeable relations 89, 178

inconsistency: lack of agreement or harmony 89, 182

incontrovertible: not able to be disputed 167

incumbent: imposed as a duty 116

indifference: lack of interest; dislike 136

indigence: poverty 76

indigent: needy 76

indispensable: absolutely necessary 117

indisputable: unquestionable 167

indomitable: incapable of being subdued 79

induct: lead in 23

inept: lacking in skill or aptitude 75

inequitable: unfair 14

inexhaustible: plentiful enough not to give out or be used up 98

inextinguishable: unquenchable 136

infallible: incapable of error 50

infinite: without ends or limits 98

infinitesimal: so small as to be almost nothing 98

infirmity: weakness 100

infixed: implanted 214

inflate: swell with air or gas 98

inflexible: not easily bent 177

inflict: cause (something disagreeable) to be borne; impose 226

influx: inflow 211

infraction: breaking (of a law, regulation, etc.) 112

infrequent: seldom happening or occurring 115

infringe: violate 167

infuriate: fill with rage 42

ingratitude: state of being not grateful 177

inherent: belonging by nature 214

inhibit: hold in check 164

inhospitable: not showing kindness to guests and strangers 178

initial: beginning; introductory 6, 115

initiate: begin; admit into a club by special ceremonies 23

initiation: installation as a member 23

inmate: person confined in an institution, prison, hospital, etc. 111

innate: inborn 193

inordinate: much too great 98

inscribe: write, engrave, or print to create a lasting record 164

inscription: something written on a monument, coin, etc. 227

insignificant: of little importance 98

insolent: lacking in respect for rank or position 79

insoluble: not capable of being solved; not capable of being dissolved 178

insubordinate: not submitting to authority 112, 165

insurgent: one who rises in revolt against established authority; rebellious 112, 165

insurrection: uprising against established authority 112, 183

integrate: make into a whole 182

intensify: make more acute 57

inter: bury 6

intercede: interfere to reconcile differences 59, 168

intercept: stop or seize on the way from one place to another 168

interdict: forbid; prohibit *16*

interlinear: inserted between lines already printed or written 168

interlude: anything filling the time between two events 168

intermediary: go-between 168

interment: burial; entombment 6

interminable: continual; endless *177*

intermission: pause between periods of activity 168

intermittent: coming and going at intervals 115

intersect: cut by passing through or across 169

interurban: between cities or towns 169

interval: space of time between events or states *168*

intervene: occur between; come between to help settle a quarrel 59, 169

intervention: intercession; interference 59

intimidate: frighten 33, 78

intramural: within the walls or boundaries 166

intraparty: within a party 166

intrastate: within a state 166

intravenous: within or by way of the veins 166

intrepid: fearless and daring *79*

intricate: not simple or easy 5

intrinsic: belonging to the essential nature or constitution of a thing *214*

intrude: come or go in without invitation or welcome *194*

inundate: flood 42, 231

invigorate: give life and energy to 101

invincible: unconquerable *79, 101*

invisible: imperceptible 232

invoke: call on for help or protection 163

involve: draw in as a participant *164*

iota: very small quantity 98

irrational: illogical; fallacious *177*

irreconcilable: unable to be brought into friendly accord or understanding 89, 178

irrelevant: off the topic *165, 178*

irrevocable: incapable of being recalled 178

isolate: set apart from others *183*

isolated: infrequent *115*

isolation: the act or condition of being set apart from others; segregation *213*

jeopardize: expose to danger 42, *66*

jeopardy: danger 42

Jolly Roger: pirates' flag 24

journalist: editor of or writer for a periodical *227*

jurisdiction: territory within which authority may be exercised *50*

jut: stick out; protrude *199*

kinship: sense of oneness *210*

kleptomania: insane impulse to steal 248

kleptomaniac: person affected by an insane impulse to steal 248

latent: present but not showing itself 86

lateral: of or pertaining to the side 214

lavish: too free in giving, using, or spending; given or spent too freely 77, *198*

lax: careless *102*

legible: capable of being read 15

lettered: able to read and write *215*

liberate: set free *136, 224*

lineage: descent 66, *251*

literacy: ability to read and write 215

literal: following the letters or exact words of the original 215

literary: having to do with letters or literature 215

literate: able to read and write 215

litigation: lawsuit 90

loathe: detest; abhor *149*

logic: correct reasoning *177*

logical: observing the rules of correct reasoning *177, 193*

loiter: hang around idly *115*

lucid: clear 216

lucrative: profitable 15, 77

luminary: famous person 216

luminous: shining 216

lurk: be hidden; move stealthily 86

luscious: delicious 91

luxurious: extravagantly elegant and comfortable 77

magnanimous: showing greatness or nobility of mind *210*

magnify: cause to be or look larger 42

magnitude: size 98

major: greater 66

maladjusted: out of harmony with one's environment 179

maladroit: clumsy 75

malcontent: discontented person 112

malediction: curse 179

malefactor: evildoer 179

malevolence: ill will *180*

malevolent: showing ill will 179

malice: ill will 180

malign: speak evil of; slander *164*

malnutrition: poor nourishment 180

maltreat: treat badly or roughly 180

mammoth: of very great size 97
manacle: handcuff 224
mandate: authorization to act; command 224
maneuver: handle; engineer 224
mania: madness; excessive fondness 248
maniac: raving lunatic 248
maniacal: characterized by madness 248
manifest: show; plain 87
manipulate: operate with the hands; manage unethically to serve a fraudulent purpose 224
manual: small, helpful book capable of being carried in the hand; relating to, or done with, the hands 224
manuscript: document written by hand, or typewritten 224
means: wealth 77
mediate: intervene between conflicting parties or viewpoints to reconcile differences 168
mediator: impartial third party who acts as a go-between in a dispute in order to arrange a peaceful settlement 168
meditate: consider carefully and for a long time 50
meek: submissive 114
meter: device for measuring; 39.37 inches 252
meticulous: extremely or excessively careful about small details 103
migrate: move from one place to settle in another; move from one place to another with the change of season 111
mind: pay attention to 103
miniature: small 59
misbelief: wrong or erroneous belief 126
mischance: piece of bad luck 126
misdeed: bad act 126
misfire: fail to be fired or exploded properly 126
misgiving: uneasy feeling 125, 126
mishap: bad happening 126
mislay: put or lay in an unremembered place 126
mislead: lead astray 127
misstep: wrong step 127
mitigate: make less severe 6
moderate: make less violent, severe, or intense 57
modify: make changes in 151
momentary: lasting only a moment 16
monetary: having to do with money 77
monogram: person's initials interwoven or combined into one design 272
monograph: written account of a single thing or class of things 272
multilateral: having many sides 214

multitude: crowd 24, 33
multitudinous: numerous 24
municipal: of a city or town 42
mutineer: rebel, insurgent 165
mutinous: rebellious 112, 165

native: person born in a particular place; born or originating in a particular place 111
necessitate: make necessary 117
neglect: give little or no attention to; lack of proper care or attention 102
negligence: carelessness 102
nemesis: person that inflicts just punishment for evil deeds; formidable and usually victorious opponent 264
neophyte: beginner; novice 6
noble: aristocrat 244
nomad: member of a tribe that has no fixed home but wanders from place to place 111
nomadic: roaming from place to place 111
nonconformist: not agreeing; dissenting 182
notable: standing out; person outstanding in some way 198, 216
noteworthy: remarkable 163
notwithstanding: in spite of 141
novice: one who is new to a field or activity 6, 75

objective: goal; involving facts, rather than personal feelings or opinions 14, 66
obligatory: required 116
oblige: compel 117
obliterate: remove all traces of 194
obscure: not clear 86, 129
obsess: trouble the mind of 194
obstacle: something standing in the way 194
obstruct: be in the way of 194
obtrude: thrust forward without being asked 194
obviate: make unnecessary 117, 194
obvious: not obscure; evident 87
odometer: instrument attached to a vehicle for measuring the distance traversed 252
offhand: without previous thought 15
omen: foreboding; presentiment 125
onomatopoeia: use of words whose sound suggests their meaning 262
opinionated: unduly attached to one's own opinion 67
opulence: wealth 77
opulent: wealthy 76
origin: coming into being; genesis 251

original: a work created firsthand and from which copies are made; belonging to the beginning 6

originality: freshness; novelty 6

originate: begin 23

orthodontics: branch of dentistry dealing with the straightening and adjusting of teeth 250

orthodontist: dentist specializing in the straightening and adjusting of teeth 250

orthodox: generally accepted, especially in religion 250

orthography: correct spelling 250

orthopedic: having to do with the correction and prevention of deformities, especially in children 249

orthopedics: the science dealing with the correction and prevention of deformities, especially in children 249

orthopedist: physician specializing in the correction and prevention of deformities, especially in children 250

outfox: outwit 128

outgrow: grow too large for 127

outlandish: looking or sounding as if it belongs to a foreign land 127

outlast: last longer than 127

outlive: live longer than 127

outlook: a looking beyond 127

output: a yield or product 127

outrun: run faster than 128

outspoken: speaking out freely or boldly 128

outweigh: exceed in weight, value, or importance 129

outwit: get the better of by being more clever 128

overawe: subdue by awe 33

overbearing: domineering over others 128

overburden: place too heavy a load on 128

overconfident: too sure of oneself 128

overdose: too big a dose 128

overestimate: overrate 129

overhasty: too hasty 79

overpower: overcome by superior force 129

overshadow: cast a shadow over; be more important than 129

oversupply: too great a supply 129

overt: open to view 87

overtax: put too great a burden or strain on 128

overvalue: set too high a value on 129

overwhelm: overpower 129, 231

palatable: agreeable to the taste 91

panacea: remedy for all ills 246

Pan-American: of or pertaining to all the countries of North, South, and Central America 246

pandemonium: wild uproar 246

panoply: complete suit of armor 246

panorama: complete, unobstructed view 246

pantomime: dramatic performance that is all signs and gestures without words 246

parallel: running alongside 214

passionate: showing strong feeling 182

patrician: member of the aristocracy 244

pauperize: make very poor; impoverish 76

pecuniary: having to do with money 77

pedagogue: teacher of children 249

pedagogy: art of teaching 249

pediatrician: physician specializing in the treatment of babies and children 249

pediatrics: the branch of medicine dealing with the care, development, and diseases of babies and children 249

pedigree: ancestral line 251

pendant: hanging ornament 225

pending: waiting to be settled; until 225

penetrate: pass into or through 195

penury: poverty; indigence 76

perceive: become aware of through the senses 24

perception: idea; conception 24

perennial: continuing through the years; plant that lives through the years 115, 195

perforate: make a hole or holes through 42, 195

peril: exposure to injury, loss, or destruction 42

perimeter: the whole outer boundary of a body or area 191

periodic: happening repeatedly 115

permanent: enduring; perennial 16, 115

permeate: pass through 195

perplex: confuse thoroughly 195

persevere: keep at something in spite of difficulties or opposition 195

persist: continue in spite of opposition; continue to exist 195

pertinent: connected with the matter under consideration 196

perturb: disturb thoroughly or considerably 196

pervade: spread through; penetrate 195

perverse: obstinate (in opposing what is right or reasonable) 113

petty: small and of no importance 98

phantom: something that has appearance but no reality 266

phenomenal: extraordinary 266

phenomenon: any observable fact or event; extraordinary person or thing 266

photometer: instrument for measuring intensity of light 252

picayune: concerned with trifling matters 98

pilfer: steal (in small amounts) 50

pittance: small amount 98

pliable: easily bent or influenced 114

pluck: courage *79*

plucky: courageous *79*

plutocracy: government, or country governed, by the rich 244

plutocrat: member of wealthy class 244

poltroon: coward 78

portal: door, entrance 24

postdate: assign a date after the true date 153

postgraduate: having to do with study after graduation from high school or college 153

post meridiem: after noon 153

postmortem: thorough examination of a body after death; detailed analysis or discussion of an event just ended 153, *243*

postscript: note added to a completed letter 153

potential: capable of becoming real *86*

precede: come or go before *34, 153,* 196

precise: very exact *103*

preclude: put a barrier before *117,* 196

precocious: showing mature characteristics at an early age 196

preconceive: form an opinion of beforehand, without adequate evidence 196

predecessor: ancestor; forebear *152*

prefabricate: construct beforehand 197

preface: introduction; introduce with a foreword *33, 125,* 197

premature: before the proper or usual time 197

premeditate: consider beforehand 197

preoccupy: engage the attention of *194*

prerequisite: something required beforehand 117

prescribe: order; order as a remedy 227

presentiment: feeling that something will, or is about to, happen *125*

presently: in a short time 67

pressing: requiring immediate attention 117

presume: take for granted without proof 197

preview: view of something before it is shown to the public 197

procrastinate: put things off 67, 115, 198

prodigal: profuse; lavish *77*

prodigious: extraordinary in size, quantity, or extent 67

prodigy: extraordinary person or thing 67, *266*

profession: vocation; occupation *51*

proficient: well advanced in any subject or occupation 198

profuse: pouring forth freely *77,* 198

progenitor: ancestor to whom a group traces its birth 212

prohibit: forbid; proscribe 16, *227*

prohibition: ban; taboo 16

project: throw or cast forward 198

prologue: introduction *33, 125*

prominent: readily noticeable *58,* 198

prompt: on time *16*

propel: drive onward 198

prophecy: prediction *125*

prophesy: predict *33*

proponent: person who puts forth a proposal or argues in favor of something 198

proscribe: condemn as harmful or illegal 227

prospect: thing looked forward to 198

prospects: chances 198

protagonist: the leading character in a play, novel, or story 267

protocol: first draft or record from which a treaty is drawn up; rules of etiquette of the diplomatic corps, military services, etc. 267

protoplasm: fundamental substance of which all living things are composed 268

prototype: first or original model of anything 6, 268

protozoan: animal consisting of only a single cell 268

protract: draw out 67, 115, 198

protrude: thrust forth 199

province: proper business or duty; division of a country 50

provoke: call forth; make angry 199

prudence: skill and good sense in taking care of oneself or of one's affairs *125*

prudent: shrewd in the management of practical affairs *192*

pseudonym: fictitious name used by an author 262

punctual: on time 16

punctuality: promptness 16

puncture: make a hole with a pointed object 42, *195*

puny: slight or inferior in size, power, or importance 98

pusillanimous: cowardly *58*

pyromania: insane impulse to set fires 248

pyromaniac: person affected by an insane impulse to set fires 248

quadrilateral: plane figure having four sides and four angles 214

quench: put out; satisfy *91*

questionable: not certain *33*

quintet: group of five 59

rabble-rouser: one who stirs up the people, especially to hatred or violence *245*

ramble: aimless walk 25

316   Vocabulary for the High School Student

rampart: broad bank or wall used as a fortification or protective barrier   *100*
ransack: search thoroughly   *42*
rarity: something uncommon, infrequent, or rare   *6*
rash: taking too much risk   *79, 136*
ravage: lay waste   *228*
ravenous: voracious   *91*
raze: tear down; destroy   *14, 181*
rebel: one who opposes or takes arms against the government or ruler   *112, 165*
rebuke: express disapproval of   *14, 16*
reckless: foolishly bold   *79, 102*
recoil: draw back because of fear   *7, 34*
reconcilable: able to be brought into friendly accord   *178*
reconcile: cause to be friends again; settle   *59, 88*
recurrent: returning from time to time   *115*
redound: flow back as a result   *231*
redundant: exceeding what is necessary   *231*
reflect: think carefully   *50*
reflection: thought; blame   *34*
refrain: hold oneself back   *150*
regenerate: cause to be born again   *212*
release: give up   *34, 136*
relent: become less harsh, severe, or strict   *88*
relevant: having something to do with the case being considered   *196*
relinquish: give up   *34, 149*
remiss: careless   *102*
remunerative: advantageous; lucrative   *15*
renounce: resign; abdicate   *149*
renovate: modernize   *139*
repress: hold back   *24, 164*
reprove: scold   *16*
repugnance: deep-rooted dislike   *261*
reserved: restrained in speech or action; aloof   *24*
resist: oppose   *141*
resolution: solving   *230*
resolve: break up   *230*
resources: available means   *77*
restrain: hold back   *24, 140, 164*
restrict: keep within bounds   *192, 211*
resume: begin again; reoccupy   *6*
retain: keep   *67*
retentive: able to retain or remember   *67*
reticent: silent; reserved   *24*
retract: draw back   *24*
reveal: make known   *87*
reverse: turn completely about; defeat   *50, 268*
reversible: wearable with either side out   *50*
revise: look at again to correct errors and make improvements   *233*
revocable: capable of being recalled   *178*
revoke: cancel   *50, 167*
robot: purely mechanical person   *242*

robust: strong and vigorously healthy   *101*
roving: wandering from place to place   *111*
rummage: search thoroughly by turning over all the contents   *42*
rural: having to do with the country   *59*

sagacious: wise; shrewd   *14*
savory: pleasing to the taste or smell   *91*
scanty: barely enough   *76*
schism: split; chasm   *89*
scorn: hold in contempt   *181*
scribe: person who writes   *227*
script: written text of a play, speech, etc.; handwriting   *227*
scrupulous: having painstaking regard for what is right   *103, 139*
scrutinize: examine closely   *103*
seasoning: something added to food to enhance its flavor   *90*
secede: withdraw from an organization or federation   *183*
secession: withdrawal from an organization or federation   *183*
seclude: shut up apart from others   *86, 183*
seclusion: condition of being hidden from sight   *229*
secure: free from care, fear, or worry; safe against loss, attack, or danger   *183*
security: safety; measures taken to assure protection against attack, crime, sabotage, etc.   *59*
sedition: speech, writing, or action seeking to overthrow the government   *113, 183*
segregate: separate from the main body   *184*
segregation: separation from the main body   *213*
semiannual: occurring every half year, or twice a year   *154*
semicircle: half of a circle   *155*
semiconscious: half conscious   *155*
semidetached: sharing a wall with an adjoining building on one side, but detached on the other   *155*
semimonthly: occurring every half month, or twice a month   *154*
semiskilled: partly skilled   *155*
semiyearly: occurring twice a year   *154*
sequester: seclude; cloister   *86, 183*
shallow: not deep; lacking intellectual depth   *51*
shrewd: clever; crafty   *14*
shrink: draw back; become smaller   *7, 34*
similarity: likeness   *228*
simile: comparison of two different things introduced by "like" or "as"   *228*
simulate: give the appearance of   *228*
simultaneous: existing or happening at the same time   *115, 228*
simultaneously: at the same time   *42*

slake: bring (thirst) to an end through refreshing drink   91

slipshod: very careless   *102*

sloven: untidy person   102

slovenly: negligent of neatness or order in one's dress, habits, work, etc.   102

sluggish: slow and inactive in movement   66

sober: not drunk; serious   7

sojourn: temporary stay   111

sole: one and only   229

solely: undividedly   *66*

solicitude: anxious or excessive care   103

soliloquy: speech made to oneself when alone   229

solitary: companionless   229

solitude: condition of being alone   229

solo: musical composition (or anything) performed by a single person   229

soluble: capable of being dissolved or made into a liquid; solvable   230

solvent: substance, usually liquid, able to dissolve another substance; able to pay all one's legal debts   230

sovereign: self-governing; independent   *242*

sparing: tending to save   *76, 264*

specter: ghost   *266*

speedometer: instrument for measuring speed   252

sphere: field of influence   *50*

spine: backbone   24

spineless: cowardly   24

sporadic: occurring occasionally or in scattered instances   115

stable: enduring; not changing   *16*

stamina: endurance   59

stealthy: secret in action or character   86

stenographer: person employed chiefly to take and transcribe dictation   272

stenography: the art of writing in shorthand   272

stress: emphasize; underscore   *138*

strife: bitter conflict   89

stroll: idle and leisurely walk   25

stronghold: fortified place   *100*

sturdy: strong and vigorous   *101*

submissive: meek   *113*

submit: yield to another's will, authority, or power   114

subscriber: one who writes his name at the end of a document, thereby indicating his approval   227

subsequently: later   *42*

substantiate: provide evidence for   *5, 232*

succulent: full of juice   91

suffice: be enough   7

sumptuous: involving large expense   77

superabundance: excessive abundance   99

superfluous: beyond what is necessary or desirable   *51, 117, 231*

superimpose: put on top of or over   226

supplement: something that makes an addition   *225*

supplementary: additional   *214*

surmount: conquer   51

surplus: excess   *51, 99, 117, 231*

survive: live longer than   *43, 127*

suspend: hang by attaching to something; stop temporarily   225

suspense: mental uncertainty   225

swarm: great crowd   *24*

swindle: cheat   77

symmetry: correspondence in measurements, shape, etc., on opposite sides of a dividing line   252

synchronize: cause to agree in time   247

synonym: word having the same meaning as another word   262

synthesis: combination of parts or elements into a whole   269

synthetic: artificially made   269

tachometer: instrument for measuring speed   252

tally: match   *193*

taxidermist: one who prepares, stuffs, and mounts the skins of animals in lifelike form   263

taxidermy: the art of preparing, stuffing, and mounting the skins of animals in lifelike form   263

technocracy: government or country governed by technical experts   244

technocrat: supporter of technocracy; technical expert   244

teem: be present in large quantity   *230*

temerity: nerve; audacity   79

tenacious: holding fast or tending to hold fast   *67, 101*

testify: state under oath   226

thermal: pertaining to heat   267

thermonuclear: having to do with the fusion, at an extraordinarily high temperature, of the nuclei of atoms   267

thermostat: automatic device for regulating temperature   267

thesis: claim put forward; essay written by a candidate for a college degree   269

thrifty: inclined to save   *76, 264*

throng: great crowd   *24, 33*

timid: lacking courage or self-confidence   *25, 78*

timorous: full of fear   *25, 78*

tolerable: endurable   34

tolerate: endure   34

toxin: poison   *261*

tractable: easily controlled, led, or taught   114

transgress: go beyond the set limits of   113

transient: not lasting; visitor or guest staying for only a short time   16
transitory: short-lived   *16*
translucent: letting light through   216
transpose: change the relative order of   226
traverse: pass across, over, or through   43
trepidation: nervous agitation   79
trespass: encroach on another's rights, privileges, property, etc.   113
trustworthy: worthy of confidence   *242*
tuition: payment for instruction   25
typographical: pertaining to or occurring in printing   272
typography: use of type for printing   *272*
tyrannical: domineering   *23*
tyro: beginner   *6, 75*

unabridged: not made shorter   135
unanimity: complete agreement   210
unanimous: in complete accord   210
unbiased: not prejudiced in favor of or against   *14*, 136
unblemished: spotless   *58*
uncommunicative: not inclined to talk   *24*
unconcern: lack of concern, anxiety, or interest   136
undeceive: free from deception or mistaken ideas   136
underbrush: shrubs, bushes, etc., growing beneath large trees in a wood   137
underdeveloped: insufficiently developed because of a lack of capital and trained personnel for exploiting natural resources   137
undergraduate: student in a college or university who has not yet earned his first degree   137
underhand: marked by secrecy and deception   *86*
underpayment: insufficient payment   137
underprivileged: deprived through social or economic oppression of some of the fundamental rights supposed to belong to all   137
underscore: draw a line beneath   138
undersell: sell at a lower price than   138
undersigned: person or persons who sign at the end of a letter or document   138
understatement: restrained statement in mocking contrast to what might be said   138
understudy: one who "studies under" and learns the part of a regular performer so as to be his or her substitute if necessary   138
ungag: remove a gag from   136
unilateral: one-sided   214
unintelligible: incomprehensible   *214*

unity: act of sticking together; cohesion   214
unmindful: careless   *102*
unnerve: deprive of nerve or courage   136
unorthodox: not in accord with accepted, standard, or approved belief or practice   250
unquenchable: not capable of being satisfied   136
unravel: solve   230
unscramble: restore to intelligible form   136
unshackle: set free from restraint   136
unsubstantial: lacking firmness, strength, or substance   *100*
untimely: before the proper time   *197*
unwarranted: uncalled for   *116*
unwary: not alert   136
unyielding: firm and determined   *101*
upcoming: being in the near future   139
update: bring up to date   139
upgrade: raise the grade or quality of   139
upheaval: violent heaving up   139
upkeep: maintenance   139
uplift: elevate; raise   139
upright: standing up straight on the feet   139
uproot: pull up by the roots   139
upset: overturn   *41, 136, 196*
upstart: person who has suddenly risen to wealth and power, especially if he or she is conceited and unpleasant   139
upturn: upward turn toward better conditions   139
urban: having to do with cities or towns   51
usher in: preface; introduce   *34*

vacancy: job opening; unoccupied apartment   7
vacant: empty   7
valiant: courageous   *79*
valor: courage   *79*
valorous: courageous   *79*
vanguard: troops moving at the head of an army   *125*
at variance: in disagreement   90
variation: change in form, position, or condition   *89, 182*
vehement: showing strong feeling   101
velocity: speed   43
veracity: truthfulness   232
verbiage: excessive wordiness   *192*
verdict: decision of a jury   232
verification: proof; confirmation   5
verify: prove to be true   *5*, 232
veritable: true   232
verity: truth   232
versatile: capable of doing many things well   75

version: account from a particular point of view; translation 25

vicinity: neighborhood 51

video: having to do with the transmission or reception of what is seen 233

vie: strive for superiority *41*

vigilance: alert watchfulness to discover and avoid danger 103

vigilant: alertly watchful especially to avoid danger *103*

vigor: active strength or force *59*, 101

visibility: degree of clearness of the atmosphere, with reference to the distance at which objects can be clearly seen 233

visual: having to do with sight 233

vocal: inclined to express oneself freely *128*

vocation: occupation 51

volition: act of willing or choosing 59

voracious: having a huge appetite 91

wary: on one's guard against danger, deception, etc. 103

wayward: following one's own and usually improper way *113*

wily: cunning; astute *14*

wince: draw back involuntarily *7, 34*

withdraw: take or draw back or away; leave *24,* 140

withdrawal: act of taking back or drawing out from a place of deposit; departure 140

withdrawn: drawn back or removed from easy approach *24,* 140

withhold: hold back 140

withholding tax: sum withheld or deducted from wages for tax purposes 141

withstand: stand up against 141

witty: cleverly amusing in speech or writing *50*

wrangle: quarrel noisily *89,* 90

PRONUNCIATION SYMBOLS

ə   banana, collide, abut

'ə, ˌə   humdrum abut

ᵊ   immediately preceding \l\, \n\, \m\, \ŋ\, as in battle, mitten, eaten, and sometimes cap and bells \-ᵊm-\, lock and key \-ᵊŋ-\; immediately following \l\, \m\, \r\, as often in French table, prisme, titre

ər   operation, further, urger

'ər-
'ə-r   as in two different pronunciations of hurry \'hər-ē, 'hə-rē\

a   mat, map, mad, gag, snap, patch

ā   day, fade, date, aorta, drape, cape

ä   bother, cot, and, with most American speakers, father, cart

à   father as pronounced by speakers who do not rhyme it with bother

aů   now, loud, out

b   baby, rib

ch   chin, nature \'nā-chər\ (actually, this sound is \t\ + \sh\)

d   did, adder

e   bet, bed, peck

'ē, ˌē   beat, nosebleed, evenly, easy

ē   easy, mealy

f   fifty, cuff

g   go, big, gift

h   hat, ahead

The system of indicating pronunciation is used by permission. From *Merriam-Webster's Collegiate Dictionary*, Tenth Edition, © 1993 by Merriam-Webster, Incorporated.

320

hw   **wh**ale as pronounced by those who do not have the same pronunciation for both *whale* and *wail*

i   t**i**p, ban**i**sh, act**i**ve

ī   s**i**te, s**i**de, b**uy**, tr**i**pe (actually, this sound is \ä\ + \i\, or \à\ + \i\)

j   **j**ob, **g**em, e**dg**e, **j**oin, **j**u**dg**e (actually, this sound is \d\ + \zh\)

k   **k**in, **c**oo**k**, a**ch**e

k̲   German i**ch**, Bu**ch**

l   **l**i**l**y, poo**l**

m   **m**ur**m**ur, di**m**, ny**m**ph

n   **n**o, ow**n**

^{n} indicates that a preceding vowel or diphthong is pronounced with the nasal passages open, as in French *un bon vin blanc* \oe^n-bō^n-va^n-blä^n\

ŋ   si**ng** \'si**ŋ**\, si**ng**er \'si**ŋ**-ər\, fi**ng**er \'fi**ŋ**-gər\, i**nk** \'i**ŋ**k\

ō   b**o**ne, kn**ow**, b**eau**

ȯ   s**aw**, **a**ll, gn**aw**

œ   French b**oeu**f, German H**ö**lle

œ̄   French f**eu**, German H**ö**hle

ȯi   c**oin**, destr**oy**, s**aw**ing

p   **p**e**pp**er, li**p**

r   **r**ed, ca**r**, **r**a**r**ity

s   **s**our**c**e, le**ss**

sh   with nothing between, as in **sh**y, mi**ssi**on, ma**ch**ine, spe**ci**al (actually, this is a single sound, not two); with a hyphen between, two sounds as in death's-head \'deths-ˌhed\

t   **t**ie, a**tt**ack

th   with nothing between, as in **th**in, e**th**er (actually, this is a single sound, not two); with a hyphen between, two sounds as in knighthood \'nīt-ˌhu̇d\

t̲h̲   **th**en, ei**th**er, **th**is (actually, this is a single sound, not two)

ü   r**u**le, y**ou**th, uni**o**n \'yün-yən\, few \'fyü\

u̇   pull, wood, book, curable \\'kyu̇r-ə-bəl\\

ue   German füllen, hübsch

ūe   French rue, German fühlen

v   vivid, give

w   we, away; in some words having final \\(ͺ)ō\\ a variant \\ə-w\\ oc-
curs before vowels, as in \\'fäl-ə-wiŋ\\, covered by the variant
\\ə(-w)\\ at the entry word

y   yard, young, cue \\'kyü\\, union \\'yün-yən\\

ʸ   indicates that during the articulation of the sound represented by
the preceding character the front of the tongue has substantially
the position it has for the articulation of the first sound of *yard*,
as in French *digne* \\dēnʸ\\

yü   youth, union, cue, few, mute

yu̇   curable, fury

z   zone, raise

zh   with nothing between, as in vision, azure \\'azh-ər\\ (actually, this
is a single sound, not two); with a hyphen between, two sounds
as in gazehound \\'gāz-ͺhau̇nd\\

\\   slant line used in pairs to mark the beginning and end of a tran-
scription: \\'pen\\

'   mark preceding a syllable with primary (strongest) stress: \\'pen-
mən-ͺship\\

ͺ   mark preceding a syllable with secondary (next-strongest) stress:
\\'pen-mən-ͺship\\

-    mark of syllable division

( )   indicate that what is symbolized between is present in some utter-
ances but not in others: *factory* \\'fak-t(ə-)rē\\